Technical Support on the Web

Designing and Maintaining an Effective E-Support Site

Barbara Czegel

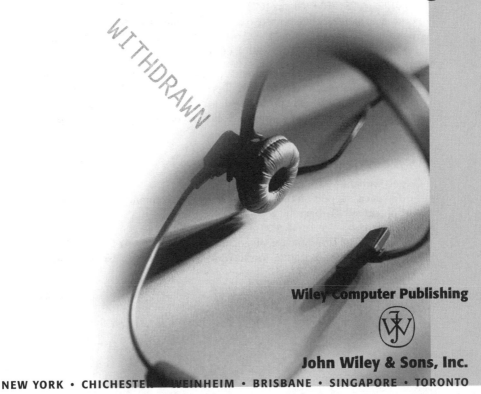

Wiley Computer Publishing

John Wiley & Sons, Inc.

NEW YORK • CHICHESTER • WEINHEIM • BRISBANE • SINGAPORE • TORONTO

Publisher: Robert Ipsen
Editor: Theresa Hudson
Developmental Editor: Kathryn A. Malm
Managing Editor: Angela Smith
Text Design & Composition: D & G Ltd, LLC

Designations used by companies to distinguish their products are often claimed as trademarks. In all instances where John Wiley & Sons, Inc., is aware of a claim, the product names appear in initial capital or all capital letters. Readers, however, should contact the appropriate companies for more complete information regarding trademarks and registration.

This book is printed on acid-free paper. ∞

This publication is designed to provide accurate and authoritative information in regard to the subject matter covered. It is sold with the understanding that the publisher is not engaged in professional services. If professional advice or other expert assistance is required, the services of a competent professional person should be sought.

Library of Congress Cataloging-in-Publication Data:

Czegel, Barbara, 1953-
    Technical support on the Web: designing and maintaining an effective e-support site/Barbara Czegel.
        p. cm.
    ISBN 0-471-39187-5 (paper: alk. paper)
        1. Web sites—Design. 2. World Wide Web. 3. Web publishing. I. Title.

TK5105.888.C79 2000
025.04—dc21   00-063309

Printed in the United States of America.

10 9 8 7 6 5 4 3 2 1

To my son the genius.

CONTENTS

Web-based support can be defined as any function accessible via the Web that provides assistance or information to users of a product or service. A support site is a configuration of Web pages that provides users with an interface to these support functions. This is a book about support sites on the Web: how to justify them, plan them, build them, market them, and manage them to ensure success.

Who Should Read This Book

This book is for you if you fall into one of the following categories:

A manager or senior staff member responsible for supporting technology-based products such as software or hardware. This book will help you move all or some of the support you provide to the Web or use the Web to expand or enhance your current support offerings.

A manager or senior staff member responsible for supporting non-technology-based products. Although the book and the examples it includes focus on technical support, the concepts can be applied directly to non-technical support. For example, if you are responsible for fielding customer questions and problems involved with the selection and installation of ceramic tiles, this book can help you plan, set up, and manage a Web site that will provide your customers with the support they need.

An owner or senior manager of a small business that has neither the headcount nor budget to provide comprehensive telephone or in-person support. This book will show you how to plan, set up, and manage a Web site that will provide the support you need without the prohibitive costs involved in increasing headcount.

A manager of an existing support site that is not working or needs to be improved in some way. This book will help you to identify the sources of your problems and areas for improvement. It will also walk you through planning and implementing solutions and improvements.

How This Book Is Organized

Technical Support on the Web: Designing and Managing an Effective Support Site consists of five sections:

- The concept of support on the Web
- Initiating Web-based support
- Design considerations
- Implementation and management
- Examples

Section One, "The Concept of Support on the Web," consists of Chapter 1, "Is Web-Based Support Worthwhile?" The answer to the question this title poses is not a binary yes or no. The answer is based on a number of factors that are discussed in this chapter along with various trends in Web-based support.

The second section in the book, "Initiating Web-based Support," contains three chapters and introduces the reader to site-planning activities. Chapter 2, "A Map for Site Creation and Management," presents a map to guide the reader through the entire process of planning, staffing, designing, building, marketing, and managing a support site. The rest of the book fills in the details outlined in this map. Chapter 3, "Establishing Scope," discusses the process of gathering requirements from all interested site stakeholders to define the scope of the proposed site. The scope summary described in this chapter is key to site success. Chapter 4, "Staff Selection," looks at the staffing required for the analysis, design, development, maintenance, and management of a support site. It discusses the creation of responsibility descriptions, skill grids, and position specifications.

The third section of the book is titled "Design Considerations" and contains two chapters. Chapter 5, "Functions, Tools, and Implementations," presents a description of many Web-based support tools that are currently available. Chapter 6, "Designing the Site," presents basic site design concepts along with samples, templates, and design processes that will help you get a design that works for your site.

The fourth section is "Implementation and Management." It contains four chapters. Chapter 7, "Processes and Implementation," discusses the development of both processes for the site and the site itself. It presents several process templates and discusses outsourcing as well. Chapter 8, "Marketing," discusses how best to market a site and includes a template and several examples. It also includes 10 suggestions for marketing at startup and a section on marketing ideas. Chapter 9, "Site Management," discusses establishing performance measurements and carrying the measurements out. It demonstrates how to put evaluation and improvement processes in place to ensure that success and improvements are ongoing. Chapter 10, "Problem Prevention and Troubleshooting," discusses how to recognize and avoid problems and ultimate disaster in the site creation process. It presents several symptoms and discusses causes, cures, and prevention.

The fifth and final section in the book contains examples of five sites, each in its own chapter. The first three sites, those for Farber/LaChance Online, Echo Online, and Strategic Connections, Inc., are ones that I have encountered in my work or day-to-day Web browsing. I don't present them as perfect sites, but rather as sites that offer ideas of value that can be used to improve existing support sites or to help design new ones.

Throughout this text, I also follow the site planning and development activities of two fictitious organizations, Education Plus and Trace Software. The final two chapters in this book contain the culmination of these examples, their support sites. The sites look terrific but are as totally fictitious as the organizations themselves.

How to Navigate This Book

The best way to approach this book is to read it from start to finish. This is particularly important for readers who fall into one of the following three categories:

You are considering setting up a support site and you want to know what is involved, how much it will cost, and how to go about it. In short, you want a plan to follow.

You've already started work on a support site, but you want to make sure you're on the right track. Basically, you want to make sure you are doing everything necessary to develop a successful site.

You already manage a support site, but it isn't working or it needs improvement. You do not understand what the problems are or what improvements are required. You might feel that the site has not been well planned and this time around you want to make sure that the work is properly planned and managed so that the improved site has a sound structure with processes in place to support it.

If you manage an existing support site and want to enhance performance or address issues in specific areas, then you might want to approach this book by first reading the chapters that address those specific areas. For example, if you are fairly satisfied with your site, but you want to do a better job at measuring performance and identifying improvements, you would go directly to Chapter 9. To get new ideas for marketing you would go to Chapter 8.

If you manage an existing support site and have a list of specific problem symptoms that you want to address, you will probably want to read Chapter 10 before you read anything else. This chapter will help you identify what you need to do next and which chapters you need to visit.

Final Words

My intention in writing this book is to give everyone involved in the process of improving, creating, or just considering a support site as much practical help as possible. I want you, the readers of this book, to avoid the expensive mistakes that are so common in the support site development process. I hope the map, templates, examples, and information provided in this book help you create a support site that meets all of your stakeholder requirements and generates a healthy return on investment.

ACKNOWLEDGMENTS

Thank you to my family for putting up with my insane working hours yet again.

Thank you to my various assorted four-legged friends for providing me with a much-needed respite from my computer.

Thank you to my students for forcing me to think so much (ouch!).

Thank you to the folks at Farber/LaChance Online, Echo Online, and Strategic Connections Inc. for allowing me to include their support sites in this book. Thank you also to the people at Control-F1 for providing screen shots of their product and for carrying out several remote control sessions with me to show me how things worked.

Thank you to my colleague Patricia Belvedere for suggesting the chapter on staffing.

Thank you to my son Chris for his help with the sample sites and for his feedback throughout the book.

Thank you to the folks at John Wiley & Sons for another opportunity to do what I love to do.

Barbara Czegel is president of SIRIUS3, a Toronto-based company that provides training for Help Desk professionals and facilitation of improvement initiatives for technology support areas. She has over 23 years of experience in both the technical and human facets of the computer industry. Ms. Czegel has been involved in planning, development, analysis, and support of retail business systems, planning systems, and manufacturing systems. She has justified, established, and managed Help Desk operations in corporate environments and is an experienced communicator and facilitator. She is the author of two other Wiley publications: *Running an Effective Help Desk* and *The Help Desk Practitioner's Handbook*.

Ms. Czegel received her Bachelor of Science in Computer Science and Mathematics from the University of Toronto in 1975. She is a member of the Association of Software Professionals and works as a professor at Seneca College in Toronto.

Barbara Czegel can be reached at bczegel@sirius3.com. The SIRIUS3 Web site is at www.sirius3.com.

PART ONE

The Concept of Support on the Web

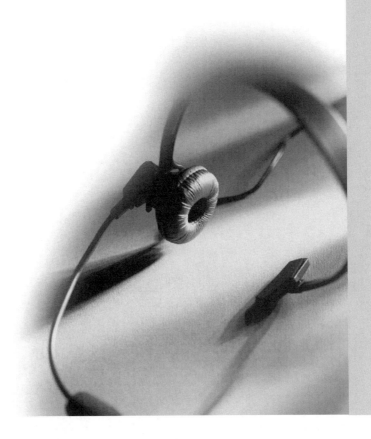

CHAPTER 1

Is Web-Based Support Worthwhile?

The Internet has truly become mainstream. Whatever business you happen to be in, chances are that most of your customers have access to the Internet. Much of the support you give to your customers is in some form of information or instruction. The Internet provides a platform that is tailor-made for information publishing and access. In other words, it is built for providing support. Countless organizations have already realized this and have jumped on the bandwagon of Web-based support, working around the clock to populate the Web with support sites of one form or another. Some sites are very successful, providing a valuable service to their customers while giving the organizations they support a good return. Others have been less successful, some are totally abandoned as ghost sites, never updated and visited, and others are visited infrequently, annoying customers by the lack of useful support they provide.

Before you consider creating a new support site or expanding the level of support you currently offer on your existing site, you need to think about how you can ensure your site is successful and how you can maximize the return on the effort you are about to expend. This chapter will help you get a start on doing just that. It will examine the potential benefits and pitfalls of setting up support on the Internet and it will look at the factors involved in determining your success. The costs involved in the process are reviewed, along with suggestions for putting a dollar value to benefits. The chapter will finish up with an example of a cost-benefit analysis for the construction of a Web-based support site.

The topics covered in this chapter are as follows:

- What is Web-based support?
- Three generations of support sites
- Potential benefits of Web-based support
- Potential pitfalls of Web-based support
- Factors affecting the return on investment
- Cost-benefit analysis

What Is Web-Based Support?

For the purposes of this book, I define Web-based support as any function accessible via the Internet that provides assistance or information to users of a product or service. The assistance or information provided is geared toward helping users solve problems with the product or service, make best use of the product or service, or select the appropriate product or service. My focus in this book is on the support of products and services related to technology—technical support.

The definition I have given Web-based support is very broad and reflects today's reality. As the technological products and services we develop become more complex and more extensive, so must the support we offer, and as our customers become more Internet-aware, we must be able to offer all or most of that support via the Internet.

The functions that support sites might offer range from the very simple, which could include email-initiated support, lists of frequently asked questions (FAQs), online documents, and searchable call-tracking databases, to an extremely complex integration of diagnostic tools that are capable of initiating interactive remote control communication sessions with support representatives. Web-based support is moving very quickly from infancy to sophistication. Sites have already evolved through three generations, as shown in Figure 1.1.

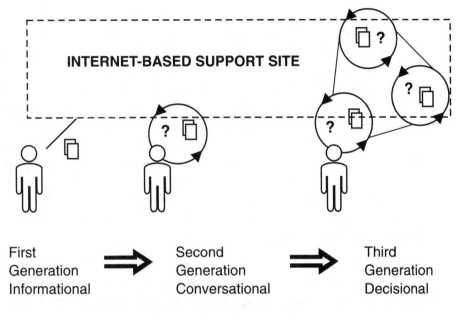

First
Generation
Informational ⇒ Second
Generation
Conversational ⇒ Third
Generation
Decisional

Figure 1.1　Evolving through generations of support sites.

Three Generations of Support Sites

Support sites in various stages of planning and implementation today can be categorized into three generations of evolution, each generation more advanced than the previous in terms of the technology used and the scope of support provided.

The First Generation: Informational

First-generation support sites are those that provide library-type support functions. As shown in Figure 1.1, customers take information from the site, while the site collects little or no information from the customer. The site has little or no information about what the customer is doing or why assistance is required. Some sites don't know who is using their services, while others might ask customers to provide some sort of identification or other information.

First-generation support sites consist of information that customers can search, view, and download. This information is published as functions or options, such as searchable knowledge bases, libraries of FAQs and technical documents, tutorials for viewing online or downloading, and patches and upgrades for downloading. The only interaction that the customer has with support representatives is via email or some form of problem-reporting software. For some products and services, if there is no phone or chat support, then email must be constantly monitored for critical support requests; the typical, 24-hour email response time is not good enough when a customer needs a quick solution to an urgent problem. Online support can be a very effective addition to phone support in that, as well as reducing the volume of calls, it can make phone support more efficient. Once a support representative determines the customer's problem, he can quickly end the call by pointing the customer to an online solution.

Organizations without a lot of money to spend, with low volumes of support traffic, or a very narrow range of support services may settle into a first-generation site quite comfortably until major changes occur either in the organization itself or in Web-based support technology. Organizations that are new at Web-based support typically start with an informational site. They can then use that site as a building block to move on to the next generation.

Most Web-based support sites in existence today can be classified as first generation. A typical first-generation structure is shown in Figure 1.2.

The Second Generation: Conversational

As organizations using Web-based support change, so do their support requirements. The technological products or services they offer may increase in complexity, necessitating more sophisticated diagnostic tools and perhaps human intervention in the support process. An increase in the number of customers using a site may mean that more and better tools are required to offer a wider variety of support functions that will redirect calls from telephone-based support areas. As customers become more sophisticated users, they will demand more sophisticated support for their increasingly complex problems. These are just some of the changes that drive the evolutionary process from first to second generation.

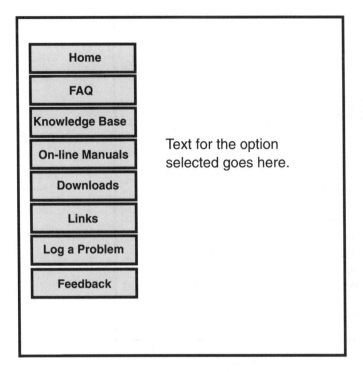

Figure 1.2   A first-generation support site.

Second generation support sites are those that allow customers to initiate and carry on some form of online conversation with technology available at the site or with a support representative. The customer may interact with a diagnostic tool that will collect symptoms from the customer, ask questions, and then suggest solutions based on the answers. Diagnostic tools typically keep trying to diagnose a problem until the customer indicates that yes, a solution worked, or no resolution was reached. At that point, the tool might simply create a problem log that it sends to the Help Desk or it might offer the customer the option of initiating an online chat session. If the customer chooses to initiate a chat session, the service representative participating in the session may have access to more tools that can be used to help the customer, such as remote control software. Within the support industry, an online chat session is generally considered to be more efficient than phone support. Using chat, a technician should be able to handle up to four simultaneous sessions, but it may require additional training to bring the technician up to this level of customer interaction.

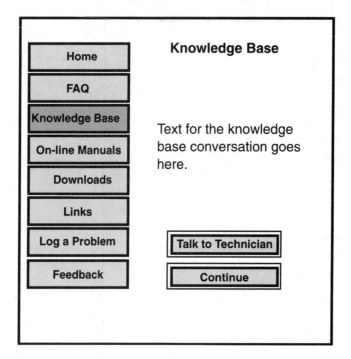

Figure 1.3 A second-generation support site.

All conversations in this generation of Web-based sites are initiated by the customer and take place across the Internet. Figure 1.3 illustrates the structure of a typical second-generation site. At the end of each round of interaction with the knowledge base, the customer has the option of requesting an online chat session with a support practitioner.

The Third Generation: Decisional

A third-generation support site uses a system made up of several tools fully integrated into a support engine that has the intelligence to make decisions to invoke specific functions based on customer activity. The support engine monitors activity on the support site. If a customer appears to be having trouble finding the right kind of assistance, the system might initiate a chat session with a support practitioner who could employ remote control tools as required to resolve the customer's problem. Alternatively, it might, based on the customer's profile, suggest that the customer schedule a service call and then go ahead and schedule the call at a time that is convenient for the customer.

Let's consider a third scenario. The customer poses a question to a problem resolution function that's part of the support engine. The support engine checks keywords in the question and decides to initiate a remote control session with the customer. After asking the customer's permission, the support engine views the customer's configuration, notices that the customer is using an incorrect version of the software, and suggests an upgrade. The customer agrees and the support engine performs the upgrade, asks the customer to test it, and ends the session. The customer's problem is resolved with no human interaction.

The move to third-generation support sites is driven by the expansion of customer bases in terms of numbers and locations. An organization works to increase its customer base and as it does, its customers become more widespread until the organization finds itself with a customer base that extends around the globe. Providing support in each specific location can be prohibitively expensive. A third-generation Web-based support site can be the virtual equivalent of having a support person sitting beside the customer. The support person in this case is the integrated support software, which will offer the customer various self-service options, converse with the customer, look over the customer's shoulder to see what is on the customer's monitor or in the customer's computer, and give the customer documentation, training, or required software. Needless to say, this capability can be very expensive and may be beyond the financial means of smaller organizations unless their international and 24-7 support requirements are very demanding.

The diagram in Figure 1.4 illustrates interaction between a third-generation support site and a customer. The support site has initiated a remote control session between itself and the customer and has discovered that the customer has an old version of the software. It asks permission to update the customer's PC with the new software.

Evolving through the Generations

Web-based support sites are not usually born as second- or third-generation sites. They typically start off as first-generation ones and evolve into second- and then third-generation sites, as shown in Figure 1.1. Let's look at an example. We'll use a fictitious organization called Business Maker, Inc. that manufactures marketing and sales software.

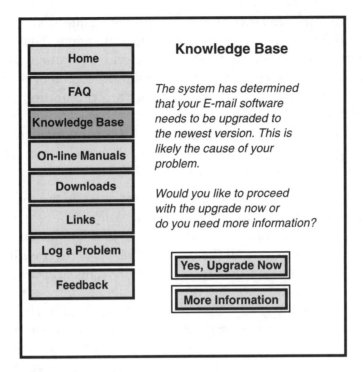

Figure 1.4 A third-generation support site.

The Business Maker Example

Business Maker's development and production activities are carried out in one city in North America, while its 20 sales offices are scattered across the world. When version 2.1 of Business Maker software was released, the organization realized it could not maintain acceptable levels of support with its current number of staff, and profit levels were such that additional staff could not be added without careful consideration.

Business Maker took a look at the calls it was getting and realized many of them were not software-specific, but rather procedural—how to use Business Maker in the business. The company created a support site with FAQs and a list of tutorials showing the areas of a business that could be helped by Business Maker. Sample procedures were also loaded onto the Web. An email option was added for questions that the site did not address, and material from these questions was used to update the Web site. Telephone support, which had previously been free, was now given a price.

The project was successful. Customers, especially those too small to afford telephone support, made great use of the support site, particularly appreciating the business tutorials. Telephone support fell to a reasonable level and the site was relatively easy to maintain.

Business Maker then made significant changes to its software, making it much more sophisticated in the process. The software was integrated with desktop suites, contact managers, telephony systems, and e-commerce systems. The beta release rolled out and what soon became very apparent was that the support provided by the Internet site was woefully inadequate. It was time to evolve.

Business Maker investigated various Web-based, diagnostic knowledge base tools and purchased one it felt best fit its requirements. Business Maker also added a Web-based component to its call management system to enable a customer to initiate a chat session with a service representative. Customers with problems could carry out diagnostic conversations with the knowledge base and if they were getting nowhere, they could ask for a chat session with a service representative. They would then be put into a hold queue until the representative was free and they could browse various documents or hints and tips while they were waiting.

The second-generation site worked fairly well, but as the Business Maker software evolved and became even more complex, the support site's problem resolution rate fell. Support representatives needed to look at customer PC configurations for certain problems. They needed to guide the customer through the support site and offer the most appropriate options, since even selecting options was becoming more complex.

Once again, Business Maker went hunting for support software. It decided on a fully integrated third-generation Web-based support system. The system included sophisticated knowledge bases and problem-resolution functions, the same Web-based, call-tracking management system from the previous generation, an automated problem-logging function, a work order and dispatch system, a remote control system, and a Web-based voice and video communication function. Business Maker offered custom interfaces to the site for different customers based on the type of business they were in. Customers could get to the most appropriate support pages faster.

When a customer logged into the site, a control module would track what the customer was doing and if certain checkpoints were reached. For example, if a certain number of solutions were rejected as unsuccessful, it would offer the customer various options, even those as complex as upgrading software or replacing files. Other options included viewing technical manuals or videos, chat sessions with a support practitioner or a business service representative, or scheduling an onsite service call or an online training session. The system would track billing information for those services that were not free. If the customer chose a chat session with a support practitioner, the practitioner could look over the customer's activity at the site and log into the customer's PC remotely to diagnose and fix the problem. The Business Maker software itself included a remote control component that the representative could use to initiate remote access. The third-generation support site put Business Maker support back on track, making it a showcase of the best practices for Web-based support.

In this case study, evolution through the generations of Web-based support mirrored the growth and complexity of the company, the product, and the customers.

Potential Benefits of Web-Based Support

Web-based support offers an extremely wide variety of benefits. These will vary depending on factors such as the generation of the support site, the tools employed, the profile of the customer base, the services offered, and so on. Benefits typically originate from six aspects of support:

- Self-service
- Remote access
- Single source access
- Information sharing
- Assisted service
- Integration

The Benefits of Self-Service

On a Web-based support site, *self-service* refers to all information, functions, and services that customers can take advantage of on their own, without having to contact a support representative. Customers might view or download information or seminars, search for solutions in a knowledge base, download a software upgrade, or check on the progress of their support log.

The primary benefit from customers performing functions for themselves is a reduction in calls to the staffed support area. This means staff might not need to be added when the number of customers being supported increases. Existing support staff would be able to use the time freed up by the reduction in calls to focus on proactive problem resolution, such as the elimination of recurring problems and the prevention of potential problems. In an over-worked support area, the staff would be able to return to more manageable call levels. The quality and accuracy of call handling and problem resolution will improve.

The more calls you are able to divert from your support area to your Web-based support site, the more benefits you will gain. This means that when you are planning your support site, you should include functions that will handle the problems, questions, and requests that your support area receives most frequently or that eat up most of your support time.

Another significant benefit of self-service is the ability to offer customers some form of support 24 hours a day, seven days a week. These extended hours of support come at no additional cost. The self-service functions you offer on your site would be available around the clock.

The self-service aspect of Web-based support also gives you the ability to expand the range of customers you serve by allowing you to offer some form of support at no cost to anyone with Internet access. Customers no longer have to pay prohibitive long-distance charges or subscribe to costly support plans to get a basic level of support. They would be able to make better use of your products and services and decrease downtime due to problems. Your products and services would thus be more attractive to a wider range of customers and organizations.

The convenience of self-service for functions such as online courses could encourage customers who would otherwise not take some training to do so. Better-trained customers make fewer calls to your support area.

Customers using email or a Web-based call management tool to report problems or ask questions will make it easier for you to schedule work. Calls coming in by telephone tend to control your schedule and the peaks and slow times are often difficult to staff appropriately. Emails and service logs that come in via the Internet can be assigned and scheduled to make the best use of your staff and make it easier to get to the most important calls quickly.

The Benefits of Remote Access

A Web-based support site can become the central source of support for an organization that is spread out across countries or continents, reducing the costs associated with having support staff at each location. Customers could use all of the self-service options and invoke an option for assisted support when necessary. When a request for assisted support comes in, support staff could use remote control software to access the customer's PC and resolve the problem or determine the next step, such as scheduling hardware support.

The support site could also help manage onsite hardware support, such as installation and repairs. Customers could use a Web-based work request option to request onsite work. The requests could be sent to a third party that is providing onsite hardware support to that particular location. All work requests could be managed and tracked from a central location with local support arranged, monitored, and adjusted as necessary.

Remote access also gives customers the ability to download software patches and upgrades from a Web-based support site. The costs involved in creating CDs, packaging, and mailing are reduced or eliminated. Customers get the software or updates they want instantly, without having to wait days or weeks for couriers or regular mail.

The Benefits of Single Source Access

A Web-based support site that contains documents such as technical manuals, user manuals, policies, FAQs, and so on will give everyone who asks for information the same answer. If you are diligent about keeping your site up to date, customers will always get the current and most accurate version of all needed information. Thus, the costs associated with problems caused by out-of-date information is reduced or eliminated.

Publishing hard-copy documents can be very costly and wasteful. Printed documents that are not purchased are tossed out, resulting in no return on the cost of printing those documents. Publishing documents to your support site allows you to provide your customers with the information they need in order to use your product without the costs involved in printing and shipping. You can then charge additional fees for those customers requesting hard-copy documents and perhaps even do your printing on an as-needed basis.

The Benefits of Information Sharing

Your Web-based support site can give your customers access to other users of the products and services you support via chat forums or discussion groups. Customers can see how others are using your products and exchange information on implementation, specific problems, integration with other products, and so on. They could make better use of your products and will experience reduced down times. They will make fewer calls to your support area and will have a higher satisfaction level with your products and services. As an aside, if your products and services suffer from poor quality, Web-based information sharing could expedite your extinction.

Information sharing on your site could take many forms. You could host chat rooms or discussion groups, or you may simply offer links to sites that offer information sharing. One computer manufacturer has an option on its support site that enables customers to see which support questions are currently being asked of the knowledge base. Access www.dell.com and navigate to the support option.

The Benefits of Assisted Service

Assisted service can be implemented from a Web-based support site in various ways. Typically, as customers navigate through the site looking for solutions, they may be offered options for human support at strategically placed intervals. These intervals are designed to encourage the customer to look for support, but to prevent them from becoming frustrated by offering them help as soon as it becomes evident that their search is not going well. Once a request for human support is initiated, the customer is put into a queue that could be chat-based or telephone-based.

If assisted service is integrated with the other support site tools, when the service representative picks up the customer call via a chat function or the telephone, most or all of the information associated with the customer's support session is available to the representative. The call is resolved more quickly than if no information had been available. The representative may even have a solution before actually talking or chatting to the customer, and the customer is saved the bother of describing the problem and the related support attempts from scratch.

Assisted service has a positive psychological effect that may encourage customers, specifically those not comfortable with Internet technology, to use Web-based support. Just knowing that human support is available at the click of a button can be very reassuring. The trick is to give this reassurance, but not give it so soon that customers are dissuaded from looking further for a solution.

The Benefits of Integration

Integrating the tools you use on your support site allows you to maximize the benefits you get from your site. Information from one tool is available to all of the others, so customers do not have to repeat or re-key information, and the support you offer can be delivered more quickly and accurately. Thus, your support site could handle an increased volume of traffic.

Integrating tools also enables a decision-making environment. Tools pass information to each other and, based on specific data in that information, specific functions are invoked automatically. For example, a customer navigating through a knowledge base reaches a predefined checkpoint that signifies that the customer probably requires a site visit. Work-order management software is invoked and a box pops up on the customer screen offering an onsite visit, perhaps even at a specific time. The software does not have to ask who or where the customer is. Other tools have collected all that information. The customer can then accept or reject the offer. If the onsite visit is accepted, the work order management software creates a work order and sends an email to the customer confirming the appointment. If the onsite visit is rejected, then another option might be offered, such as remote control access by a support technician with an accompanying chat session.

The Potential Pitfalls of Web-Based Support

The potential pitfalls in Web-based support come from poor planning and implementation. A site that offers little actual value to a customer, no matter how visually perfect it is, is worthless. Sites that are difficult to navigate, that contain out-of-date information, that do not offer help for the most common problems, that are designed at too advanced or too simple a level for the customer base they support all fall into the worthless category. You can spend a fortune on support tools, but if you haven't done a thorough job in planning and implementation, your support site will fail and you will get no payback on what you invested. Customers will go to alternatives such as telephone support, and getting them back to the Internet would be difficult.

Unfortunately, getting little or no payback is not the worst result that a poor support site can have. Your site can actually cause the organization you support to lose customers and associated revenue. The Internet makes it very easy for customers to find and do business with those of your competitors who have superior support offerings.

The following sections describe some of the most common pitfalls in putting together a Web-based support site. Avoid them.

Not Enough Consideration Given to Customer Profiles

Who are your customers? Are they sophisticated users of the products you support, able and willing to navigate through problem diagnostic software, or are they beginner users, perhaps uncomfortable with Internet technology and self-support? The former group will appreciate information geared to their level of use and will not be afraid of tools that involve them in the problem-solving process. The latter group may never visit a site that caters exclusively to the former. Similarly, the more sophisticated users would get very little benefit from a site that only offered solutions to simpler problems or help for beginner-level users of the product.

What if your customers consist of both types of users? Your site will have to cater to both profiles—that of the sophisticated, more advanced user, and that of the tentative beginner. Neglecting to address the requirements of either group could cause your site to fail.

Inappropriate Functions or Information

The functions you put on to your support site should be those functions that are most requested by your customers. If you currently have a call management tool, you can get that information from the call database. It will identify your most frequently occurring calls. You will know which questions are asked most often, which problems are experienced most often, and which services are requested most often. This information is your blueprint for the functions and information that will make your site most useful to your customers.

As an example, your call statistics may indicate a frequently occurring problem that can be resolved by a software patch. You can put the problem, the resolution, and the patch itself onto your support site. All calls for this problem can be rerouted to the support site. If, however, you do little or no research before putting functions or information on to your site, you won't necessarily be addressing the problems and solutions that will give you the biggest return. Very simply, your site will not have the answers your customers are looking for, so your customers will stop visiting it.

Lack of Processes

The information you put on to your site is only useful when it is current. The minute it becomes out of date it loses its usefulness and gains the potential to start annoying customers who are looking for current information. You can work very hard populating your new site with good information, but if you do not have the processes in place to review it and keep it current, then your site will fail. Customers will label it as out-of-date or unreliable and will stop using it.

Along with processes for keeping your site up to date, you need processes for handling email, support logs, feedback, and any other forms of communication that are generated from your support site. Customers who have to wait a long time to get a response to an email will abandon that option and start using the telephone. Your hoped-for benefits of reduced calls to the support area will not materialize, and even worse, the calls you get from customers who have been waiting for answers to emails will not be friendly.

The processes for maintaining and managing your site are essential to its success. Once a site has been labeled as unresponsive or not useful, convincing customers otherwise will take a long time. Chapter 7, "Processes and Implementation," will show you how to create effective processes.

Inappropriately Skilled Staff

If you assign the task of collecting and designing knowledge for an interactive problem diagnostic tool to someone whose previous experience consists of setting up FAQs, you are inviting disaster. The tool will not be set up and maintained properly, it will not provide value to the customers, and, worse, it could actually become a problem generator. Problem generators tend to have a negative impact on return.

People who work with Web-based support sites must have the appropriate skills and training. Otherwise, they cannot help but do a poor job, which can result in decreased site return or lost customers. Hotshot Internet coding experts are not necessarily the people you want controlling the design, implementation, or management of your Web-based support site.

Poor Marketing

If people don't know your support site is there, they won't use it. Poor marketing can make even a good site fail through disuse. Registering your site with search engines isn't enough, since too many sites exist on the Internet. Yours might not come up until the twentieth page of sites returned by a search and few Internet users have the time or patience to look that far.

Find out which media your customers access on an ongoing basis, and use those media to let them know about your site. Marketing your site is discussed in Chapter 8, "Marketing."

No Measurement of Ongoing Improvement

If your support site does not change as the organization you support changes and as the customers you support change, it will lose its effectiveness and usage of the site will decrease. If you are not regularly measuring performance, collecting feedback, changing support offerings as the business and customers change, or looking for other ways to improve your support site, the benefits it once generated will start to shrink. Worse, since you aren't taking measures, you may not even know that your site is dying until it is dead. Chapter 9, "Site Management," shows you how to measure site payback and monitor performance on an ongoing basis.

Inappropriate Tools

Knowledge bases that are difficult to navigate or poorly organized will not be used. Likewise, functions that have prohibitively long response times when accessed via modem will not be used by customers with modem access to the Internet. Tools that do not match the intended function, audience, or widely used transmission media will put a support site into decline. The functions the tools support will simply not be used. See Chapter 5,"Functions, Tools, and Implementations," for more on this topic.

Poor Site Design

Sites that are difficult to read, are poorly organized, or have too many heavy-duty graphics are sites that will not be used. Customers do not have time to try to figure a site out, decipher hard-to-read fonts, or wait for complex graphics to load. Don't forget that most customers will only visit your site occasionally and will not be familiar with its layout, so navigation must be "intuitive." Ease of navigation is absolutely critical to the success of your site, and customers must always be presented with a clear link to live support if they become frustrated or feel their problem is urgent. Designing a usable site is not difficult, but it does take some thought. Chapter 6, "Designing the Site," covers the topic of site design in more detail.

Negative Impact on the Bottom Line

Sites must enable customers to resolve their problems quickly. Otherwise, providing online help will end up being more costly than phone support. What is the cost to the bottom line if a problem that could be solved with a one-minute phone call to the Help Desk takes five minutes or longer to resolve online? With regards to internal support, it may cost an organization a great deal in lost employee productivity. As far as external support is concerned, longer turn-around times may result in losing customers to a competitor. All ancillary costs for providing Web-based support must be carefully examined to make sure that they don't outweigh the benefits to the bottom line.

Factors That Determine Return on Investment

In the section entitled *Potential Benefits of Web-based Support*, we discussed some potential sources and forms of return, such as cost savings generated by a drop in call traffic or by avoiding an increase in call traffic. Return can be defined as the benefits you get from the implementation of your support site and can be translated into a dollar value. In this section, we're going to look at the factors that determine how good that return is.

Factors that determine how much return you receive on the investment you put into setting up or improving your support site fall into three categories: management, functions, and tools. When problems arise in any of these categories, your site will not realize its return potential and could even generate significant losses for your organization.

In the following sections, we will examine individually and in combination the impact management, functions, and tools have on the return that a Web-based support site generates.

Management

The category of management encompasses the processes of controlling the support site. A site that is being managed well with information updates, traffic control, and ongoing improvement initiatives is a site that has the potential for good return. A site that has no real management and is supported in a haphazard way has little or no potential for return but does have potential for generating losses.

In order to show how the management category interacts with the functions and tools categories to affect return, I have created a simple binary rating system. A rating of MG denotes a site that is managed well, while a rating of MP denotes a site that is managed poorly.

Good Management: A Rating of MG

In order to achieve the coveted MG rating, a site must follow the best practices of Web-based support site management as outlined here:

- The information and functions on the site are kept up to date. This means that all FAQs, knowledge bases, technical manuals, online seminars, and so on reflect the most current information available. The processes for keeping these information bases up to date are supported, understood, and followed by the people managing and maintaining the site.

- The procedures for managing and responding to all communication generated by the site are in place and followed, and response times have been established and are adhered to. Site users are also notified of the response times that they can expect.

- Any new functions, software, or major changes are well planned and tested before being added to the site.

- People working on the site, either responding to customer communication, managing the software tools, or updating information, must have the appropriate skills and experience. This means that someone whose only exposure to knowledge bases has been the creation of a FAQ will not be found working on the knowledge design for an interactive problem diagnostic tool.

- Procedures are in place for monitoring and evaluating site performance. Trends and statistics from site tools are watched carefully, and feedback is solicited regularly from site users.

- The site is marketed so that potential users are aware of its existence, what it offers, and how it can help.

- Initiatives are established for ongoing improvements. The staff managing and maintaining the site stay informed of Internet and industry trends as well as changes in the direction of the supported business. Opportunities for improved or expanded site offerings are actively pursued, and competitor's sites are scanned for ideas.

Poor Management: A Rating of MP

The not-so-coveted MP rating is somewhat easier to achieve than its MG counterpart. An MP rating is given to sites that have few or no real management processes in place. Updates are performed on an ad hoc basis, perhaps only when someone has some free time. Site visitors are frustrated by the length of time it takes to get a response from emails sent to the site. If you recognize your site in any of the following descriptions, then you can rate your site an MP:

- The knowledge base provides answers that were current last year. The FAQ is based on questions that your support area received six months ago.

- No procedures exist for maintaining or managing the site. Responsibility is passed from person to person, with no priority attached to it. Your support area often receives calls prefaced with "I sent you folks an email, but no one answered," while your site boasts, "We will respond to your email messages promptly."

- When changes are made to the site, they are made quickly and without very much thought. Testing means little more than "upload it and see what it looks like." No consideration is given to testing the different versions of browser software or modem speeds that customers use to access the site.

- "Monitor and evaluate performance" are words you read in a book. They are for huge organizations, not for your support site. You don't ask for feedback from customers using your site, but sometimes you do get it and it is not positive.

- One day you're going to improve your site, but not right now, you don't have time.

Functions

The processes involved in selecting the functions and information that are available on your support site have a huge impact on the return that the site generates. The more calls your site can eliminate, the more work it can take off the shoulders of your support staff, and the greater the return would be. A site that provides functions that were selected without much thought will never reach the return it could potentially have.

Using the rating system that was introduced in the previous section, we give a rating of FG, good functions, to a site that has selected functions well and a rating of FP, poor functions, to a site that has selected functions without much thought.

Good Functions: A Rating of FG

Organizations that earn a rating of FG for their support sites take the time to understand the support calls they are getting and to understand the profiles of their customers. FG-rated sites contain information that has already proven to be useful. The staff managing and maintaining these sites searches and analyzes data in the call database to identify those calls that occurr most frequently and take the most time of any call-based support areas. The information required to solve users' problems is placed on the support site, and this process is repeated at regular intervals.

The staff running FG-rated sites encourages customer feedback concerning functions and information and pays close attention to what is received. FG-rated sites often include an easy-to-use customer feedback form somewhere on the site. Feedback is collected frequently, analyzed carefully, and then the appropriate changes are made.

FG-rated sites reflect the knowledge and understanding of their customers. In organizations with internal support areas, the site staff visits customers regularly, collecting their support requirements and getting an understanding of how they access the support site. For external or remote customers, the staff develops and encourages discussion groups and virtual user groups so that it can understand what the customers need in terms of support. The staff is then able to learn about the software and hardware customers use to access the site, when they access it, and how comfortable they are using various Internet functions.

Poor Functions: A Rating of FP

Organizations that do not believe in or have no time for planning and analyzing customer requirements and call patterns will have support sites that drop easily to a rating of FP, poor in the category of functions. Organizations with FP-rated sites tend to take shortcuts. They don't have time to analyze and understand their support call profile, or they are not posting functions that reflect this call profile to their support site. Planning for their site might involve scanning a few competitors' sites and designing a site based on what they find, their philosophy being "Hey, if it works for them, it will work for us."

This shortcut has a few problems. First, the sites they copy might not be working. Sites that look great could be total failures, getting very little return. Next, scanning competitor sites is a great way to get free ideas, but these ideas should be for newer, better implementations, not for exactly the same implementations. You need to be thinking ahead of your competitors. Finally, your customers may not be after the same information and assistance as the customers of your competitors. This means you are giving them information and functions that are either not useful or not as useful as they could be. Your return will consequently suffer.

Simply put, organizations with FP-rated sites do not know their customers. They do not consider customer feedback essential. They feel that looking through and analyzing feedback is too time-consuming and besides, "It's usually bad, so why bother. Customers are never satisfied." These organizations prefer to take the shortcuts that lead them to owning support sites that are not very useful to their customers.

Not surprisingly, another philosophy that organizations with FP-rated support sites follow is "We aren't in the business of managing user groups for our customers." Thus, opportunities for understanding customers, finding ways to improve, and developing more informed customers are lost.

FP-rated sites generate little or no return for their organizations. In strictly financial terms, this may not appear significant, especially if the site investment is minimal. The real danger in this situation comes from the negative impact on profitability that the FP-rated site might cause. Customers that are not getting the support they need will go elsewhere. They might call the organization's support line, generating more call traffic to a probably over-extended support department. External customers may go to a competitor, taking their business with them. Internal customers may go to a peer for support, a very expensive option that can tie up two or more employees for a significant and unproductive time.

Tools

The wide variety of Web-based support tools that are currently available can dramatically increase the return of a support site. These tools can provide fast, easy-to-use self-service or assisted service in varying ranges of functionality and price. Even small one- or two-person businesses can find Web-based support tools that fit into their budget.

This does not mean that every tool will generate a good return. If you have an acre of lawn in front of your house, you would not use garden shears to trim your grass (unless you were really, really bored). Similarly, you would not cut the postage stamp-sized lawn of your town house with a lawn tractor. You would select your grass-cutting tools with more care.

On a support site, things are no different. If you don't invest time in researching and selecting appropriate tools, they can reduce or eliminate return and perhaps even negatively impact profitability.

Using our now well-established system, we assign a rating of TG, good tools, to a site that has selected tools appropriate to the customers and organization it supports, and a rating of TP, poor tools, to a site that has selected inappropriate tools.

Good Tools: A Rating of TG

Support sites with a TG rating take tool selection seriously. They look at what functions the tool must provide for maximum return and consider only the tools that provide those functions. They select tools with an ease of use that matches the technological sophistication of their customers, so that the customers will feel comfortable using them. A good support site researches all the costs involved in purchasing a tool, including installation, maintenance, and training, and select a tool they can afford. They don't skimp on training costs to get a tool with greater functionality. They also make sure that the tool is compatible with their technological platform, so that they aren't creating maintenance or performance headaches.

Organizations with TG-rated support sites not only choose their tools carefully, but they also make sure that their staff has the skills and training to install and maintain the tools properly. Vendor training is provided to all staff who set up and maintain a tool, so that the full functionality of the tool can be understood and implemented, and the maximum benefit is realized. The staff who implement or support the tool is selected based on their skills. For example, experienced knowledge workers would be chosen to design and assemble the information required for a knowledge base used in a sophisticated problem diagnostic tool.

Tools used in a TG-rated support site are well maintained. The knowledge or information used by the tools is kept up to date, and new releases and patches are tested and installed in a timeframe that maximizes functionality and ensures stability and accuracy.

Poor Tools: A Rating of TP

Support sites with a TP rating typically do not devote enough time to tool selection; practice false economy by skimping on tool costs, maintenance, or training; or buy technology for technology's sake. Organizations that are too busy to spend time on making the right tool selection are prime candidates for a TP rating. They don't know which functions a tool should provide, which tools are the most appropriate for which functions, and which tools their customers will actually use. They end up purchasing quickly, without much planning or analysis. If they discover that the tool purchased does not have the required functionality, they either put it aside without implementing it or implement it and watch it die a quick death through disuse.

Tools aren't very useful if they're not used properly, and chances are they won't be used properly if the people using them don't get the required training. Organizations with TP-rated support sites don't believe this. They believe every penny of the budget allocated to purchase support tools should be spent on technology and functionality, not on support or administration functions such as training. They feel that training is a non-issue for their support staff and that their staff is paid to be able to learn how to use any piece of technology fairly quickly. Perhaps even the employees themselves think this. This philosophy may be fine for very simple technologies, but for more complex tools, it leads to longer than necessary learning and implementation curves, errors, and poor return.

Purchasing technology for technology's sake can be very damaging to an organization in terms of decreasing returns on the technology investment and negatively affecting the profitability of the business. Support groups that are technologically knowledgeable but overenthusiastic and at the same time undermanaged have a tendency to buy the "latest and the greatest" rather than "what our customers really need," a trend that can earn a Web-based support site a TP rating. This overenthusiasm brings with it the tendency to purchase tools that are so new as to be unstable, tools that are totally unsuitable to the technological sophistication of their customers, or tools that do not provide the required functionality.

Management, Functions, and Tools in Combination

In the previous sections, we examined the individual impact of management, functions, and tools on the return a Web-based support site generates. We now look at the impact of these factors in combination.

To keep things simple, we will only consider the values of good and poor for each of the factors. We will also consider all the possible combinations of factors and values. Table 1.1 summarizes this analysis.

The first combination in Table 1.1, MG FG TG, describes a Web-based support site that is well managed with good coverage of the functions that offer the best return and use the tools that are most appropriate. The staff managing the site is constantly looking for ways to offload support from telephone-based support areas and make the site more

Table 1.1 Factors That Affect Return on Investment

RATING	MANAGEMENT	FUNCTIONS	TOOLS	POSSIBLE RETURN
MG FG TG	Good	Good	Good	Significant
MG FG TP	Good	Good	Poor	Below Potential
MG FP TG	Good	Poor	Good	Loss
MG FP TP	Good	Poor	Poor	Significant Loss
MP FG TG	Poor	Good	Good	Below Potential
MP FG TP	Poor	Good	Poor	Loss
MP FP TG	Poor	Poor	Good	Significant Loss
MP FP TP	Poor	Poor	Poor	Significant Loss

interesting and useful to customers. An opportunity exists here for significant savings on current and future support costs. MG FG TG is where you get an optimal return and is where you should aim to be.

The second combination, MG FG TG, indicates a site that is not making good use of tools. Perhaps inappropriate tools have been selected, perhaps staff did not get the appropriate training, or perhaps customers don't like using the tool. The site is not experiencing the return that it could be.

The third combination, MG FP TG, indicates a problem with functionality, and this could be serious enough to generate a negative return or a loss. The support site does little to eliminate calls to telephone-based support areas. It is in the red in terms of return.

The fourth combination is serious trouble: MG FP TP. Here problems are occurring with both functionality and tools. Not only is this site in the red because it has not eliminated calls, the loss has been significantly increased by too much money being spent on inappropriate tools that are not used.

In the fifth combination, MP FG TG, management is the only sore spot. The functions and tools are in place, but they are not being managed and maintained as well as they could be. The site might not be undergoing consistent improvements, and if it continues in this state for long, the "below potential" could turn into a loss.

The sixth combination, MP FG TP, has only one good performer: functionality. The right functions are on the support site, but either too much money has been spent on tools or the tools are not appropriate, don't do enough, or are difficult for customers to use. Once again, because good management is absent, functionality could deteriorate. This site is in the red and dropping.

The seventh combination, MP FP TG, describes a support site that has just about hit rock bottom. It has good tools but can't do anything useful with them because it does not offer the right functions and is poorly managed. The organization that owns this site should have saved the money it spent on tools. In terms of return, it is significantly in the red.

In the final combination, MP FP TP, the support site has hit rock bottom. It offers useless functions and information that are out of date or incorrect, and the tools provided to get at this useless information are totally inappropriate. The organization that owns this site has thrown away all the money it invested in the site and it is still probably paying some site maintenance while getting nothing in return except perhaps decreased profitability.

Figure 1.5 displays the information in Table 1.1 in bar chart format. The best and worst combinations become very quickly obvious, as does the fact that there is really only one combination that lets you realize a significant return. In order to have a successful Web-based support site

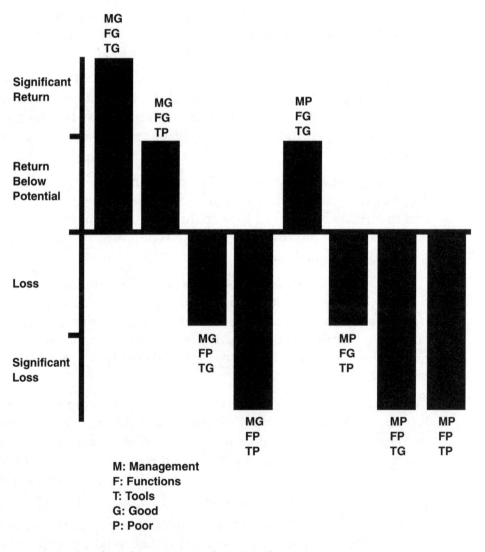

Figure 1.5 Bar chart showing factors that affect the return on investment.

with a maximum return, you must do a good job of site management and maintenance, selecting and maintaining functions and information, and selecting tools.

You are now ready to consider creating a cost-benefit analysis for the support site you are intending to build or upgrade.

Putting Together a Cost-Benefit Analysis

In this section, we will examine how to calculate the costs involved in setting up a support site and how to determine the dollar value of the benefits. We will then look at a simple example of a cost-benefit analysis in which we justify the creation of a Web-based support site by calculating the payback interval and the return on investment.

Costs

As with any system implementation, when you are creating or improving a Web-based support site, you will have both one-time and ongoing costs to consider. Your one-time development costs will include the following:

- Web hosting, domain name registration, and Internet access, if your organization doesn't already have these in place. These costs will vary depending on how large your organization is, whether you will host your own site or use an Internet Service Provider (ISP), how you will access the Internet, and so on. These costs also need to include any hardware, software, and communications equipment you need to become Web-enabled.

- The time and resources to gather requirements for your Web-based support site and to determine the scope of your site. You need time to plan exactly what support options you will offer.

- The time and resources involved in support tool selection. I have kept this as a separate cost since tool selection can be a very complex and lengthy process depending on the type of tool you are purchasing.

- The cost of the support tools you select.

- The time and resources involved in gathering, formatting, and loading the data for your site; building any required knowledge bases; coding Web pages; and implementing the final system.

Once your site is up and running, you will have ongoing maintenance costs to consider. These costs include the following:

- The time and resources involved in keeping data up to date, managing the site, and supporting any customer-initiated communication

- The extended support contracts for the support tools purchased

- The administration and maintenance costs involved in maintaining your Internet connection, hardware, and software

- The cost of having customers performing their own online support, particularly self-help. As far as internal support is concerned, employees who attempt to solve technical problems aren't performing their intended functions and so their productivity is lost while the problems are solved. This is true for phone support as well as Web-based support. If employees who utilize online help require more time than when using your current method of support, then the cost in lost productivity of that additional time should be factored in. As far as external support is concerned, you may lose customers who become frustrated with online support. This could be a problem if your customers are not Internet-savvy. If this is a concern, survey your customers beforehand.

Benefits

In order to be able to use benefits in a cost justification, you must assign a dollar value to them. The benefits you can quantify include the following:

A reduction in calls to a support area. This means a reduction in support time and cost. You can show how many calls are eliminated and you can estimate the average time saved per call. A dollar saving can be calculated by using a standard hourly wage, such as $60 per hour, and applying it to the time saved.

Hiring that is no longer necessary. Putting a Web-based support site in place may mean that you can put off hiring additional staff for a specific time or indefinitely. To calculate the savings, simply apply your standard wage to the time frame. For example, if you can put off hiring someone for one year and you use an hourly wage of $60 per hour, which translates into $2,100 per week, your savings is $109,200.

The time saved for internal customers. If you support internal customers, then the time you save for the customers will positively impact the profitability of the business you support. You can estimate the time customers save by helping themselves or by experiencing lower wait times. You can then apply a standard hourly wage against this time. Statistics from your call-tracking software will help you with these numbers.

An increase in business. If you support external customers, you can estimate the impact of your support site on the spending habits of your customers. For example, will the additional support offerings or the 24-hour support available from your site entice new customers? Will sales increase? Will current customers buy more of what you sell? You can use statistics from organizations similar to yours to formulate estimates for potential increases in business that you feel the support site will generate.

A reduction or elimination of costs involved with supporting remote locations. If you support remote locations, you may be paying for onsite support staff and offices or for frequent onsite visits. Your Web-based support site can reduce these costs dramatically. Self-support along with assisted support options involving remote control software can eliminate much of the onsite support required. Remote customers can even use your site to dispatch support technicians when onsite support is required, such as in the case of hardware replacement. You may set up a contract with a third party close to the remote site to provide the dispatched support.

Savings in publishing costs. You can determine how much your current publications are costing you and which costs you can eliminate by publishing directly to your support site. Customers can then download the information they need.

Some benefits are difficult to quantify, such as increased customer satisfaction, more knowledgeable customers, or an enhanced business image. Even though you can't quantify them, you can list them as additional benefits. They may help make a decision if the justification is not conclusive.

The Analysis

The process of identifying and analyzing costs and benefits and determining return on investment is illustrated in the following example.

Your Web-based support project may look very different from that pro-filed in the example, but you should be able to use at least some of the concepts presented to strengthen your own analysis.

Introducing Sales Generation Software, Inc.

Sales Generation Software, Inc. (SGS) is a very young (and fictitious) company in an early growth stage. In its very early days, our previous example company, Business Maker, probably looked very similar to SGS, but it did not have the advantage of the Internet to alleviate the product support process.

SGS does not have a lot of money to spend and its management has decided to ease up on hiring in the support area until it can establish some kind of fee-based support. Currently, SGS customers are wan-gling free business consulting during onsite support visits. The SGS product necessitates several business decisions and those SGS cus-tomers who don't have the business knowledge they need want help with the decisions. This stolen consulting increases support time and cost considerably. SGS wants to give customers the option of getting business consulting or enhanced support, but for a fee. SGS does not want to do this until a comprehensive set of free support options is in place.

A Web-based support site has been chosen as the vehicle to provide comprehensive self-support for SGS customers. The planned site includes online FAQs, manuals, business tutorials, problem-reporting and resolution capabilities, software downloads, and email.

Assumptions for SGS, Inc.

In order to keep things simple, we'll make some assumptions. First, labor costs, including overhead, are $60 per hour. That translates into $2,100 per a five-day, 35-hour workweek. I have made no differentia-tion between work by contract staff and internal staff. In reality, SGS might want to hire contract staff to do the complete implementation while they continue on in their daily work. In terms of the financial analysis, I have not differentiated between capital costs and expenses. In real life, each is treated differently.

One-Time Costs for SGS, Inc.

One-time costs for the Web-based support project include the purchase, installation, and training costs for the software and the labor costs involved in data gathering, design, and loading. SGS has just completed gathering and analyzing information for the support site project and has selected a support tool that provides a variety of functions in a centralized online package. The structure of the software, as shown in Figure 1.6, enables it to become the whole support site. It will enable SGS to provide the following functions and information online: user, administration, and business manuals; simple business tutorials; a FAQ; a searchable knowledge base; an incident-logging function; downloads for software patches and upgrades; and feedback or questions via email.

The cost for a two-seat license with assorted extras is $10,000. SGS has chosen to purchase the extended support agreement, which is 12 percent

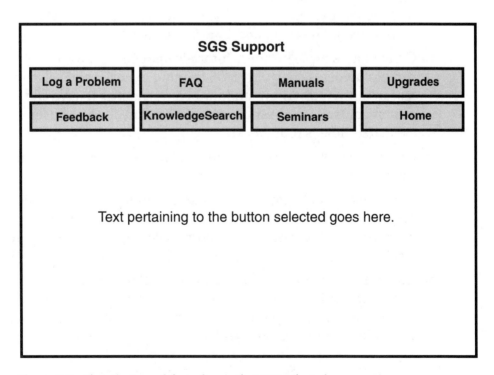

Figure 1.6   The structure of the software that SGS selected.

of the purchase price, or $1,200. SGS also selected to have the software vendor come on site for two days to do some analysis and the software installation, configuration, and training. The cost is $3,000.

The requirements analysis and software selection is performed by one SGS support person over three weeks. The cost is $6,300.

The work that the SGS staff will have to perform to get the site up and running is as follows:

- Prepare three manuals: the User Manual, Administration Guide, and Business Guide for online access. The estimated time is three weeks.

- Assemble a FAQ for online access. This is not a huge task because support staff are already maintaining such a document. The estimated time is one week.

- Assemble a knowledge base to be used by the new software. This process involves taking their current call database, converting it, and adding in business problems and solutions. The call database only contains problems and solutions for technical problems, but SGS wants customers to be able to get answers to business problems as well. The estimated time is four weeks.

- Create four simple business tutorials in document form. This process involves analyzing SGS training material and selecting, researching, and writing up four business topics that would help customers make the best use of SGS software in their business. The estimated time is four weeks.

- Prepare the software patches and upgrades for the download option. The estimated time is one week.

- Determine what business and technical information the bulletin page will contain. Also determine the format and how it should be maintained and create the first entry. The estimated time is one week.

- Create and document a management process to ensure that the site, actually the information contained in the software tool, is updated on an ongoing basis and that someone is responsible for this task. The estimated time is one week.

All the work that the SGS staff has to perform comes to approximately 15 weeks, or $31,500.

Ongoing Costs for SGS, Inc.

The ongoing costs for the SGS support site include $1,200 for the extended support contract SGS negotiated with the software vendor and the labor costs involved in keeping the information and functions up to date as well as installing any software upgrades.

SGS estimates that maintaining information and functions and installing upgrades will take four days per month. Over one year, this is 48 days, or approximately 10 weeks. At $2,100 per week, this becomes $21,000 per year.

Benefits for SGS, Inc.

The benefits for SGS from the Web-based support site stem from a reduction in calls to the support area and a reduction of onsite visits, especially visits that turn into free business consulting sessions. SGS also figures that by implementing the support site, they can put off hiring another support person for a year.

The new support site will also enable SGS to begin offering customers fee-based support. SGS feels that they could not offer fee-based support until they have something to offer clients who do not need or could not afford the extra support. Support obtained from the new support site is free, but customers can purchase various additional support options, including business analysis and consulting.

SGS estimates the new site will save 100 calls per month. SGS support calls tend to be long since customers typically want help with the business decisions that SGS software necessitates. At a conservative 15 minutes per call, the 100 calls would take 1,500 minutes or 25 hours per month. In one year, this is 300 hours or $18,000 of a support person's time.

The business tutorials and online manuals available on the new site will also enable SGS to reduce its onsite visits to customers. SGS estimates a reduction of 20 three-hour site visits per month. This translates into 60 hours or $3,600 per month, which becomes $43,200 in one year.

Publishing and distributing spiral-bound manuals currently costs SGS approximately $6,000 per year. The new site will eliminate this cost by enabling customers to access the manuals online. If they want to purchase a manual, they will pay a fee that will cover publication costs.

The reduction in human support requirements that the new site enables means that SGS can put off hiring another support employee for at least half a year, possibly more depending on business growth. At the $2,100 per week labor cost, this translates into a saving of $52,500 over 26 weeks.

Fee-based support will start out as a break-even activity. Fees are structured such that all SGS support staff costs are covered, including the acquisition of any additional contract or full-time staff required. SGS will use the information it gathers from this support to improve their software products and plan the future consulting infrastructure. In the future, once the SGS product has a stable installation base, SGS plans to turn fee-based support into a revenue-generating activity. Estimated future revenue could be included in the cost-benefit analysis, but SGS has chosen to exclude it simply because it is not needed to justify the cost of the support site.

Cost-Benefit Analysis for SGS, Inc.

The analysis for the justification of the new SGS support site is shown in Table 1.2. This is a very simple justification. The site not only pays for itself in the first year, but also has a projected return on investment of 64 percent. The second year projects a return on investment of 96 percent.

SGS has done a careful job selecting the functions and tools it needs to get the greatest benefit from its site. Whether it actually gets a 64 percent return the first year depends on how well the implementation is carried out and how well the site is managed.

Key Points

This section provides a quick reference to the key points covered in this chapter. Web-based support is defined as any function accessible via the Internet that provides assistance or information to users of a product or service. The assistance or information provided is geared toward helping users solve problems with the product or service, make the best use of it, or help select the appropriate one.

Table 1.2 Cost-Benefit Analysis for the SGS, Inc., Support Site

		YEAR 1	YEAR 2
One-Time Costs			
Software (Two seats)	$10,000		
Installation and Training	$3,000		
Software Selection	$6,300		
Site Creation	$31,500		
Ongoing Costs			
Software Maintenance (12%)		$1,200	$1,200
Site Maintenance		$21,000	$21,000
Total	$50,800	$22,200	$22,200
Cumulative Costs	**$50,800**	**$73,000**	**$95,200**
Benefits			
Support Calls		$18,000	$18,000
Onsite Calls Saved		$43,200	$43,200
Publishing		$6,000	$6,000
Put Off Hiring		$52,500	
Total		$119,700	$67,200
Cumulative Benefits		**$119,700**	**$186,900**
Return On Investment		64%	96%

Support sites can be categorized into three generations of evolution. First-generation support sites, called *informational sites,* are those that provide library-type support functions. Customers take information from the site, while it collects little or no information from the customer. Second-generation sites are conversational. They enable customers to initiate and carry on some form of online conversation with the technology available at the site or with a support representative. Third-generation sites are decisional. They use software that integrates several tools into a support engine that has the intelligence to invoke specific functions based on customer activity.

The benefits associated with support sites come from several sources. The self-service aspect of Web-based support generates a reduction in calls to the support area and enables organizations to provide expanded support functions 24 hours a day, seven days a week. Internet-initiated requests allow better control over scheduling.

The remote access and control aspect of Web-based support means that the site can become the central source of support for an organization that is spread out across countries or continents, reducing the costs associated with having support staff at each location.

The single-source aspect of Web-based support enables organizations to provide a current source for any documents that customers can download. Publishing costs and the costs associated with problems caused by out-of-date information are reduced or eliminated.

The information sharing enabled by a support site means that customers can exchange information on implementation, specific problems, the integration of products, and so on. Customers can then make better use of an organization's products and will experience reduced down time.

Assisted support provided by a site encourages customers to search for solutions on their own, asking for help when they can go no further. Thus, the support person who gets a call from such a customer is dealing with a customer who is at least somewhat knowledgeable about the problem.

When you are creating and managing a Web-based support site, you can get into trouble if any of the following are true: Your site does not cater to your customers' requirements; you don't have processes in place to keep information up to date, handle customer communications in a timely fashion, and manage the site; your staff does not have the required skills; you select tools too quickly; you don't market your site.

Factors that determine how much return you get on your investment of setting up or improving your support site fall into three categories: management, functions and tools. Each of these categories has a significant impact on the return a site earns and when problems occur in any of the categories, the site will not realize its return potential and could even generate significant losses for the parent organization.

As with any system implementation, when you put together a project to create or improve a Web-based support site, you will have both one-time and ongoing costs to consider. Your one-time development costs will include Web hosting, domain name registration, and Internet access, if these aren't already in place. These one-time costs also include the time and resources dedicated towards gathering requirements; determining the scope; selecting the support tools; and gathering, formatting, and loading the data for your site. Your ongoing costs will include the time and resources involved in keeping data up to date, managing the site, supporting any customer-initiated communication, extending support contracts for the support tools purchased, and the administration and maintenance costs involved in maintaining your Internet connection, hardware, and software.

PART TWO

Initiating Web-Based Support

CHAPTER 2

A Map for Site Creation and Management

C reating a Web-based support site is a project and needs to be managed as a project. As we saw in Chapter 1, "Is Web-Based Support Worthwhile?," we need to work on maximizing the return of the site while avoiding the many potential pitfalls. This is just not possible if we run our project in a haphazard way. In order to put the right functions, management processes, and tools into place to get the return that our cost benefit analysis promised, we need to do some careful planning in order to manage the entire project. The resulting site also needs to be managed as any support area would. Performance measures need to be set, and evaluation and improvement initiatives need to be an ongoing part of the project. The site also needs to be monitored constantly to see how effective customers find it.

The Association of Support Professionals (ASP) has published two publications entitled *The Year's Ten Best Web Support Sites, 1998 Edition* and *The Year's Ten Best Web Support Sites, 1999 Edition* (they can be purchased from their site at www.asponline.com). In these publications, the organizations awarded best Web site statuses and discussed the design, implementation, and management of their sites, including their failures and successes. The following observations kept coming up again and again:

- The process of creating a support site needs to be managed as a project.

- The site needs to be planned carefully with input from customers and any stakeholders within the organization.

- You need to have the people with the right skills developing, maintaining, and managing your support site.

My intention is not to drown you in project management concepts, but to give you a map to follow from the initiation of the support site project through to completion and management. Use the map as a reference or checkpoint as you get your site up and running.

Figure 2.1 shows the processes involved in creating and managing a Web-based support site. This is the map you will use to navigate through the various processes of the project. Each box in the diagram represents a phase of the project. The chapters that describe the work involved in each phase are listed under the boxes.

THE INTERNET-BASED SUPPORT SITE PROJECT

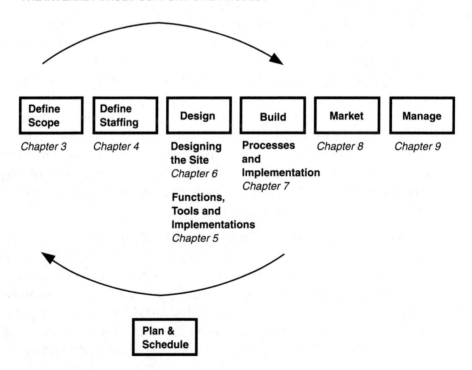

Figure 2.1 A project map.

Table 2.1   The Project Tasks Involved in Defining the Scope

TASKS	DETAILS
Collect requirements.	Identify the site users as well as the business and support stakeholders. Also collect requirements from the business, stakeholders. Also collect requirements from the business, support, and site users.
Define data sources and processes.	For each requirement, research the data sources and define how the required information is put together.
Create a scope summary.	Create a table summarizing the requirements, sources, information required, and possible implementations. Then apply the budgetary considerations to this table.

Planning and scheduling activities start at the beginning of the project and continue until the site has been built. Plans and schedules are constantly being updated as decisions are made and details are worked out. These are the activities that control the project and that make sure that it is delivered on time, on budget, and with the agreed-upon scope in place. Planning and scheduling should not be a phase. They are controlling activities that should be carried out throughout the life of a project.

The first phase in the support site project is outlining the scope, covered in Chapter 3, "Establishing Scope." This involves defining what the site must deliver and what must be included in the support site project. The tasks involved in defining the scope are shown in Table 2.1. The scope summary, which is the deliverable of this phase, will help you plan the work required in the rest of the project.

Once you have an idea of the work involved in the project, your thoughts must turn to staffing. You need to decide what skills you need and where you can get them. Chapter 4, "Staff Selection," looks at the work involved around building, managing, and maintaining a support site and the skills required to perform this work. It may make sense for you to outsource work that requires skills that available employees do not have. Chapter 4 deals with this topic as well. Table 2.2 shows the project tasks involved in selecting staff.

At the end of the Determine Staffing phase, you should have work, positions, responsibilities, and hiring specifications defined for the creation, management, and maintenance of your support site. You are ready to start acquiring staff.

Table 2.2   The Project Tasks Involved in Selecting Staff

TASKS	DETAILS
Determine staffing requirements.	Based on the scope summary and the required work in the project, determine the skills and numbers required.
Define responsibilities.	Define the responsibilities for each position.
Create hiring specifications.	Create a list of required skills to test potential employees.
Hire or outsource.	Carry out the resource acquisition process.

In the third phase of your project, the design work is carried out. The format of the site is designed and functions, tools, and implementations are selected. The site design process must use the scope summary, created in the first phase of the project, to drive the design. The output from the design phase of the project includes a series of site prototypes and a decision on which tools should be used. Chapter 5, "Functions, Tools, and Implementations," can assist you in the site design process, which is covered in Chapter 6, "Designing the Site." Tasks in the site design phase are shown in Table 2.3.

Once the site has been designed with tools, functions, and implementations, the build phase can be initiated. This involves defining processes around managing and maintaining the site, actually creating the site, and putting the final product into place. Table 2.4 displays the tasks

Table 2.3   The Project Tasks Involved in Site Design

TASKS	DETAILS
Find out which factors are constraining the site design.	Identify the human, monetary, and technological factors constraining the design decisions. Also define the affect of the constraints on design.
Select site functions.	Use the requirements and suggested implementations to select and design the site functions.
Create site prototypes.	Using information from the previous two tasks, create the initial site layouts and the navigation strategy. Also get feedback from all stakeholders and revise until an agreement is reached.
Research and select tools.	Work with analysts and developers to research the tools required to satisfy the functions selected. Then integrate the tools into this site.

Table 2.4 The Project Tasks Involved in the Build Phase

TASKS	DETAILS
Identify the required processes.	Outline the processes required for the site along with info maintenance, customer communication, and specific site functions.
Define each process.	Assign responsibilities for each process to a specific position. Also define and document (or automate) each process.
Create an implementation and testing checklist.	Create a list of tasks involved in completing the site. Also create test criteria and test plans.
Establish the initial site support team and procedures.	Assign a team to support the site in its early stages. Then create backup plans for identified risks.
Implement the site.	Carry out the implementation and testing. Make the site available to customers.

involved in this phase. Chapter 7, "Processes and Implementation," describes these in detail.

At the end of the build phase, you should have a site that is up and running and being monitored very closely. For the next month or two, you will monitor and make adjustments to the site.

Following its implementation, the site should then be marketed and managed. The marketing of your site can be matched to its implementation. You may want to hold off on running a full campaign until you make sure that your new site can handle the traffic such a campaign might generate. Chapter 8, "Marketing," discusses how to market your site in its initial stages and on a day-to-day basis. Effective marketing is marketing that is planned, measured, and adjusted on an ongoing basis. You need to constantly be looking for new, more effective ways to promote your support site in order to attract your target market. The more customers use your site, the higher the potential payback. Table 2.5 shows the tasks involved in the marketing cycle.

Once the site is up and running, it needs to be managed with processes in place for ongoing evaluations and improvements. Performance measurements need to be set up so that you can see how the site is performing from both an organizational perspective as well as from the customer's viewpoint. Table 2.6 outlines the tasks of establishing a site

Table 2.5 The Project Tasks Involved in the Marketing Cycle

CYCLE OF TASKS	DETAILS
Identify or reclassify your customer segments.	Divide your customers into segments that make sense for your product. These are customers that are using your site or that could use it in the future.
Create or update your marketing plan.	Decide what you want to accomplish through marketing. For each goal, define your target audience, activities, schedule, and how the initiative is to be measured.
Carry out activities and gather data.	Carry out each activity and gather the resulting data.
Measure effectiveness.	Analyze the results of marketing activities to see which were successful.
Determine the required adjustments.	Identify which adjustments should be made to your customer segmentation, your marketing activities, or your site. Then start again.

management process. Chapter 9, "Site Management," discusses how to effectively manage a support site.

In building, maintaining, and managing your site, you may encounter a number of problems. Chapter 10, "Problem Prevention and Troubleshooting," can help you resolve these or avoid them completely. The chapter examines the causes, symptoms, effects, and preventative measures for a number of common problems. Taking a careful look through the material in Chapter 10 can keep you and your support site on track and out of trouble.

Table 2.6 The Project Tasks Involved in Establishing the Site Management Processes

TASKS	DETAILS
Define the performance functions.	Define the site objectives, service levels, and the most critical measures. Then determine all the components of site performance.
Set up the site-monitoring processes.	Decide which statistics or processes need to be monitored, how frequently, and who should monitor them.
Set up the evaluation processes.	Create forums for evaluating the ongoing performance and decide who should participate.
Set up the improvement processes.	Take the the evaluation results and create site improvements.

Key Points

This section contains the key points covered in this chapter's description of a support site creation and management project.

In order for your support site to be successful, its creation and management must be carefully planned through a series of phases. The first phase is to establish the scope by defining what the site must deliver. The second phase involves defining which skills are needed to create the site and how to find them. The third phase is design. Here the format of the site is designed, and the functions, tools, and implementations are selected. The fourth phase is the build phase in which decisions are made regarding managing and maintaining the site. At this stage, the site is also created and put into operation.

Once the site is built, it needs to be marketed in a planned fashion on a day-to-day basis to ensure that the traffic required to get the planned return on investment actually materializes. The site also needs to be managed effectively. Management processes need to be defined and put into action so that the site's performance can be evaluated and any possible improvements can begin.

CHAPTER 3

Establishing Scope

In Chapter 1, "Is Web-Based Support Worthwhile?," we were introduced to the three factors involved in maximizing the return of a Web-based support site: management, functions, and tools. In Figure 1.5, we saw how important the function factor is. If functions are implemented poorly on a site, the site cannot generate any return, regardless of how good the management or tools are. In this chapter, we will examine how to select the functions that will generate the best return for your specific site. We will also cover the topic of establishing your site's scope.

This chapter will initially focus on the tasks involved in defining a site's scope. We will then specifically discuss the following topics:

- Collecting requirements
- Defining data sources and processes
- Scope summary

Tasks Involved in Establishing Scope

Scope definition is the first phase of a project to build or improve a Web-based support site. Table 3.1 shows the tasks that need to be performed in this phase of the project. The tasks in your list may be more specific to reflect the particular requirements collected.

In the Collect Requirements task, you must first identify everyone who has an interest in or is affected by the new or upgraded support site. You must also ensure that you obtain input from the business, support organizations, and from the people who will use the site. You'll have to take some time to decide how to receive this input. Once you identify key business and support stakeholders, you can simply talk to them, but getting input from the site users is more challenging. You want to be careful to get requirements without setting unreasonable expectations.

The second task of defining the scope is determining which information and processes are needed to satisfy the requirements identified in the first task. For each requirement, you need to research all of the potential data sources and then decide how you will transform that data to meet the requirement. For example, if the data source is a call-tracking database, you need to define how you will select data from the database. You may only be interested in the problems or requests that account for the highest number of calls.

The third task in creating the scope is summarizing. For each requirement, you will list which data or processes are required and which potential implementations you might want to consider. In addition, you

Table 3.1 The Project Tasks Involved in Defining the Scope

TASKS	DETAILS
Collect requirements.	Identify the site users as well as the business and support stakeholders. Also collect requirements from the business, support, and site users.
Define data sources and processes.	For each requirement, research the data sources and define how the required information is put together.
Create a scope summary.	Create a table summarizing the requirements, sources, information required, and possible implementations. Then apply the budgetary considerations to this table.

can weed out options that are too expensive for your budget. Thus, your scope summary defines the size of your project in terms of work, content, and costs.

Collecting Requirements

You're at the very beginning of your Web-based support site project. You need to select the information and functions that you will offer on your site, but you have some work to do before you can make these decisions. As Figure 3.1 shows, you need to start by getting input from the people who have a stake in the site: people in the business, support people, and site users. The following questions need to be answered:

What do you want this site to accomplish for the business and for the support organization?

Who are the intended users of this site and what do they need?

The answers to these questions, tempered by budget, will determine the initial scope of your Web-based support site. Once you have the

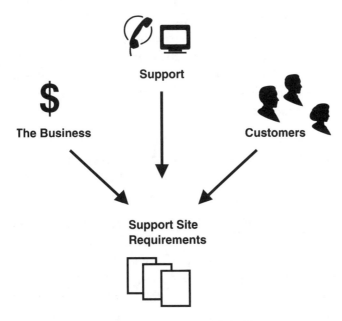

Figure 3.1 Getting input from site stakeholders.

answers, you can research which data, processes, and functions are
needed to meet the requirements.

What Do You Want This Site to Accomplish?

The answer to the question, "What do you want this site to accomplish?" is the key driver in your Web-based support site project. Everything that follows hinges on this answer and everything that eventually makes its way to the site should be part of the answer. When you ask this question, you are really asking it of two areas: the business and support. If you are a small company, these areas might be the same. If you are a large company, these areas won't necessarily be the same and each area may answer the question in a very different way.

What Does the Business Want?

Your support site is being built to furnish support for the products and services provided by a specific organization. The organization might be a for-profit business, a government office, or a non-profit agency. It might support external customers, internal customers who would typically be employees of the organization, or both. Site requirements would vary for each of these cases. In order to determine what these requirements are, you need to identify and contact the appropriate people in the organization. Before you contact them, you might want to put together an inventory of what a Web-based support site could offer. This may help them with their answers.

What do organizations typically expect from an Internet based support site? They may want it to enhance their image, promote products and services, generate revenue, reduce costs, save employee time, or, in the case of smaller organizations, provide sole source support.

A business with a professional, useful support site is a business that looks like it has its act together and will attract customers. Customers feel more confident buying from such a company. Many examples of organizations doing a great job of supporting products and services can be found on the Internet. I'll give you a few examples that you might want to look at. Go to the technical support option of www.rational.com, which contains everything from product-specific technical notes to knowledge bases and online user groups. You might also want to visit www.lucasarts.com and www.corel.com. The products and services that each of these sites support are quite different, as are the support sites themselves, but all of the sites portray very professional and capable organizations.

You can also find many examples of very shoddy support sites—I'll leave you to find your own—that do nothing good for the organizations that own them. Some of the worst support sites are those that display a "Site under construction" message when you try to access them, which makes one wonder if the product or service being supported is also still under construction.

Support sites are a good place to promote products and services. When customers are choosing which product they need help with, they can be shown new, related products that might be appropriate for them. Support sites are typically navigated according to the user's search for a product or service, so at any point on the site, you know what the customers who have reached that point are looking for. This knowledge enables you to advertise a product or service that would appeal to those customers. For example, if customers have asked to access support on Drawing Package 1.0, the support page for that software would be an excellent place to advertise Drawing Package 2.0 or an add-on to Drawing Package. A support site for technology products and services offers great opportunities for target marketing.

Going one step further, organizations might want to use the support site to sell products or services. The support site might sell upgrades and related software, or services such as installation, consulting, or fee-based support. You'll see an example of this in the support option of www.corel.com. Be very careful when adding other functions. If your site becomes too cluttered or complicated, it may defeat your efforts to provide excellent online support. Don't forget that many customers want to quickly find solutions to their problems. The last thing you want is customers calling in because they found the site navigation to be troublesome.

A reduction in costs is almost guaranteed to be on the list of requirements you get from your organization. However, you will need some details about which areas will generate the reductions. Support sites can lead to cost reductions in several areas, the most significant of which is staffing. The site may offload enough calls from an overworked Help Desk to enable traffic to return to manageable levels, making additional hires unnecessary. The site may also eliminate the need for a remote support organization, or it may reduce or eliminate off-hours staffing. Another area for potential cost reductions is in publishing. The site can eliminate or drastically reduce the costs involved with hard-copy publishing and transporting materials such as manuals, CDs, and product brochures.

Web-based support sites serving internal employees can go far in reducing the down time of those employees. Employees can access the site to get answers to commonly asked questions or to perform tasks such as password resets. The site can be set up to provide business-specific information about the best use of technology.

If an organization is very small or if support requirements are minimal, then having staff dedicated to the support function may not make much sense. Smaller organizations may look to the Web-based support site to be the sole source of support for products or services. The information and functions offered would have to be selected carefully in order to satisfy most customer support requirements, and some communication medium, email at the minimum, would have to be provided.

What Does the Support Organization Want?

The answer that support organizations most often give to the question, "What do you want from this Web-based support site?" is "We want to offload calls from our Help Desk!" Help Desks struggle constantly with the situation of too many calls, too many projects, and too few employees. Offloading calls could mean many things and result in a variety of support site offerings, so you must gather specific information about what the support area wants to offload. Does it want to free staff up from the monotonous task of answering frequent, easy-to-satisfy queries or requests such as password resets or simple questions? Does it want more than this?

Other requirements for a support site might include the following:

- The online logging of problems, requests, and questions
- After-hours support
- Full-support for remote customers
- Training options that customers would actually use
- Software downloads, online forms, and documentation

- Resource and link lists to help customers do their own research
- The replacement of initial levels of support such as call screening or short responses

In offloading calls, the biggest win from the point of view of cost, staff morale, and employee satisfaction typically comes from automating frequently requested functions or providing FAQs for common questions. Automation and online functions tend to be more cost-effective than having the same tasks performed by humans. Support practitioners will appreciate being freed from the mundane task of answering the same questions over and over and carrying out the same simple process again and again. They can focus on more complex and interesting issues, which is a much better use of their time from the point of view of the organization paying them. Customers, once they get used to the technology, are very happy to find what they want at the support site quickly without any phone calls or waiting. A support site also tends to be anonymous, which some timid customers who are embarrassed by their lack of knowledge might appreciate.

Non-telephone-based options for problem logging, questions, and requests take the heat off of Help Desk staff. Work generated by emails and support logs can be planned and carried out offline, unlike the instant service that a phone call demands. Staffing levels can then be projected and scheduled more accurately.

Support organizations may want to use the support site to provide unattended off-hours support. They would want the site to satisfy most off-hours support requirements with an emergency option, such as a page for issues that cannot wait until the start of the next business day.

Developing both self-support and assisted support for remote offices might be another requirement of a support organization. To satisfy this requirement, the Web-based support site must offer functions that not only enable customers to solve problems and perform various tasks for themselves, but allow remote support practitioners to step into the problem-solving process when necessary as if they were there in person.

Some support organizations might look to the Web-based support site to provide customers with the means to take effective training whenever their schedule permitted. Training could be as simple as very targeted documents and graphics, or it could be full multimedia. The content and audience would have to be considered carefully, however, before investing either time or money in acquiring or building the training materials. Yet the more successful the training, the fewer calls to the Help Desk.

Publishing hard-copy documentation, forms, and software is not only costly in terms of materials and shipping, but also in terms of effort. Administrating these processes is also overwhelming. Fortunately, the requirements for publishing material on the support site are relatively easy to satisfy. Documents can be either viewed online or downloaded for viewing later, and software can be selected and downloaded. The complexity would vary, depending on the formats and safeguards required.

Customers will often call a Help Desk to request information that they could get on their own if they knew it was available. Support organizations that have such customers may set up a Web-based support site to channel these customers to the appropriate resources. A set of links categorized by subject might be an appropriate implementation. Subjects would have to be determined by customer demand.

Some support organizations have levels of support that screen calls or provide support for problems or requests that can be resolved easily and quickly. More complex requests are sent to a second level of support. These organizations may want a support site to replace these processes. The support site would guide the customer through the problem resolution process until a certain threshold was reached, perhaps based on time, the number of searches, or the specific positions in a knowledge base. At that point, the site would offer the customer the option of connecting to a support representative or it would connect the user automatically. The support staff then would only get those calls that could not be resolved by the support site. Implementating such a function could take several forms, depending on how much money the budget allows. Communication could be implemented via chat software, teleconferencing, or by phone.

Who Are the Intended Users of the Site?

Who will use your support site: internal customers, external customers, or both? If you manufacture hardware or software, will resellers and systems integrators be using your site along with end users? Will your customers be beginner-level users, sophisticated users, or both? Will customers be paying or will they be getting support for free? You need to know who your site users are before you can research what they want. Each group of users may have very different requirements.

Specialized site users such as resellers or system integrators will need information to help them sell, install, and configure your product. They will also current need information about any and all patches, problems, solutions, and cautions involved with using your product. They will want to know all planned product activities such as upgrades, beta releases, beta testing, and new product developments. It may make sense for these users to have a separate site with secure login access. You do not want end users to have access to all this information.

Customers who are paying for support will have very specific requirements that will typically be defined in a contract or service-level agreement. The services to be provided and the response times to be met are part of this agreement. Customers will also require some kind of secure sign-in procedures. The services provided may include downloads of full upgrades (perhaps as part of a maintenance package), higher priorities for interactive support sessions with support representatives, and so on. Paid support is often initiated from a support site by clicking a button that brings up a paid support login screen.

Internal customers will require support specific to your organization. They might need access to internal policies, procedures, information, and software, and their problem domain is very different from that of your external customers. Problems internal customers have are typically generated by systems they use to do their day-to-day work, while problems external customers experience are those encountered by using the product or service your organization produces or provides. Separate support sites may be in order, and the support site for your internal customers will probably be situated on your Intranet.

What Do the Site Users Want?

Based on the different profiles that your site users might have, their requirements may include some or all of the following:

- Fast responses to email or other forms of online communication
- Problem-resolution capabilities

- Interaction with a support representative via the Internet
- Access to emergency services
- Notifications of new product information
- Access to current documentation or technical information
- The capability to download upgrades or patches
- Links to more information, discussion groups, or user groups
- High security
- Access to all site functions all the time
- The delivery of everything that is promised
- Current information and updates

Site users do not send email messages to the site thinking, "well, it may take the people a week to reply, but that's okay." They send messages to the site expecting a prompt response. You have to determine what *prompt* means for your specific users, decide on the response time you can actually manage, and change your customers' definition of prompt to be just that. You need to analyze which response time works best for you and your customers and then market it on the site. An example would be, "Contact Us—All Email Messages Will Be Responded to Within 24 Hours."

Not surprisingly, site users want to be able to go to your site to get their problems solved. But this could mean many things depending on who your site users are. FAQs might satisfy the requirements of users that have procedural questions, typically internal users. Users with more complex problems or a wider range of potential problems will have different requirements. They will want searches, access to one or more knowledge bases, perhaps even diagnostic tools, and they may want to know where they can go for further information. As a user, it is very frustrating to go to a Web-based support site and see only simple FAQs that do not begin to answer the more complex problem you have. On the other hand, an unsophisticated user who finds a support site full of acronyms and technical terms will quickly abandon online help and pick up the phone.

Some site users, such as those paying for support or those in remote locations, may require assisted support. They may want the ability to have a support representative intervene when they cannot resolve the problem on their own. Paying customers may want immediate online access to a support representative or at least the highest priority. They will expect to get the terms that the service agreement promised.

If a Web-based support site is to be your sole support for customers, then customers will want some kind of emergency support or some way of getting immediate help. You could provide this by setting up some kind of page initiation function. The function could include a chat or message component to enable customers to fill in a short description of the problem, which would be sent to the service representative along with the page.

External customers for organizations manufacturing hardware or software as well as integrators and resellers will want information about new products as soon as that information is available. Integrators and resellers will want to sell it, and it may meet demands or outstanding requirements that their customers have. External customers may be waiting for it to satisfy an outstanding requirement or provided needed functionality.

Internal customers may have a requirement for documents that provide them with procedures on how to perform specific functions, such as ordering equipment upgrades, or they may want to be able to view procedural business documents. External customers will want to see all documentation, technical specifications, service packs, and so on. Integrators may need procedural documents, such as what analyses they must go through with their customers to have a successful installation.

Site users also count on support sites to be able to provide downloads, software patches, fixes, and so on. They don't want to have to wait for CDs in the mail. Paying customers will want the ability to download upgrades as soon as they are available, as will system resellers and integrators who will want to be notified of any new bugs or problems as soon as they are discovered in the software.

Internal or external customers of your products and services, and perhaps even systems integrators or resellers, may want to use the site as a springboard to other sites or discussion groups that teach, host discussions, and provide relevant information. Customers, system integrators, and resellers might all want the ability to join online groups to talk to others who are using, selling, or installing your products or services.

Site users who are interacting with your site and disclosing sensitive information, such as resellers or system integrators, may have to disclose issues involving their customers and how they do business. These site users have a requirement for high security, and that security must be included in the scope of your Web-based support site project.

All site users want your site to be constantly available. This means any planned site maintenance needs to be carefully scheduled and done in such a way as to cause minimum disruptions. Any time someone cannot find your site, you could be losing a potential customer or tarnishing your organization's image.

All site users also want your site to deliver what was promised. None of your planned site benefits can be realized if you do not keep promises you make on your site (unless one of them involves irritating customers). This means all buttons should work. All links should exist. All data should be current. Email should be answered on time, and calls that are logged via online logging functions should be handled within the promised time.

All site users demand current information. They want to know about any significant upcoming events, such as service outages, conferences, and user group meetings. They want to know about new product releases and they want all of the information on your site to be up to date. They also want to be able to send questions via email and get a response back in a reasonable time and certainly within the advertised time.

Lastly, all site users want information tailored to their needs and presented in a language they understand. Sophisticated users want to get right to the meat of the matter and don't want to waste time navigating through a lot of introductory material, while general users appreciate FAQs that are clearly presented without unfamiliar technical terms and acronyms.

Merging and Prioritizing Requirements

Once you have gathered requirements from the business, the support organization, and potential site users, you need to analyze the requirements as a whole and prioritize them. You will identify any potential conflicts in the requirements and analyze ways to resolve them. You

Table 3.2 The Requirements Table for Education Plus

PRIORITY	SOURCE	REQUIREMENT
Mandatory	Business/support	Provide all customer support requirements.
Mandatory		Promote professional image.
		Market new products.
		Attract new business.
Mandatory	Customers	Quick responses to email.
Mandatory		Download copies of courses.
Mandatory		High security.
		Request and track course changes online.

will identify duplicate requirements and merge them, ensuring that they really are duplicates and no functionality is lost in the merging.

Putting the requirements information in a table such as Table 3.2 or 3.3 will help you see the overall picture and help you start your analysis. The examples that follow will give you an idea of how this process occurs.

Example 1: Education Plus

Education Plus is a fictitious business that provides pre-built online training packages. Education Plus develops custom training packages and then distributes them to customer organizations electronically. The

Table 3.3 Requirements Table for Trace Software

PRIORITY	SOURCE	REQUIREMENT
	Business	Reflect new international image.
		Promote international business.
Mandatory		Remote support for European office.
		Eliminate necessity for hiring.
Mandatory	Support	Offload support.
		Customer training.
		Online problem logging.
Mandatory	Customers	Emergency support.
Mandatory		Improved email support.

business recognizes that it needs to provide some kind of formal support but does not want to staff a support line. It wants all support to be provided by a Web-based support site. A requirements gathering process is initiated by Johnston Reeves, one of the four Education Plus employees. Johnston polls colleagues and customers for input into what the support site should contain.

Since only four people compose Education Plus, the business and support organizations are the one and the same. Education Plus' goal is for the support site to provide all the customer support requirements. They are willing to answer email but hope that there is not too much. They want the site to promote the professionalism and quality of Education Plus, to market new services, and to attract new business. They also want the site to provide some way of gathering information from customers to help improve the training products and expand the course offerings.

It has been determined that Education Plus customers, who are the future support site users, do not mind accessing support online. In fact, they appreciate the 24-hour access, but they want assurance that the support site will quickly respond to email quickly. They want to be able to download copies of their particular courses in the event that their own copies are corrupted or if backups are unavailable at a particular location. The customers want to be able to request changes online, and they want to be able to track the changes' progress. They also want to be sure that other organizations cannot look at the courses that were designed specifically for them.

The prioritized requirement table for Education Plus can be seen in Table 3.2. The requirements that constitute the absolute minimum basis for a site have been marked as mandatory. A site that does not meet at least these mandatory requirements is not worth accessing. All other requirements are considered more or less equal.

One potential conflict exists in Table 3.2. Education Plus may have underestimated how important email is to customers. A support site that collects input from customers still needs to have a human support component behind it. Education Plus is hoping for minimal email use and its support is casual. Customers want formal, timely support, however, which will not happen unless processes are in place. The people at Education Plus must be willing to invest time and money into formalized email processes.

As part of planning the support site, Johnston Reeves must answer the following questions: How much time will email handling take? How will the responsibility be shared among the four employees? What email volumes might be expected now and in the coming months? Is a part-time support representative needed?

Customers have indicated that quick responses to email are mandatory, so these questions must be answered before Education Plus goes any further in its site creation.

Example 2: Trace Software

Trace Software is a fictitious company that manufactures virus and Internet security software for homes and businesses on both single PC and network platforms. The company currently has a Web-based support site but feels the site no longer meets its needs. Trace Software nominated the head of the support organization, Jesse Kim, to carry out the task of creating a new site. Jesse talked to Trace Software management and to people within the support organization to come up with a list of requirements.

Management wants the support site to reflect Trace Software's new international image, since the business recently opened an office in Europe. Management wants the support site to promote international business and to provide support for the Trace Software employees stationed in the European office. The European staff needs the same level of support as the staff in North American. Management also wants the site to provide expanded support offerings and traffic-handling capabilities to eliminate the need for additional hiring of support staff. Competition is rampant; new players in the security software market are being introduced almost on a daily basis, and the company wants to keep its money in product development and target marketing.

Jesse's support organization has its own requirements as well. Jesse wants to offload as much support traffic as possible to the new Web-based support site. The current Trace Software support site offers online documentation, a simple, searchable knowledge base, a FAQ organized by software products, and an online customer meeting room made up of a discussion group, a chat function, links, downloads, and a message board updated by a volunteer customer. Jesse wants to expand the information available on the site, specifically the FAQs and knowledge bases, to increase the site resolution rate. The support site is currently diverting about 30 percent of calls from telephone support. Jesse wants to increase this to at least 50 percent, yet she realizes this might necessitate purchasing a more intelligent knowledge base or some kind of diagnostic problem resolution tool.

Jesse also wants to provide customers with training in Internet security concepts and basic networking. Since Trace Software caters both to larger organizations and home businesses, a growing number of Trace users are home-based and somewhat non-technical. Simple instructions would go a long way toward making these users more comfortable with installing and using the software and less apt to call for support.

The people working out of the remote office need full support during their working day and emergency support outside of regular working hours. The time difference between the locations makes this a challenge. Jesse is looking to the support site to bridge the gap by providing all the required support when the North American office is closed for the day.

Jesse wants customers to be able to log and track problems online via the Web-based support site. This will allow for improved planning and scheduling of support work and staff. Logs that are not urgent can be scheduled into the working day.

Trace Software customers have some input for the new site. They tell Jesse that they will only increase their use of the new support site if they get faster responses to their emails. They currently have to wait almost three days for a response and often they do not wait; they phone instead. They also want some kind of after-hours emergency support. They point out to Jesse that although Trace Software telephone support shuts down at 7:00 P.M., their businesses do not.

Table 3.3 summarizes the requirements that Jesse has collected and prioritized. She only marked as mandatory those things that would make the support site fail. She will prioritize everything else once she has a better understanding of which data, processes, and costs are involved with each requirement.

A potential conflict Jesse has to keep an eye on lies between the customers' demand for improved email support and off-hours support versus Jesse's wish to push more functions on to the Web. If she isn't careful, the customers might feel like they are being pushed out onto the Web without support and they will react by increasing their use of telephone support.

Defining Data Sources and Processes

When you have completed your requirements table, merged duplicates, and analyzed potential conflicts, you are ready to move on to the next step in establishing the scope of your Web-based support site. You need to define the data and processes you will need to implement each requirement in your table. This information will help you determine how much work is involved in each requirement and help you start identifying possible implementations for each requirement. Figure 3.2 illustrates this process.

Table 3.4 contains the key requirements we have talked about so far in one form or another. Let's navigate through this table identifying the data sources and processes that might be involved in each of the requirements.

Call Reduction

We'll start with the requirement to reduce telephone calls to the Help Desk. In order to meet this requirement, you need to understand your call profile. You also need to look at data from your call tracking software. It will tell you which problems or requests are generating the

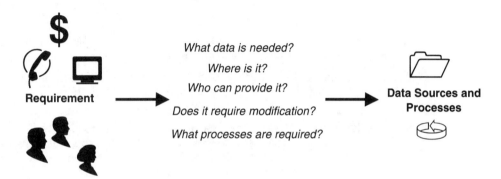

Figure 3.2 Defining data sources and processes.

Table 3.4 Defining Data Sources and Processes

REQUIREMENT	DATA AND PROCESSING REQUIRED
Reduce calls to other support areas	Analyze call information to determine sources of the highest percentage of calls. Also identify resolutions to the problems and define the processes to be automated.
Self-service problem resolution	Here you will define the scope of customers' problems, investigate solutions, identify the data conversion or translation required, and define the process required to keep the solution data up to date.
Self-service problem logging	Analyze problem-response capabilities, investigate the Web capabilities of current tools and any necessary conversions, and research alternate tools and required conversions.
Replace initial level(s) of support	Analyze the call data to define all calls handled by the initial level being replaced, determine which data is required to resolve problems and carry out processes, and determine where assisted support should be suggested.
Assisted support	See "Replace initial level(s) of support."
Respond quickly to customer-initiated options	Determine the response times that can be met, analyze the content communicationof email traffic and the data required for resolution, and determine the email traffic that can be diverted to self-service.
After-hours support	See "Sole support."
Remote support	See "Replace initial level(s) of support and sole support."
Sole support	Analyze call data and get customer input to determine which information and functions must be covered, estimate volumes and set up contingency plans for excessive volumes, and provide emergency support options (see "Emergency support").
Emergency support	Define what constitutes an emergency and set up staffing and processes to handle emergencies; then market it to customers. Also monitor the emergency services to determine what resolutions can be moved to self-support and to identify abuse.
Security	Analyze customer profiles, customer input, and call data to identify the need for increased security.
Self-service training	Get feedback from customers and analyze call information to determine what training is required. Then put a process in place to keep everything current.
Self-service documents	Analyze call data and customer input to identify what documents to provide and where the source is stored. Set up processes for maintaining the documents and ensure all documents are available and current.

REQUIREMENT	DATA AND PROCESSING REQUIRED
Self-service software download	Analyze call data, customer input, and new product development to decide what downloads to provide and where the source for the download comes from. Set up processes for maintaining the download function to make sure all software is current and that the correct versions are available.
Information sharing	Analyze call data, user profiles, and user input to determine which topics, user groups, or information sharing would be appropriate.
Links to more information	See "Information sharing."
Fee-based support	Analyze call information as well as customer and traffic projections to determine which service levels you could provide for paid support.
Market products and services	Research where marketing information should be placed on the site. Collect information about products and services and put a process in place to keep it current.
Sell products and services	If someone in your organization is providing this function, set up a link to it. If not, create a new project.

highest percentage of calls. These are the calls you will target for elimination. Once you identify these calls, you need to collect resolution data. If this information is in your call database, you need to analyze it to see if it can be used as is, if it needs updating, or if it needs to be converted in some way before it can be used. If you don't have this information in your call database, you must identify the sources of this information. These might be other databases, online sources, or expert colleagues.

If elimination of a call indicates some kind of process automation, such as a password reset, you need to define the steps in the process being automated. If you can't define the process, you can't automate it.

Identifying calls that can be diverted to your Web-based support site is not a one-time process. You need to keep reviewing your call-tracking data to constantly keep on top of the calls that creep up in frequency so that you can get rid of them, channel them to your support site, before they start affecting the performance of your support group.

Self-Service Problem Resolution

If you want customers to be able to solve their own problems by using your Web-based support site, you must offer them enough information to cover their problem domains. First, you must anticipate your customers' possible problems. What types of problems might they experience? Second, you must identify the sources of information that can provide solutions to satisfy the problems. Does your call database have the necessary information? Will you have to modify the information to make it more suitable for less or more sophisticated users? Can you purchase a pre-packaged third-party knowledge base to provide some or all of the information? Do you have to build the information from scratch? Who are the experts who can help you? Who are the laypersons who can help you evaluate the usability of this information for general users? Getting this information may require significant effort. Third, you must analyze the translation or conversion involved in any existing information sources, such as your call database. Finally, you must think about how this information can be kept up to date. Information that cannot be dated becomes useless very quickly.

Self-Service Problem Logging

Customers will only use online problem logging if marketed resolution or response times are met. If no resolution or response times are marketed, then customers will expect instant responses and they are going to be disappointed.

In order to successfully host customer online problem logging, you need to first analyze how quickly you can respond to the logs. You need to estimate the traffic levels and staff time that can be allocated to the logs. If the logs back up and customers get no response, they will start complaining and stop logging. A good idea is to plan for overflow time in case you get more logs than you planned for.

You will also need to do some research on the capabilities of your current call logging tool. Is a Web interface available? If so, is it appropriate for your support site? If no, you have to research what is available. If you need to replace your current call logging tool, you need to determine the conversion work involved.

Replace the Initial Level(s) of Support

The initial levels of support are those that screen calls or provide support for problems or requests that can be resolved easily and quickly. To provide the same service via a support site, you need to first go to your call data to define which calls were handled by these initial levels. Next, you need to research the resolutions to determine where the resolution data is coming from and which conversions or processes are necessary. You then need to think about a process that enables customers to ask for help if they cannot find a resolution, the equivalent of sending a call to the second level of support. If customers simply leave the site and place a call, you have lost valuable problem-solving data that could shorten the resolution time considerably. Ideally, you want to capture information that identifies what the customer has done on the site. You also need to define where in the problem-solving process the customer should be offered help. This could be a threshold based on time, the number of searches, or specific positions in the knowledge base. Finally, you need to decide what form this help might take and consider potential implementations. Resolutions that are offered on your support site will require a process to keep them up-to-date.

Respond Quickly to Customer-Initiated Communication

In order for customers to be satisfied with communication response times such as email, you need to first reach an agreement with your customers on what constitutes a satisfactory response time. Before you start negotiating with your customers, you need to know what response times you can actually meet. This will involve estimating email traffic levels and how many hours it would take to handle those levels. If you come up with a time that is greater than 24 hours, then you need to reconsider the situation. Either you have to add more people to handle the traffic or you need to channel the traffic to other parts of your support site. This means researching reasons for customers sending you communications and then finding resolutions. If you make this an ongoing process, chances are that you won't find yourself in a situation in which you have too much email to handle. And don't settle for 24-hour email response times if you think you can do better. The faster you can reply to a customer, the happier they are with your service (and company) and the less likely they are to pick up the phone when they need help again.

Sole Support

If your Web-based support site is to provide the only source of support for your customers and you have no telephone support, then you must do a thorough job in analyzing call data and determining the problem domain your site will need to cover. It is crucial that you find sources for all the information required to resolve the potential problems. You must also try to anticipate all the possible requests for information, documents, or software and find sources for these as well.

No matter how well you build your site, occasionally customers will need to contact someone. At the least, your support site should provide email support. Depending on the products and customers you support, your sole support site may have to offer some kind of emergency or instant response service. In order to do this effectively, you need to identify what constitutes an emergency and put a support structure into place for it, such as having staff on call to handle emergency pages from your support site.

You may want to charge for extras such as email support and emergency support. This will help cover your costs and will help prevent abuse of these functions.

Emergency Support

If the users of your Web-based support site need occasional emergency support, you first need to define very specifically what constitutes an emergency. You may have to negotiate this with your customers. You must then put the staffing structure and processes in place to handle emergencies and give customers a way of initiating a request for emergency support. Marketing the emergency service to ensure customers understand what it is for and how to invoke it should be part of this process.

Emergency support typically means 24-hour support, so you may have to set up an on-call status for staff if you do not already have one. Once emergency support is in place, you need to monitor it carefully, moving as many resolutions as possible to the self-service portion of your site and addressing any abuse of the emergency service. You may want to consider fee-based emergency support. This will go a long way towards ensuring that only emergencies get through.

Security

The users of your Web-based support site may have varying security requirements. You need to analyze the profile of each user group and associated call data. One example might be systems integrators who, in asking support questions, might divulge confidential information about their clients' business. Another example might be customers asking for help with a product customized for their very competitive business. They would not want other companies to know anything about the customization. Once you understand the security requirement, you can design a security structure for the site.

Self-Service Training

Your call data will go a long way towards defining the kind of training you need for your site. It will tell you what your customers have been calling about and what areas they lack knowledge in. The profiles of your customers will also help you with this information. For example, internal customers may need training in standard desktop software or internal business software, while external customers may need training in using your product. You can conduct customer surveys to determine what kind of training is most desired.

Once you understand which topics should be covered in your training, you need to investigate the possible training sources and implementations. If you decide to create some of the training yourself, you will need to identify the experts who will provide the training information and the support staff who will then develop the training Web site. You will also need to keep the training up to date and look for new training opportunities.

Self-Service Documents

In order to decide which documents you should publish on your support site, you need to analyze all the documents you currently produce to support your products, such as user documentation and technical specifications. You also need to go to your call data and user profiles to see what else your site users might need. For example, internal customers may need access to technology standards documents, technology-ordering procedures, or service-level agreements.

It is also important to research the original sources of all documents, the changes or conversions required, and the implementations. You need to set up processes for ensuring a single source and for updating. If documents need to be created, you need to decide who or what source can provide the content. Quite often, several different sources of the same information exist within an organization. Duplication of online self-service information must be kept to a minimum, as it creates more work when the content is updated. Repetitive material will also frustrate users who are searching through self-service documents.

Self-Service Software Downloads

Software that site users might download should include new releases, patches for known problems, interim releases, plug-ins, or other related software. To decide which software should be available for download, you need to look at call data, customer profiles, and new product development. The business should be involved with this decision and it should also decide on what is free and what should be offered with some kind of fee-based support. Processes should then be set up for adding the software to be downloaded.

Information Sharing

Your call data and your site user profile will tell you which topics your site users need to know more about or which topics they are interested in. These topics would include any areas of interest or Web sites related to the products and services you provide. Once you have an idea of the topics that site users need to know more about, you need to research sources of information for these topics, typically other Web sites.

You may also get relevant sites from your customers. They may have already done your research for you. You can do this by interviewing customers or by encouraging input via your support site.

In the same way, site users should be the ones to decide which forms of information sharing they want to participate in with other site users.

You can collect this data via a page on your support site, from any user groups that may already exist, or by interviewing customers directly. Once you know what your customers want, you can think about various implementations.

Fee-Based Support

Before you embark on fee-based support, you must have an excellent understanding of the service levels you can provide. You need to research call data and estimate the number of potential paying customers and site traffic. Management, the support organization, and possibly customers will decide which functions should be included in the fee-based structure and will design the structure and service-level agreements. You will also need to research how to offer and administer the service.

Market Products and Services

If your Web-based support site needs to market products and services, you need to determine where on your site would be the best place to reach people most interested in your products and services. For example, people accessing support for a specific product version would be the ones most interested in a new upgrade of that software or in some kind of plug-in for it. You also need to collect the information to be marketed and put a process in place to keep it current. Although marketing products and services via the support site can be very effective, don't let this interfere with the primary function of the site. Users are less likely to use online support if too many features reduce the ease of navigation or intuitive *feel* of the site.

Selling Products and Services

If your organization already sells its products and services via a Web site, your support site can do its part in generating sales by simply offering a link to the sales site. You may want to keep track of how many sales are made by people coming from your support site.

If you are setting the sales structure up from scratch, you will need to create a separate project. It is crucial that you research the scope of the sales application, the security implications, the interfaces with other systems, and the technology required. Don't try to lump your online sales project in with your Web-based support site project. They are two very different projects and need to be carried out separately.

No Shortcuts, Please

Earlier in the chapter, Table 3.4 summarized the data that must be looked at and the processes that must be established in order for the various Web-based support site requirements to be put into place. If you have started thinking about taking short cuts, I beg you to stop. Short cuts result in poor support sites. For example, while I was writing this book, I purchased some software from the Web. I could not get it working. I went to the support site, navigated through the knowledge base, read all of the relevant articles, and could not find a resolution to my problem. As a last resort, I took advantage of the email support and sent in my problem. I immediately got an automated reply that stated, "We have received an unexpectedly high volume of support requests, so we will not be answering this email. Please go to our support site for help." The reply also included instructions for specific cases, one of which was "Request Refund," which is what I did.

The Scope Summary

A *scope summary* is an outline of the requirements your support site must meet, the information and processes required, and the potential implementations of the requirements (see Figure 3.3). This summary will help keep your project on track in terms of making sure that you are delivering what is required and that you have a good understanding of the work and costs involved. In the following section, we go back to Education Plus and Trace Software for examples of putting together a scope summary.

Education Plus

As you may recall, Table 3.2 listed the initial requirements Education Plus received from its customers and from the business. The business wants all customer support to be handled through the support site with as little assisted support as possible. Customers are willing to use a

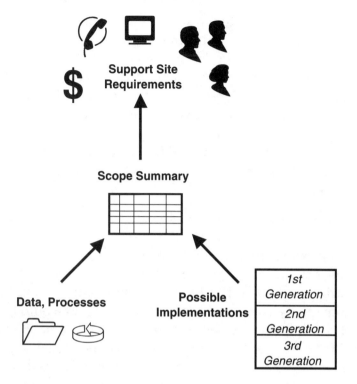

Figure 3.3 A scope summary.

Web-based support site; in fact, they want to log and track their own change requests, but they do want quick response email support. Customers also want a secure way of downloading copies of courses that were designed specifically for them. The business wants the support site to promote products and portray a professional image.

Johnston Reeves, the Education Plus employee responsible for creating the support site, must consider these requirements. Education Plus does not have a call-tracking system. Orders for new courses are treated as contracts and are kept in an online contract folder. Any calls received are recorded for the contract they pertain to. The contract file needs to be analyzed to determine which functions and information must be provided on the Education Plus support site to eliminate the need for those calls.

Education Plus is going to have to purchase some kind of call or product management system with a Web interface. Customer requests and contracts could be stored in the system, which could then be made accessible via the support site. Customers could then enter and track requests themselves. The system could also include security information for courses so that only pre-authorized users could download a course. In fact, the system's sign-on and security procedures could be used to control security for the whole site. Education Plus' customer base is growing quickly, and the current system of using the online contract folder could soon be outgrown. Even if Education Plus had not been in the process of creating a support site, new software would have been required sooner than later.

Johnston also must consider the email issue. Customers are demanding email, but the people at Education Plus are afraid that the volume might necessitate extra staff, something they are not willing to consider right now. Johnston decides that more information is needed on this issue; a pilot project might be just the thing. He would ensure that the support site contained as much self-help as possible and would encourage the use of the online call or order management system. He would monitor email from the site for a month to determine the volume, content, and work involved in responding, and he would then set up a process to ensure that all email is answered within 24 hours. After a month, he would analyze the results, anticipating that with everything the site has to offer, email volumes would not be an issue. If problems occur before the end of the month, perhaps he would have to convince his colleagues to hire temporary help until a permanent resolution is found.

Table 3.5 gives the scope summary for Johnston's support project. Some possible implementations for the self-support requirements are FAQs, a searchable knowledge base, and course downloads. Data for the FAQs and knowledge base could come from the contract folder, could be stored in the call or order management system, and would need to be updated by a designated person as required.

To promote a professional image, Johnston will research other sites and present some examples to his colleagues to get an agreement on what constitutes a professional image. Johnston plans to outsource the work involved in designing the site; no one at Education Plus had the required skills or experience.

Education Plus will market new products at strategic points throughout the site, such as the FAQ. Some research will have to be carried out to

Table 3.5 Scope Summary for Education Plus

PRIORITY	SOURCE	REQUIREMENT	DATA AND PROCESSING REQUIRED	POTENTIAL IMPLEMENTATIONS
Mandatory	Business/ Support	Provide all customer support requirements.	Analyze contract file to determine which information and functions must be covered. Put a process in place to keep data current.	FAQ, searchable knowledge base, and course download.
Mandatory		Promote professional image.	Research other sites to see what look is desired.	Hire site designer.
		Market new products.	Research where marketing information should be placed on the site and who should provide it. Put a process in place to keep it current.	Online ads in locations accessed by current customers.
		Attract new business.	Market new products, plus collect customer testimonials as well as research and create course samples.	Separate the products page with product descriptions, samples, and customer testimonials.
Mandatory	Customers	Quick response to email.	Estimate volumes and determine what response times can be met and what email traffic can be diverted to self-service options. Then create the processes required.	Implement one-month pilot.
Mandatory		Download copies of courses.	Need the process to ensure that only owners of courses get access to them. Also need to store courses on secure server.	Special customer-only function to access course downloads that could be part of call or order management.
Mandatory		High security.	Secure server and enable sign-in procedures.	Sign-in could be part of the call or order management system.
		Request and track course changes online.	Research the available call or order management systems.	Web interface to the call or order management system.

determine exactly where these points are. Johnston wants to target the marketing at customers who would most be interested in the product involved.

New business could be attracted with features such as customer testimonials and perhaps some sample courses. Someone would have to research which courses would be best for this and how much data would have to be changed so that no actual existing customer course is used. A separate page could be devoted to marketing products to new customers.

Johnston now has a good idea of what it will take to meet the requirements and for the Education Plus Web-based support site to be implemented successfully. He knows that a first-generation site, an informational one, will suffice. His budget will dictate how much he can spend on any software he needs, but he knows he must be at least somewhat flexible with this budget. Education Plus is growing and purchasing software that will not accommodate growth but will almost certainly prove to be a false economy.

Trace Software

In Table 3.3, we saw the requirements from staff, support, and the business for Trace Software's improved Web-based support site. We'll now look at how Jesse Kim, who is heading up the site improvement project, will develop a scope summary based on the list of requirements.

Jesse feels that one of the best ways to develop a good international image is to see how other businesses are establishing themselves worldwide. Someone is going to have to do some research on the Web, and the European staff will have to be on the design committee so that they can approve or negate any designs. To attract new business, Trace Software will probably have a product page on the site with product details, customer lists, and downloadable trial versions. One of the products was selected as a best product of 1999 by a technical magazine, and a link to that article could be placed on the product page. Jesse knows she will have to put processes in place to keep the page up to date.

Two of the most critical requirements for the site are to have it provide remote support for the European staff and to offload 50 percent of Help Desk calls. Jesse must find a way to put as much self-support on the Web as possible and give the remote sites assisted service when required. Jesse will have to define, based on current call logs and input from the European staff, the current calls that can be eliminated to reach the 50 percent goal, the calls can be expected from the European staff, and where to get the data to resolve all of them. FAQs must be updated and a process must be put in place to keep the problem-resolution information up to date. A good interactive, knowledge-base tool will most likely be necessary. This tool will have to be integrated with any remote tools the support practitioner will use when supporting the European office. These need to be defined as well. Jesse has a tool in mind that will enable the customer to indicate that help is required and then give the support practitioner control of the customer's PC with a chat function in place to allow the two to communicate. Jesse's support site will probably end up as a second-generation site, a conversational one.

For European customers outside of normal North American business hours, the customer could generate a page and the person on call would use the Internet to access the tools required to support the European location. Remote customers would need a way to sign in so that all the data from their session is collected along with the customer information before they start interacting with the support practitioner. This same process of paging could also be used for emergency support for customers that are registered users of Trace Software products. Jesse must ensure that emergencies are well defined and the boundaries are marketed. She will use the data of the first few months to see if perhaps fee-based emergency support makes sense.

Jesse must consider the requirements of online problem logging and email support together. She needs to do research on a possible Web interface for Trace software's current call-tracking tool as well as make sure all the tools she will need to purchase can work together. She will assign someone to research email content so that as many emails as possible can be eliminated by self-help options. She thinks that the best way to implement email support is to use the Web interface for the call-tracking tool. Instead of sending an email, customers would log calls. Processes and priorities would have to be put into place to ensure that all the calls logged at the site are handled in an appropriate time frame. Perhaps the online call-tracking tool could be used as a method of entry for requests for assisted support or emergencies. The tool's sign in procedure could be used to gather customer information and authorize access. Special problem types or separate functions could be set up specifically for assisted support and emergencies.

Customer training is another requirement that Jesse must address. Potential training topics must be identified. Someone would have to look at the call logs and talk to both the current support staff and the European staff. Once topics are identified, sources of training would have to be researched. Training for Trace Software's own products could be put together simply in the form of documents, or perhaps Jesse could get Education Plus to design some training for them and then post it to a training page on the new support site. The more informed Trace Software's customers are, the fewer calls the Help Desk would get, but Jesse feels it does not make sense for Trace Software to be in the training business. She would look into getting Education Plus to come up with some quotes.

Table 3.6 shows a scope summary for Trace Software's support site project. Jesse now knows what her site will contain and has an idea of the work involved and the tools that must be purchased. She thinks her budget is adequate, but even if it isn't, she believes she has the data necessary to convince management to increase that budget. Jesse's ready to start thinking about the people she needs to do the work and about the design of the site.

Key Points

In this section, you will find a summary of the key steps involved in defining scope.

The first step in defining the scope is to obtain input from the people who have a stake in the site: people in the business, people in support, and site users. You need to answer the questions, "What do you want this site to accomplish for the business and for the support organization?" and "Who are the intended users of this site and what do they need?" The answers to these questions, tempered by budget, will determine the initial requirements the support site must satisfy. Before you go any further, you must prioritize this list, consolidate similar requirements, and resolve any conflicts between requirements.

The second step in defining the scope is to define the data and processes you will need in order to implement each requirement identified in the first step. This information will help you determine how much work is

Table 3.6 Scope Summary for Trace Software

PRIORITY	SOURCE	REQUIREMENT	DATA AND PROCESSING REQUIRED	POTENTIAL IMPLEMENTATIONS
	Business	Reflect new International image.	Research support sites of similar companies.	Create site design committee including international group to ensure acceptance.
		Promote international business.	Research other sites and obtain information from international marketing staff.	A products page including descriptions, customer lists, and trial versions.
Mandatory		Remote support for European office.	Define the issues that the support office will most likely have and the data required to resolve them.	Have assisted support options on top of self-service and provide a support practitioner with adequate remote support tools.
		Eliminate the necessity for hiring.	Accomplished by offloading support.	See Offload support.
Mandatory	Support	Offload support.	Analyze call data to see which calls can be eliminated to reach the 50-percent goal, which data is necessary to eliminate the calls, and where it can be obtained.	FAQs, an interactive knowledge base, and improved processes for updating resolution information.
		Customer training.	Get input from call data and support practitioners to define the required training. Also define the data source.	Have Education Plus develop some training modules to be posted to a training page.
		Online problem logging.	Research Web interfaces for current call-tracking product.	Implement Web interface.
Mandatory	Customers	Emergency support.	Define boundaries around emergency calls: what is an emergency and who can call.	A page can be initiated from the support site.
Mandatory		Improved email support.	Analyze current email content and traffic and decide what can be offloaded.	Have customers use an online call-tracking system for all communication: problems, requests, and questions.

involved in each requirement and will help you start identifying possible implementations for each requirement.

The third step involves consolidating all of the information you gathered in the preceding three steps and considering potential implementations. A scope summary is an outline of the requirements your support site must meet, the information and processes required, and the potential implementations of the requirements. This summary will help keep your project on track in terms of making sure that you are delivering what is required and that you have a good understanding of the work and costs involved. It will help you eliminate less important requirements.

Your scope summary, ideally a table like those in Tables 3.5 and 3.6, is your blueprint for the rest of your project. The scope summary will help you plan and control the rest of the project and select the appropriate staff. It will help ensure the site that you design and build is the site that brings you the highest return on your investment. The scope summary will also help you manage and market your site once it is implemented.

4

Staff Selection

This chapter will discuss the staff you'll need to carry out the work involved in setting up and running your Web-based support site. I will divide the work into categories, discuss the skills required for each category, and present how to use these work-and-skill classifications to determine staffing requirements. I will also talk about defining responsibilities and creating hiring specifications to lessen the impact of turnover and will address the hire versus outsource issue. Throughout the chapter, I will present various examples and templates.

I will start off by presenting a checklist of tasks involved in selecting staff and will continue with discussions of the following topics:

- Categories of work and skills
- Determining staffing requirements
- Defining responsibilities
- Creating hiring specifications
- Hire or outsource?

Tasks Involved in Selecting Staff

Whether you plan to build a new support site or simply want to formalize the process of staffing for your existing site, you will need to execute the series of tasks listed in Table 4.1. These tasks will help ensure that you get the right people to work on your site and that you have a process in place to bring new people on board to handle ongoing turnover, a fact of life in support.

The first task is to determine the staffing requirements. To decide on the people you need, you will use the scope summary for your support site (review Chapter 3, "Establishing Scope," if you've forgotten what this is) as well as the following section, *Categories of Work and Skills.*

The second task is to define the responsibilities for each of the staff so that there is no confusion about who does what and to ensure that all required work is covered.

In the third task, you create hiring specifications: a skill grid and a position specification. The skill grid describes the various skill people involved with the support area, suggests how to test for them, and lists sources of training. The position specification groups together the skills and level of mastery required for each position. You can use these tools to acquire staff for your support site project and to respond to ongoing growth and turnover.

The final task is to actually do the hiring or outsourcing of staff. The section in this chapter entitled *Hire or Outsource?* will help you decide

Table 4.1 The Tasks Involved in Selecting Staff

TASKS	DETAILS
Determine the staffing requirements.	Based on the scope summary and the categories of work and skills involved in the project, determine the skills and numbers required.
Define the responsibilities.	Define the responsibilities for each position.
Create the hiring specifications.	Create a grid of skills, responsibilities, and questions to test for the skills.
Hire or outsource?	Carry out the resource acquisition process.

which tasks, if any, to outsource and which tasks to keep within your organization.

Categories of Work and Skills

As illustrated in Figure 4.1, the work involved in creating and running a Web-based support site can be divided into the following six categories:

- Site analysis
- Site design
- Site development
- Site management
- Site maintenance
- Site support

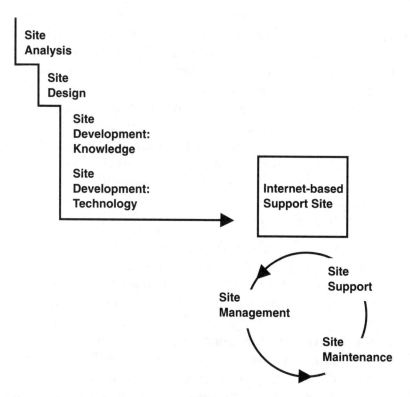

Figure 4.1   Categories of work for Web-based support sites.

This does not mean you will have separate staff to do each type of work. If you are a small organization, you may have one person doing everything. Alternatively, you might have one or two people doing site analysis, design, and development and another one or two people performing site management, maintenance, and support. You may choose to assign one person to do site analysis, outsource site design and development, and then have someone else do site management, maintenance, and support. The combinations are endless and the work split is not the most important issue. What is most important is to understand the work involved in each category and the skills that are required to perform the work. As long as you have those skills covered, you can allocate staff in any number of ways and still get the required work done satisfactorily. In this section, I will cover the tasks and skills involved in each category of work.

Site Analysis

Analyzing a site or a potential site involves developing the scope and investigating the data sources. The tasks initiated during site analysis include gathering requirements from all stakeholders, typically management, the support organization, and customers, and then determining which requirements are most important. The site analysis also involves investigating sources of data for the requirements and determining the work involved to transform the data into a usable format. The site analyst also typically looks at potential implementations for the requirements to determine rough cost estimates. Non-essential requirements that are too costly can be eliminated from the scope, and any budget increases needed for essential requirements can be initiated. The work involved in creating the scope summary described in Chapter 3 falls into the site analysis category.

The person playing the role of site analyst requires a good grounding in analytical skills. The site analyst must understand how the organization works and where it is headed. A person in the site analyst role will talk to management, support staff, and customers and needs to understand what questions to ask and how to ask them. As well as a good understanding of the organization, good interviewing skills are essential, as are good communication skills. The site analyst will write documents, verify facts, and collect approvals. Poor communication could very easily lead to incomplete or incorrect information, misunderstandings, and faulty decisions. A poor job at site analysis could mean that the wrong functions are implemented, which, as we saw in Chapter 1, "Is Web-Based Support Worthwhile?," precludes an acceptable return on investment.

Site analysis builds the foundation of your support site. If you gather the wrong data or incomplete data, your foundation will become very weak and your site will fail, as Figure 4.2 illustrates.

Site Design

Site design involves taking the requirements generated by the analysis and translating them into a workable physical design for the site. In terms of tasks, this means deciding what support site functions should be implemented and how, how the various parts of the site will interact,

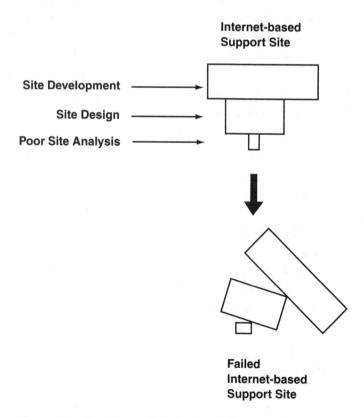

Figure 4.2 Poor site analysis leads to failure.

and participating in the research and selection of support site tools. The site designer will also plan the physical appearance of the site and ensure that it promotes the image the organization wants to get across.

In Chapter 1, we saw the importance of functions and tools in the success of a support site. If functions on the site are not the right ones, the site cannot be successful and if tools are poor, the site can have only minimum success. The site designer shares the responsibility for functions with the site analyst and the responsibility for tools with the site developer. In short, the site designer has a significant impact on the return on investment of the support site.

The site designer also requires good design skills. This person must know what colors, text, photographs, graphics, and arrangements of Web page components will appeal to customers and make the site easy to use. The designer must have enough technical knowledge to be able to determine whether a certain design is possible and to understand how specific components, such as graphics and downloads, affect the speed of customer access and wait times. The designer must also have enough technical ability to be able to research and understand what functions and tools are available for the support site. He or she must also determine the site's compatibility with various operating systems and the current Internet environment. The site designer needs to keep abreast of current technology in order to know what is available, what works, and what to stay away from.

The person in the site designer role must also have some understanding of the business the organization is in to be able to design the appropriate look for the site and to take future directions and growth into consideration. This person must also be able to see things from a customer's point of view to understand what a customer wants to see when accessing the support site. A visually dramatic site bursting with multimedia might be impressive and fun to watch once, but to a customer who is accessing the site on a regular basis to get information or to resolve problems, a much simpler, faster site would be preferable. Dramatic sites can become very tiresome very quickly.

The site designer must also have good usability skills. This is especially important when designing a site that supports users who may not be accustomed to using the Internet. A site that is intuitive for an experienced Web surfer may be a nightmare for a novice seeking technical support. It's very important to spell out navigation features in a clear language for novice users. This can be something as simple as a hypertext link with the phrase Frequently Asked Questions instead of the acronym FAQs. Also, don't ask your users to click through many levels to find solutions, and ensure that the pages that they view always indicate their navigational context.

Site designers must typically collaborate with analysts and developers on different aspects of the design and implementation of the support site. They must also get feedback from individuals on initial design ideas or prototypes. Good communication skills are a requirement.

Site Development

Site development involves translating a site design into a working Web-based support site. This might involve coding programs, creating various software and hardware interfaces, installing components such as firewalls, installing packaged tools, interfacing with existing sites, coding new software functions, creating knowledge bases, and so on. People developing knowledge bases must have specialized skills and are typically not the same people that develop the rest of the site. For this reason, I will separate the discussion of site development into two components: knowledge development and technology development.

Knowledge Development

If the development work for your site includes designing and building some kind of knowledge base or problem resolution tool, then you will need someone with the required specialized skills to create this database or tool. This person must define the boundaries of the problem domain being serviced by the problem resolution function. The possible resolution sources must be identified, and information must be collected. These sources could be call databases, subject matter experts, documentation, and so on. The knowledge developer must have enough technical knowledge to be able to understand the data and to validate that the knowledge base provides the correct information. The knowledge developer must also have good communication skills to interact with the subject experts and technology developers as well as to make any modifications to the content. The knowledge developer must also have an excellent technical knowledge of the tool being used to store, manage, and control access to the information. The knowledge developer must understand how the information needs to be structured to allow for optimal problem resolution by the end user. In large database design projects, the category of knowledge development can be broken down further with the knowledge development staff in a much more specialized way than can be described here.

Knowledge developers must always keep in mind the kind of terminology that users are familiar and comfortable with. Whether working on a simple list of FAQs or a sophisticated knowledge base, the developer must not use terms that would be arcane to an average user. This can make knowledge development a very tricky task for sites that are accessed by both sophisticated and novice users. Each group will want to use the terminology they are most familiar with.

Technology Development

In site development, any tasks that don't fall into knowledge development can be categorized as technology development. The staff developing a site's technology must have excellent technical skills. It also must have a very detailed understanding of the Internet and its interfaces. This staff will be depended upon to create the programming required for the site, which will vary depending on the technology the site uses. They will need to install and test various software tools and components, and they will need to focus on functions such as server hosting and firewalls if the site is not a branch of an existing one. Depending on the specific environment, the technology developers may also need to have strong communications skills for interacting with knowledge developers, site designers, and any other people involved in the project.

Also, a good customer focus is necessary to help understand how critical a robust, problem-free site is to customers. Developers must be able to see how the mistakes they make impact their customers, such as scripts that won't run on specific machines, files that can't be accessed, or programs that crash.

It is also important for technology developers to understand the technological direction of the business and how the technology infrastructure might change in the future. In general, they must realize the importance of the support site to the business.

Site Management

Managing a support site involves monitoring the ongoing performance of the site, making any adjustments that are necessary, setting up and maintaining the site's processes, and driving the ongoing cycle of evaluation and improvement.

The role of a site manager is typically given to an existing Help Desk manager or a manager of another support area. In a very small organization, the role may be assigned to someone in another capacity. Any of these situations can work well, but care must be taken that this role is given adequate importance and not forgotten.

A site manager requires good management skills to supervise and direct the processes and people involved in the site. He or she must be proactive, someone who makes things happen. A site manager also needs good problem-solving skills to deal with the technical, customer, and business issues that will arise on a daily basis.

In short, a site manager needs a good business focus. A clear understanding of what is going on in the business ensures that the site keeps up with the business and reflects the changing business or organizational needs. For example, a business might be phasing one product out while trying to encourage customers to use a replacement. The support site would be an excellent place to market this change, but it wouldn't necessarily happen unless the site manager is aware of this business direction and its importance. Similarly, if the organization were a government agency, the site manager would need to have a good understanding of what is going on in terms of changes in organization or legislation. This would allow the site manager to plan changes and post any required information, documents, or forms as soon as the change happens.

As well as a good business focus, a site manager needs a good customer focus and can see things from a customer's point of view. A site manager needs to know how to interact with customers and must have excellent communication skills, both oral and written. He or she must also understand the customer's familiarity with the Internet. It can be very easy to forget that something that appears obvious or transparent to the manager is often not evident to the unsophisticated user.

Site Maintenance

The site maintenance staff carries out site updates, keeping any supporting software or information such as FAQs and knowledge bases up to date, and they also makes any requested changes. The technical skills involved here are similar to those of the site developer. People maintaining a site must also have good communication skills to receive and validate information about what needs to be maintained. A strong customer focus is also required in order to be able to understand the impact of changes or a lack of changes on the customers using the support site. For example, if site maintenance involves taking a site offline for a few hours, someone who is not customer-focused may not realize the impact this will have on customers. People maintaining a site must also understand the terminology that customers are most familiar with. They must avoid using terms and acronyms that will not be understood or explain them if they are required.

Site Support

Work in the site support category revolves around handling all customer-initiated communication coming from the site. This could be as simple as offline support, such as responding to email or working on problems logged by customers from the site, or it could involve online support, such as remote interaction with a customer. Remote interaction will vary depending on the functions and tools in use, but it could involve running various diagnostic tools on the customer's PC and performing other remote functions, such as software downloads, while carrying on a dialog with the customer via some kind of chat function.

Practitioners not involved with any live support who respond to email and handle problem logs must have the technical expertise to be able to resolve the problems of their customers. They must have excellent communication skills. When they are writing a response, they have only words, no tone or body language. They must choose words carefully with professionalism and tact. They must understand their customers and be able to focus on their needs.

Practitioners involved with remote support must have all of the skills just described plus an excellent user's knowledge of the remote tools they are using; some of these can be very complex. They must have an excellent customer focus as well.

In most organizations, site support practitioners would performing both online and offline support. The work would be similar to that of a traditional telephone-based Help Desk. The best Help Desk practitioners are focused on the needs of the organization they support. They are proactive and are strong in problem-solving, communication, and customer service. Their technical skills are also good. You can find detailed descriptions of the roles and skills involved in Help Desk work in another book I have written entitled *Help Desk Practitioner's Handbook*, also published by John Wiley and Sons, Inc.

Work and Skill Grid

Table 4.2 summarizes the most important skills of each work category of a Web-based support site and shows how each is used. As mentioned previously, people working on a site will not typically stay in one category of work. Many times this is simply uneconomical. The people doing site analysis may be the same ones doing site design and site development. Site managers might do the work involved in site maintenance as well as site support. In a small organization, one person could be doing everything. If one person is doing work from more than one category, ideally that person will have the required skills for each task. Ensuring that people doing the work have the right skills will go a long way towards making the support site successful and realizing an acceptable return on investment.

How to Determine Staffing Requirements

To determine the staffing requirements for your particular site whether it's already in place or just being built, you need to consider the size of your project, the categories of work you are going to be carrying out, and the details of what is done in each category. You can use Table 4.2 to help you determine the skills you should be looking for and the section titled *Creating Hiring Specifications* can help you decide what, if anything, you should outsource.

Let's return to our two examples from Chapter 3, Education Plus and Trace Software. I will use these companies to illustrate the process of determining staffing requirements.

Table 4.2 How Key Skills Are Used in Each Category of Work

	BUSINESS SKILLS	TECHNICAL SKILLS	CUSTOMER SKILLS	COMMUNICATION SKILLS	OTHER SKILLS
Site analysis	Determine business requirements.		Determine customer requirements.	Carry out interviews, get information, and clarify requirements.	Analytical skills
Site design	Ensure site communicates business image and business direction.	Research and select appropriate tools, as well as determine compatibility.	Understand customer requirements and plan site usability.	Collaborate with analysts and developers, present prototypes, and get feedback.	Design skills
Site development: Knowledge	Understand the business problem domain and how it may change	Design and build the knowledge base structure.	Understand problem solving from the customer's viewpoint.		
Site development: Technology	Understand the technology direction of the business and the importance of site to the business.	Develop program, communication, and security structures. Install required software and hardware.	Understand the impact on customers if the site is not built or tested properly.	Interface with designers, knowledge developers, and others.	
Site management	Ensure the site meets the changing needs of the business.	Recognize when updates are required and understand the impact of technological issues.	Understand customer requirements to ensure the site is meeting them.	Interface with other workers, managers, and customers.	Management skills, problem-solving, and being proactive
Site maintenance	Same as for site development.	Same as for site development.	Understand the impact of maintenance on customers.	Same as for site development. Also interface with site manager.	
Site support	Understand the impact of each problem on the business.	Support the problem domain, plus use all the support tools effectively.	Understand the impact of problems on customers.	Interface with customers, other workers, and the site manager.	Problem-solving and being proactive

Education Plus

Much of the site analysis for Education Plus has already been done. Johnston Reeves has created a scope summary, as shown in Table 3.5 in Chapter 3. What's left to do is to analyze the contract file in which all calls are tracked to determine what information and functions must be provided on the site to eliminate the calls. The work must include a process to keep information current.

In terms of design, Johnston has decided to research other sites and pass them by his colleagues until a desired look is agreed upon. Someone will have to design the final look for the site, the functions, and the physical layout. That person must also research and select tools such as a Web-enabled call or order management system. Marketing information needs to be positioned on the site in such a way as to target the appropriate customers. The site designer must work with the person doing the knowledge development work to determine the appropriate locations on the site for this marketing information. Johnston plans to outsource the design work since no one at Education Plus has the skills or time required to create the site's design.

Knowledge development work for the Education Plus support site project will include designing and building a FAQ and a knowledge base. The person doing knowledge development will also have to work with the site designer to research where marketing information should be placed and design a process to keep it current.

The technology development portion of the site development work will involve actually building the site. The developer will need to work with the site analyst to estimate site volumes, determine security requirements, and design site sign-on procedures. The developer will work with the site designer to ensure that any software selected is appropriate for the environment and will perform any software and hardware installations, communication configurations, coding, or any required integration.

Johnston believes that all site management work needs to be done by someone within the business, and he and his colleagues agree that he should take this job. He could be able to keep a close eye on trends and initiate any improvements required. He will get a good feeling for what the site is doing or can do for the business. Site maintenance will involve troubleshooting technical problems and making any required content or design changes.

Site support is an interesting issue. Johnston wants to get any maintenance requests that come from the customers. He's not ready to hand that over to anyone yet because much of the communication involved requires pricing and business decisions, but he is leery of the time involved in answering less important email questions. Johnston and his colleagues discuss the issue and one of the colleagues, Kelly Rana, volunteers to handle email for a month as a pilot to see if its volume necessitates alternate staffing.

Investing in a permanent staff for design, technology development, and site maintenance work does not make a lot of sense for Education Plus. The skills required for these work categories are not skills that Education Plus will require often and they are skills that are fairly expensive to keep in place.

The work involved in analysis and knowledge development is another matter. Johnston and his colleagues want to understand the organization's data and any associated problems. They want to have total control over the creation and maintenance of that data. They don't want to do anything that moves them further away from that data. Kelly will do the work required to gather data from the contract files. She will work with an outsourced resource, a knowledge expert, to design the FAQs and knowledge base as well as to select software. Kelly and the knowledge expert will set up a process to update the information, a process Kelly can carry out on her own or pass on to another Education Plus employee.

The final result of Johnston's staffing planning, summarized in Table 4.3, is as follows:

- Education Plus, specifically Kelly, will complete remaining site analysis work.
- Outsourced resources will do the site design and site technology development as well as any future maintenance.
- Education Plus, Kelly again, will work with an outsourced resource to design FAQs and knowledge bases, select a knowledge tool for problem resolution, and build processes to allow Education Plus to maintain the information.
- Johnston will perform site management tasks as well as manage the support site project and particularly the outsourced resources.
- Kelly will handle all email messages and Johnston will handle maintenance requests coming from the call or order management system.

Table 4.3 Staffing Requirements for Education Plus

WORK CATEGORY	STAFFING REQUIREMENT
Site analysis	Education Plus: Johnston and Kelly
Site design	GSS's site designer working with Kelly
Site development: Knowledge	GSS's knowledge expert working with Kelly
Site development: Technology	GSS's technical expert
Site management	Education Plus: Johnston
Site maintenance	GSS, as required, with Kelly, who will do the knowledge maintenance
Site support	Education Plus: Kelly and Johnston

Johnston does some research on companies that can provide the work that he has decided to outsource. He asks various business associates for recommendations and gets very favorable comments about a firm called Gold Standard Sites (GSS). He meets with GSS, provides his requirements, does some interviews, gets a quote, and makes his decision. GSS will provide all of the outsourced services for the Education Plus support site and three GSS people are to be involved: a site designer, a knowledge expert, and a technical expert.

Trace Software

Unlike Education Plus, Trace Software won't be outsourcing any of the work involved in creating its Web-based support site. The required skills are all available in-house, but Jesse Kim does need to select the appropriate staff and make sure that staff is available when required for the support site project.

The site analysis work that remains to be done in the project includes working with the European support office to make sure all the support issues and requirements are covered. This also includes performing an analysis of current call and email data that needs to be analyzed to determine how best to reach the target of having 50 percent of all calls handled by the support site. Based on all this information, the site analyst must also select the training that would most benefit site users and determine the sources and formats of the training. Emergencies are another responsibility of the site analyst. Potential emergencies must be researched so that parameters making up an emergency can be defined and the appropriate handling procedures put into place.

The site designer will have to research other sites and work closely with design committee members from both the North American and European locations and with the marketing staff to come up with a design that is accepted by all. The designer will also have to do a fair amount of research on support tools and must be involved in the final selection.

The site's knowledge development will involve identifying sources of all the data required for the site, designing the structures of FAQs and knowledge bases, determining the configuration of knowledge tools, overseeing data, and carrying out extensive testing. Knowledge developers will also need to set up processes for keeping knowledge current.

The technical developers will work with designers to ascertain the suitability of the support tools selected. They will design the site's technical infrastructure, install the software and hardware, and configure the communications, coding, and integration. They will also be responsible for carrying out extensive testing of all of the site's remote capabilities.

Currently, site management is being performed in a haphazard fashion. The new site needs a full-time manager and Jesse thinks a good start for this person would be to manage the support site creation project. The site manager will have to watch trends in assisted, offline, and off-hours support and make sure that both North American and European customers are getting the support required. The site manager will also have to support the European office working closely with staff there to respond to any changes required. The processes for all work revolving around the site must be put into place as well as an initiative for ongoing evaluations and improvements.

Most of the ongoing site maintenance will focus on the knowledge content of the various tools employed. All information accessed by the knowledge tools—for example, knowledge bases and FAQs—must be kept up to date. Additional maintenance might include upgrades to the tools and functions being used, design changes, and so on.

Two types of site support are required: offline and online. Offline support will involve handling communications from site email or the site call-tracking system. Online support will involve handling requests from the site for assisted support and emergencies. Staff will use remote support tools to interact with customers to get a resolution. Each of the offline and online support will require an after-hours component.

Jesse looks at the work that needs to be done and decides she will have to draw resources from the following groups:

- Help Desk practitioners
- Help Desk manager
- Web development team
- Web technology specialists

Jesse calculates that for the duration of the project she will need two people to do the site analysis and knowledge development, two site designers, one site technology developer, and a site manager. Two current Help Desk practitioners could do the site analysis and knowledge development with some training, but Jesse wants the knowledge and skills involved with analysis and knowledge development to remain in the support area. She is also willing to allocate the necessary training budget.

She will need two people from the Web development team to do the site design and will use one of the Web Technology specialists for the technical development work involved in the site. She also has some thoughts about permanent staffing once the project has been completed.

Jesse feels the site manager should be the current Help Desk manager. She believes that merging Web-based and traditional support will maximize effectiveness of resource usage and quality of support. The Help Desk manager is responsible for reducing the call load to the Help Desk and moving it to the Web site. The goal is to move as much as possible to self-service and provide live or offline support for the rest. Jesse doesn't want to create a separate Web support team. She wants Trace Software customers to experience consistent, speedy, and accurate service and feels that separating teams or functions would hamper these objectives.

The offline support being generated by the site could be integrated with the current call management. The processes for current call management are in place and working well. A separate type could be used for reporting site-initiated problems and a separate priority could be set up

Table 4.4   Staffing Requirements for Trace Software

WORK CATEGORY	STAFFING REQUIREMENT
Site analysis	Two people from the Help Desk
Site design	Two people from the Web development team
Site development: Knowledge	Two people from the Help Desk (same individuals in site analysis)
Site development: Technology	One Web technology specialist
Site management	Help Desk manager
Site maintenance	Technology-related changes are performed by the Web technology specialists. Knowledge-related changes are performed by Help Desk practitioners.
Site support	Responsibility will rotate throughout the Help Desk. Offline support is absorbed into the system. Online and after-hours support is rotated through the Help Desk.

if necessary. Existing Help Desk practitioners could also provide online and after-hours support, perhaps on a rotating basis. All practitioners would need to be trained to use the remote tools required to provide online support. This would create a pool of people that could be drawn upon as required to ensure that peaks in traffic or staff absences would not affect the customer services.

Table 4.4 summarizes Jesse's staffing requirements for building, managing, and maintaining the support site.

Defining Responsibilities

The more clearly you define the responsibilities for setting up, maintaining, and managing your site, the less chance you will have of forgetting certain tasks or of making mistakes. During the initial project, clear responsibilities will give you an improved ability to manage the project. Employees will have less confusion about who should be doing what, less duplication of effort, and fewer instances of tasks falling through the cracks. Once the site is up and running, defining responsibilities will help ensure that the management and maintenance of the site is not on the back burner. The staff can also be much more comfortable and more effective knowing what they are responsible for, which is what they are measured on. Resolving site problems becomes easier, along with staff performance assessments. Having clearly defined responsibilities will facilitate the acquisition of employees, and when staff do come on board, they will become productive more quickly.

Responsibilities are typically assigned by position and they define the categories of work in each position. To give you an idea of what you may want to include in staff responsibilities, three examples of responsibility definitions are provided. The first is for a temporary site designer position that is required during the creation of the support site. The second example is for the permanent position of support site manager for a site that has already been created. The final example is for a permanent position of support practitioner for a site that involves both offline and online support.

Site Designer Responsibilities

Table 4.5 describes the responsibilities of a site designer. This position is temporary; it will end once the design work on the site has been completed.

Table 4.5 Site Designer Responsibilities

RESPONSIBILITY	DESCRIPTION
Prototype design	Create the initial site design prototype using input from analysts and then validate the prototype with technical developers.
Support tool selection	Work with technical and knowledge developers to research and select the support tools required for the design.
Site infrastructure design	Create the support site HTML shell, including all header and navigation items.
Project communication	Track and record the time spent on the project. Also keep the manager informed of progress and any problems or delays.

Site Manager Responsibilities

Table 4.6 describes the responsibilities of a site manager. If the person in this position is also responsible for managing a Help Desk, as in the Trace Software example, the responsibilities in Table 4.6 would be merged with Help Desk manager responsibilities.

Site Practitioner Responsibilities

Table 4.7 describes the responsibilities of a practitioner who provides both offline and online (assisted) support to customers initiating requests from the support site. The practitioner could very well be working for the manger described previously.

Table 4.6 Site Manager Responsibilities

RESPONSIBILITY	DESCRIPTION
Monitor site activity.	Monitor traffic volumes and function use. Also identify and address negative or dangerous trends.
Keep site current.	Ensure that knowledge maintenance processes are carried out and that product information on the site is current. Also ensure all links are current.
Manage site performance.	Ensure all email messages receive prompt responses as per marketed times. Also ensure all assisted service requests are completed satisfactorily. Carry out regular customer surveys and make any adjustments necessary to address performance issues.
Ongoing evaluations and improvement.	Carry out an ongoing process of evaluation and improvement. Work with the Help Desk, product development, and marketing to define how the support site can meet specific goals of each of these areas. Use site performance data to research and implement new tools and methods to improve performance.
Staff management.	Ensure that the responsibilities for support practitioners are clearly defined and communicated to the staff. Also ensure that the staff has all the information and training required to carry their responsibilities out. Develop quarterly performance appraisals based on assigned responsibilities. Provide management with monthly performance reports and respond to management requests or concerns regarding the site's performance.

Table 4.7 Site Practitioner Responsibilities

RESPONSIBILITY	DESCRIPTION
Responding to email	Respond to site-initiated email messages as per defined priorities and time frames, escalating when necessary.
Offline problem analysis and resolution	Monitor the call-tracking tool as per procedures, accepting calls from the queue in priority order. Analyze and resolve problems according to defined priorities and time frames, escalating when necessary.
Online problem analysis and resolution	Respond to site-initiated requests for support in a priority sequence. Use remote tools to resolve customer problems, escalating when necessary.
Technical knowledge	Keep current on all the support tools used and take all the training required for optimal tool use. Keep current on the trends and technology within the problem domain being supported. Again, take all the training required in order to provide the required levels of support.
Problem prevention	Fix causes, not just symptoms, doing what is necessary to prevent problems from recurring.
Communication	Provide manager with weekly status reports and keep him or her informed of all problems and issues on an ongoing basis.

Creating Hiring Specifications

Staff turnover is a fact of life. Even if you currently have the staff you need, you should have a plan in place to facilitate acquiring staff when the need arises. Staff resignations or the need for new positions can come about very suddenly, leaving you with the task of defining what you need and then going through the time-consuming process of interviewing and hiring. If you have a skill grid and position specifications in place, you can make the whole process shorter, easier, and more successful.

A skill grid is a table of the required skills to create or support your site. The table includes a description of each skill, training that is available to enhance or build the skill, and questions or observations that can be used to test for the skill. A sample skill grid is shown in Table 4.8. A position specification lists the skills and levels of skill mastery required

Table 4.8 Sample of a Skill Grid

Communication	Good at listening and getting ideas across to peers, management, and customers
Training	Communications 101 training from Communications, Inc.
Sample questions, observations	Describe your strongest qualities as a communicator. Give examples of how you have used them in the past.
	Describe a communication problem you have had to face when working with another person or team. How did you resolve it?
	What do you consider your biggest communication mistake? How did you handle it or resolve it? Is there anything you do differently as a result?
	Does the candidate listen actively?
	How good is the candidate at getting his/her ideas across?
	How does the candidate use body language?
	You could also add position-specific scenarios to test how a candidate would react.
Customer skills	Believes customers are of critical importance, is able to see things from a customer's viewpoint, is respectful of customers, is tactful, and is able to handle challenging behavior
Training	Customer Skills 101 training from Communications, Inc.
Sample questions, observations	Describe the profile of the customers you served in one of the previous organizations you worked for. Explain who they were and what they did. What role did these customers play in the success of the organization?
	Give an example of things you did to ensure that the end user of the product you were working on was satisfied with the product.
	Describe the most challenging customer interaction you have had. How did you handle it?
	Does the candidate refer to customers respectfully or disrespectfully?
	Use position-specific scenarios to test how a candidate would react.
Business skills	Must have a general understanding of business and consider how the business affects all activities
Training	Business Skills 101 online training from Education Plus
Sample questions, observations	How does your role (or your department's role) impact the performance of the organization?
	Describe how the organization you worked for functions.
	What business or operational areas have you interacted with in your work? Describe how you interacted with each.
	What do you consider the most important aspects of your job? Why?

Site design skills	Understands and is able to apply the concepts of effective Web-page design
Training	Online training on Internet site design from Education Plus
Sample questions, observations	Describe your biggest site design success and explain why you feel it was such a success.
	Describe your poorest site design or a design mistake and explain why you think it was bad.
	What are some of the factors you take into account when you are starting the design of a site?
	Who do you get input from before you start the design of a site?
	Give some example of good/bad design practices.
	As an option, give the candidate some requirements for a simple site and instruct him/her to draft a rough design and then describe it.

for a particular position. A sample position specification is shown in Table 4.9.

A skill grid can be approached in several ways. You can create one for each position or you can create one skill grid that contains all the skills required for a group of positions and then build each position specification by listing the skills required. The latter method offers you more flexibility. You have a menu of skills to choose from and if you need to build or change a position, you simply add or remove skills.

When you are preparing to interview prospective candidates for a position, you can use the position specification to tell you which skills and levels of skills you require. You can then go to the skill grid to see which questions to ask to test for a particular skill. You can also get an idea of the training that a candidate will require if all or part of a particular skill is missing. You may not always find someone who meets one hundred percent of your skill requirements.

Table 4.9 shows an example of a position specification with two sections. The first section describes skills that are drawn from the skill grid shown in Table 4.8. These tend to be generic and fairly static. The second section describes the specific technical skills that this position requires. These skill requirements will tend to be dynamic since the pace of technological change is very rapid. Structuring a position specification in this way makes it easier to maintain.

Table 4.9 Position Specification Sample

Position title	Site designer
Standard skills	Site design skills: excellent
	Communication: excellent
	Business skills: basic
	Customer skills: good
Specific technical skills	HTML: excellent
	General knowledge of Internet technologies: excellent
	Also must know what technologies can be used in putting a site together and must understand how they are used. The candidate does not necessarily have to be able to apply them.

You may choose to set up your skill grids and position specifications in other ways. You might include all the technical skills in your skill grid and then just have one skills section in your position specification. There is no right way to do this, so do whatever is easier for you to set up and maintain.

Hire or Outsource?

If you are building a Web-based support site from scratch, the decision to hire people or to use outsourced staff can usually be determined fairly quickly. You would typically outsource skills that you have an infrequent need for or for which you have no hiring budget. You would typically not want to outsource positions that involve working with key business and customer data.

If you are a very small business with no other requirements for Internet skills and no one in the business has adequate skills to perform the required work, then outsource. You may want to ensure that the out-sourced resources leave you with a site that you can maintain yourself.

If you want to outsource part of the work, outsource technology-related tasks in design, technical development, or maintenance before you out-source anything else. If possible, stay away from complete outsourcing of the analysis, management, or knowledge work involved with your site. You could lose valuable business and customer knowledge when your relationship with the outsourcer ends.

Steps to Successful Outsourcing

If you do decide to outsource, you need to follow four steps to ensure success (see Figure 4.3). First, check out several organizations that provide the services you need. Ask colleagues for referrals. If the work you are outsourcing is fairly major, you may want to create a Request for Proposal (RFP) and distribute it to those organizations you are considering for provision of work. The RFP should include a very detailed description of all the work you require and any specific positions you require.

Second, find out as much as possible about the organizations you are considering. Ask for sample sites they have worked on and ask for references, which should be checked. If possible, interview the staff that is responsible for performing the work. Also use skill grids and position specifications to test for skills.

Third, draw up a clear agreement. The outsourcer needs to understand what you require and you need to know that the outsourcer is willing and able to provide what you require. Be sure to define responsibilities for each party clearly. If the outsourcer is filling specific positions, include the position descriptions in the agreement. If you have interviewed specific people for the work, you may want to ensure that the people you interviewed are the ones who will actually do the work, and

Research several organizations	✓
Check sample sites, references and interview staff	✓
Draw up a clear agreement	✓
Manage the work	✓

Figure 4.3 Checklist for successful outsourcing.

this should be specified in your agreement. Also include performance measures in the agreement so both parties will understand how the outsourced work is measured.

Finally, manage what you outsource. Monitor the work closely and resolve any issues with the outsourced work as soon as they occur. Have status meetings frequently to review how the outsourced work is progressing. Outsourcing a function does not mean that it will perform itself. It needs to be managed, so allow enough time for this or you may be unpleasantly surprised. The first piece of work I ever outsourced was a total disaster. I made assumptions, I did not do frequent quality checks, and I did not do enough to ensure that the outsourcer understood the requirements. What I got was what I deserved—garbage. Expensive garbage. You need to manage outsourcers more closely than your own employees, because outsourced employees may not have access to the same information that in-house employees do.

Key Points

This section provides a summary of the key tasks involved in support site staffing.

The work involved in creating and running a Web-based support site can be divided into the categories of site analysis, site design, site development, site management, site maintenance, and site support. Each of these categories requires key skills, as shown in Table 4.2.

To determine staffing requirements for your particular site, whether it is already in place or just being built, you need to consider the size of your project, which categories of work you are going to be carrying out, and the details of what is to be done in each category. Examples of requirements are shown in Tables 4.3 and 4.4

The more clearly you define the responsibilities for setting up, maintaining, or managing your site, the less chance there is of forgetting tasks or making mistakes. During the initial project stages, clear responsibilities will improve your ability to manage the project. Once the site is up and running, establishing priorities will help ensure that the management and maintenance of the site is not relegated to the back burner. Responsibilities are typically assigned by position. Some examples of responsibilities are shown in Tables 4.5 through 4.7.

Hiring specifications, in the form of skill grids and position specifications, provide you with a plan to facilitate acquiring staff when the need arises. The information stored in a skill grid includes a description of the skill, suggestions for testing for the skill, and the training available for obtaining or enhancing that skill. A position specification lists skills and skill levels required for a specific position. Refer to Tables 4.8 and 4.9 for examples.

Once you're ready to acquire staff, you must decide whether to hire or outsource. You would typically outsource work that you have an infrequent need for or for which you have no hiring budget. You would typically not want to outsource work that involves working with key business and customer data. If you decide to outsource, be sure to research several organizations, check sample sites and references, interview the staff, draw up a clear agreement, and then manage the work.

PART THREE

Design Considerations

CHAPTER 5

Functions, Tools, and Implementations

In Chapter 1, "Is Web-Based Support Worthwhile?," I discussed tools and functions as factors that affect a support site's success. In turn, implementation is a factor that affects the success of tools and functions. In the ASP's publication *The Year's Ten Best Web Support Sites, 1999 Edition*, the Iomega Corporation's support site provides an interesting example of the impact of implementation. Instances of *no resolution found*—a situation that indicates a failed attempt to find a resolution—on the Iomega support site dropped by 55 percent when information and solutions were written in non-technical language so that customers could understand them more easily.

The intent of this chapter is to provide you with an overview of support site tools, functions, and implementations that work. I will start by examining self-service tools such as online problem logging and personalized support site interfaces. The subject of problem resolution will also be covered by first looking at individual sources of knowledge and how they can be pulled together by a problem-resolution tool. I will also discuss the use of downloads, discussion groups, online training, e-newsletters, email, and customer feedback. Our discussion will then focus on assisted support options such as online chat and remote control options. I will conclude the chapter with discussions on site log analysis tools and the move to third-generation support sites. Some further references are provided that I hope will help facilitate your tool research. Specifically, the sections presented in this chapter are as follows:

- Customized support site interfaces
- Online problem reporting and tracking
- Self-service problem resolution
- Online training
- Downloads
- Discussion groups
- Email
- Customer feedback
- E-newsletters
- Assisted support with online chats
- Assisted support with remote control
- Site log analysis
- Moving to third generation?
- References and resources

Customized Support Site Interfaces

One thing I noticed when I was researching (and researching and researching) support sites was how many sites gave customers the ability to customize the interface to the site based on the customer's profile. This is a wonderful idea, especially on sites that are very large or support a large number of products. A customized Web interface can cut down the amount of time a customer spends getting to the required functions and can remove extraneous information and keystrokes. The customer can go directly to support functions dealing with a specific product or suite of products, and material sent to the customer such as software alerts or newsletters can be focused on those things the customer is interested in. I have seen the customized

Web interface implemented in a variety of interesting ways. I'll present two of them here.

Microsoft, which has a vast network of support sites, provides customized Web interfaces via a Custom Support Site option, accessible from the main support page at support.microsoft.com. Customers can choose from eight interfaces, each of which provides a very different view of the site. If you haven't been there, I suggest you at least have a look at the Home Customers interface and the IT Professionals interface just to see how well each caters to its intended audience.

Sybase Inc. takes a different approach. You are given a login ID based on a name and password that you provide. You are then asked to choose which products and services you are interested in. The interface you see when you log into the site reflects your selections in everything from the What's Hot section to the information that your searches return. You can even specify which notifications you want to receive, such as technical documents or changes in documentation. Sybase has called this customized interface *Mysupport* and you can access it from mysupport.sybase.com.

Online Problem Reporting and Tracking

Most call-tracking systems offer some kind of Web interface that enables customers and support practitioners to log and track problems or requests via the Internet. Customers enter identification information and a description of the problem and may be prompted to select a problem type and a priority. The system puts the problem into a queue and issues the customer a ticket number. The customer can then use this number to check on the status of the problem. Once the problem is resolved or the resolution identified, the customer is notified via email or telephone (if any more information is required) and any supporting documents are emailed out.

The main advantage that this function provides is that it takes calls out of the *resolve-me-immediately* mode that telephone-based calls have. It puts these calls into a queue that can be scheduled and handled based on priorities, the skills available, and so on, rather than simply on which call comes in first. Customers don't have to wait in a telephone queue; they can simply report the problem and, if the problem has not shut them down, continue with their work. Of course, in order for online problem reporting to be successful, customers must understand how long the response time is, and the support system must then respond within this time.

An online problem-reporting system can offer another advantage if it provides a series of fields within a form to guide customer input. When a customer uses regular email to request help, the problem is typically described in free-flowing text that is entered into the body of the message and vital information may be omitted. This will result in a time-consuming email dialog because the support technician has to request more information from the customer. This is less likely to happen with an online reporting system that uses forms that contain fields to direct customer input. The customer can be guided through the description of the problem by being presented with a series of options or simple questions that narrow down the nature and urgency of the problem. The technician is also saved a lot of data entry as the information is automatically entered into the appropriate database fields when the service request is submitted.

Depending on the type of organization involved and the customer profile, online problem reporting and tracking may be open to all customers or it may be a restricted function. For example, it may be only open to registered users of a product or for customers who have paid for a specific level of support.

Implementation Options

In this section, I will discuss three options for implementing problem reporting on your Web site: simple reporting available to all customers, reporting and tracking available only to registered customers, and a front end for problem reporting and tracking.

Let's look at the first option: offering all customers simple problem reporting without giving them any tracking capability. You could do this through the use of email or by using a call-tracking Web interface. If you use email, you could set up a form that customers would fill in and email to the ID that corresponded to their problem. Each ID would be the responsibility of a specific group of practitioners to process. Alternatively, you could use an email tool that would automatically create an entry in your call-tracking system. This would help ensure that all email statistics are captured and that no emails fall through the cracks. Support practitioners would respond to email messages with a resolution, perhaps attaching appropriate documents or Web addresses to give customers as many sources of help as possible.

If you choose to use a call-tracking Web interface, you could set it up so that the customer need only provide an email address (unless you wanted to gather specific customer information) along with a problem type selected from a dropdown list and a problem description. The problem would be sent to the appropriate queue based on its type. The Web interface could automatically set the priority of each problem to a value reserved for Web-generated problems. This would allow you to track Web-generated problems and ensure they were responded to within a specific amount of time.

The second implementation option is to give logging and tracking abilities to registered customers via the call-tracking Web interface. Customers would have to log into your call-tracking system and be validated as registered users. They could then report a problem or search through any knowledge bases made available via the Web interface. They could also track the status of their logged problems or requests. Giving customers access to the call-tracking software would help ensure all customer interactions are logged. Customers would have access to solutions as soon as support practitioners entered the solutions.

One caution with this process is that it would expose the call-tracking system to the customers. Strict processes would have to be put into place for support practitioners using the system to control the information and keywords entered, the quality of information entered, and an adherence to agreed-upon service levels. Security would have to be implemented to ensure customers could not look at other customers' data. For example, they should be able to look at the resolution to a problem, but not at information about the customer who experienced the problem. Web interfaces to call-tracking systems would typically take these types of security requirements into account.

The third implementation option involves trying to prevent the need for the logging by providing the customer with a final chance to resolve the problem before presenting the logging window or email form. When the customer indicates an intent to report a problem, the support site could display a list of potential problem resolutions based on the type of problem the customer is having (see the section titled *Problem Resolution Implementations* for details on how this might work). The customer would have the option of reviewing the information or continuing with the reporting process.

Symantec Corporation does something similar on their Web support site at www.symantec.com/techsupp. If the customer selects the Contact Customer Support option while navigating through the various support options for a specific product and version, the Symantec site displays potential resolutions under the heading *Save Time! Read These Hot Topics Before Contacting Support!* before continuing on to fee-based options such as online chats or telephone support. The Hot Topic selections and the buttons for fee-based support appear on the same page. Customers who have already checked out the displayed Hot Topics would not be forced into using extra mouse clicks to get where they wanted to go.

Self-Serve Problem Resolution

A support Web site typically has several sources of information that provide knowledge to the problem resolution process.

Sources of Knowledge

These sources of knowledge on a Web site can include the following:

- FAQ documents
- Logged problems and solutions
- Documents describing known issues or bugs
- Technical documents
- Product documentation
- Knowledge base of cases

A caution: using multiple sources of data can result in a lot of duplication. This can lead to two problems. First, a customer searching online for a solution may be frustrated by being presented with repetitive information. This becomes an issue when the solution being presented is not the answer the customer needs, yet the customer encounters multiple instances of this answer. Second, keeping multiple sources of the same data up-to-date is time-consuming. Having overlapping sources of information is a common occurrence in most organizations and utilizing all of these sources of knowledge is the best way of assuring that the online knowledge base is complete. Thus, a conflict exists between the needs of avoiding duplication and providing the customer with the most complete information. Careful consideration needs to be taken when providing multiple sources of knowledge for online customer self-help. Now let's examine each knowledge source individually and then we'll look at how they can be combined in various implementations of problem-resolution tools.

FAQ Documents

A FAQ, which stands for Frequently Asked Questions, is a document that contains solutions or answers to common questions. These questions are typically selected based on the frequency with which customers ask them. Such documents may contain diagrams or even video clips to relay the instructions necessary to solve the problem or answer the question.

FAQs are probably the most common Web support site offering and there is a reason for this. If you set them up based on the most common questions you get, organize them in a way that makes the most sense for your customers, and update them faithfully, they will solve most of the problems that customers bring to your site. In ASP's *The Year's Ten Best Web Support Sites, 1998 Edition,* a Microsoft representative claimed that 100,000 Help Desk calls for a specific product were eliminated in one year by a FAQ, a simple Top Ten list, for that product. That's a pretty hefty payback for the lowly FAQ.

FAQs can be incorporated into one or more documents, or each question and answer can be a separate document. Putting each question and answer into a separate document makes it easier to use FAQ information in various problem-resolution implementations, which in turn makes it less complicated when the information requires updating. FAQ documents can be presented as part of the results of a search, they can be included with product information, and they can even be part of interactive problem-resolution sessions.

FAQs offer two main challenges. The first is organizing the data. This may not be a consideration if you have one FAQ composed of 20 question and answer combinations, but when you have thousands of FAQ documents, organization becomes a major issue. How do you organize the information to make it easier for customers to access? The second challenge is keeping the information up to date. Again, 20 entries may not be a challenge, but thousands certainly are. How do you ensure the information is as current as possible, accurate, and in a language that customers can understand?

Different organizations have solved the problem of organization in various ways and it is worthwhile going to some sites to have a look. Cisco Systems had the challenge of a very wide product range to support and therefore a very wide range of FAQ topics. If you go to Cisco's online support site, accessible from the main site at www.cisco.com, you can see how the challenge was met. Their FAQs are organized by product. For example, to browse FAQs for high-end routers, you would select a high-end router category and then from the list displayed select the high-end router product you needed help with. At the product level, you would be presented with a list of subcategories of documents. These might include hardware specifications, software installation, and software configuration, including a Samples and Tips section, troubleshooting, and product documentation.

Another interesting FAQ implementation can be seen at Cambridge-Soft's support site accessible from the www.camsoft.com site. You select the product you are interested in and you are then presented with a table that lists FAQ topics down the side and specific platforms (Windows, Macintosh, or Unix) across the top. A dot in a table cell indicates the availability of the topic for the specific platform. The tables are similar to the tables in automotive brochures that list vehicle options. Clicking on a dot will list all the FAQ documents available for that topic.

Macromedia includes a FAQ at the top of most product pages on its support site. You can look at the support option at www.macromedia.com site and see the Top Technotes or Learn topics for each product you select.

All three support sites, Cisco, CambridgeSoft, and Macromedia, have organized their FAQs by product because they have learned that customers typically navigate support sites by product.

Creating HTML code for each new FAQ that you create can be a tedious process. Many organizations opt instead to use Web development tools such as Java or Perl to create applications that will enable them to key in the text for a new FAQ and store it in a database where it is immediately available to the online support site. They maintain and delete documents in the same way. Customers using the support site get new information as soon as it is discovered and keyed in.

If you give your support practitioners the ability to create or correct FAQ documents as soon as they notice the requirement or as soon as they come upon a problem that they know many users will have, your FAQ documents can be kept current with a minimum of effort. You can also create processes to search for and eliminate defunct FAQ entries. Before you let your practitioners loose on your FAQs, however, you need to make sure that they have the required skills. The FAQs need to be in a non-technical, easy-to-understand language and need to be technically and grammatically correct. One person should probably be given the responsibility of approving/editing them so that the language is consistent.

FAQs will probably offer the highest return on investment of any function on your support site. Use the Web to get ideas on how to maximize your FAQ's effectiveness. Take some time to look at how other organizations in your business area have implemented their FAQs.

Logged Problems and Solutions

Another source of knowledge for your Web site is the database of logged problems and solutions that your support practitioners create. You could make this data directly available to your customers as solved cases to be searched. You can see an example of this at Sybase's support site, accessible from the home site at www.sybase.com. Customers can choose to search solved cases using keywords. Matching cases are returned in a list and customers can select specific cases to see details of causes, resolutions, or work-arounds.

The challenge with this information source is that the information would be viewed exactly as it was keyed into the tracking tool. Support practitioners typically do not have time to worry about how the resolution or problem description they are keying will read to Web customers.

They may not ensure everything is written in easy-to-understand English. The result is that your customers may get to look at some rather rough text. This won't matter to your more technical or more knowledgeable customers, but you probably would not want to make this the sole or recommended source of solutions for your less technical or less knowledgeable customers.

You also must train your practitioners on how to present technical solutions in clear, non-technical language. You can also assign someone to review or edit the practitioner's problem resolution descriptions, rather than taking away from their support time with grammatical and descriptive issues. Logged problems and solutions can be a valuable addition to the support offering on your Web site, but it should not be the prime source unless you are willing to spend considerable time and effort editing and checking the data.

Documents Describing Known Issues or Bugs

A list of bugs that have been detected in the products you manufacture or support can be a valuable resource to your customers. If you publish these as soon as you know about them and include patches or workarounds, you may be able to save your customers much time and grief.

You can provide bug reports as a separate site resource such as a Hot Items List or Bug Alert. You can also have them appear with your FAQs or other knowledge sources. If this is to be the case, then it is best to have each bug on a separate page so that there is only one source to revise when the information needs updating.

Technical Documents

Technical documents typically include technical specifications, diagrams, interfaces, compatibility information, and so on. They can pertain to hardware or software and might include installation or connection instructions. The content of technical documents will vary depending on the product involved, but they are usually aimed at the very technical user, such as someone who actually puts hardware together. If some of your customers need very detailed and technical information about the products you support, then this information should be located in an easily accessable place. A section of your site could be dedicated to technical documents, or users could access this information by specifying a product. They would then get all the necessary information, such as FAQs, known bugs, technical and documents, for that product.

Product Documentation

The product documentation might include user documentation, information on getting started, and so on. You may choose to store the documentation as files to be downloaded or you may present it as it would be displayed in the product itself, such as the online documentation file with the same capabilities. You can do it both ways. You will probably at least have to make it available for download. Having an understanding of your customer base will help you decide which options you have to offer for product documentation.

As an example, to download a copy of Using Freehand documentation from Macromedia's support site, which is accessible from www. macromedia.com, I selected the Freehand product and then simply chose the documentation from the displayed options. The .PDF file containing the documentation was downloaded in zip format. The whole process was very easy. Along with the documentation, several other support options were available to be accessed, such as Top 3 Technotes.

Knowledge Base of Cases

If you support products that you do not manufacture, many prepackaged knowledge bases are available to be included on your support site for searching and as input to more sophisticated problem-resolution tools. If you manufacture a software or hardware product or if you want to provide information specific to your environment, you may choose to create a knowledge base for customers to access from your support site. A variety of knowledge tools is available to help you out with a wide range in complexity and price. Various tools can also help you author knowledge, while others enable you to store and then access knowledge in an interactive or reasoning fashion. Some organizations choose to author and store knowledge using tools they have in-house and then use a more sophisticated access tool such as a case-based reasoning tool to enable customers to carry out interactive problem-resolution sessions with the knowledge base.

A knowledge base created for a specific product or environment is typically composed of cases. A case might consist of a problem description, symptoms, keywords, and a resolution. The knowledge base of cases can be searched or it can be navigated with more sophisticated tools that help customers reach solutions by having them answer questions or select options to narrow the problem down. Less technical customers may find this interactive process easier than executing a search.

Problem-Resolution Implementations

As you can see from the examples we have discussed so far, Web-based support sites typically include several sources and forms of knowledge. All these sources can provide information for search engines or for problem-resolution functions that you can implement on your site. Instead of duplicating information, which can lead to a horrific maintenance nightmare, your tools can simply include all of your information sources, as shown in Figure 5.1.

Problem-resolution functions have two goals: provide a solution quickly and provide the correct solution. The resolution functions I will present here are of three types. The first presents a list of potential answers immediately and the second tries to narrow down the problem by getting more knowledge about it by asking the customer to answer questions. The third is a little different and may merit its own section because of its remote control component, but I include it here for completion. The third type of problem-resolution function, which I will call Immediate Fix, actually looks into the customer's PC, compares what it finds with a checklist of what should be there, and then fixes what it can. The remote control of the function is triggered by support site software, not a human being.

Immediate Answers

The most common implementation of immediate answers is a search. The customer enters search information and the search engine returns a series of documents that match what was entered. Search engines vary in sensitivity and complexity and can include all knowledge sources on

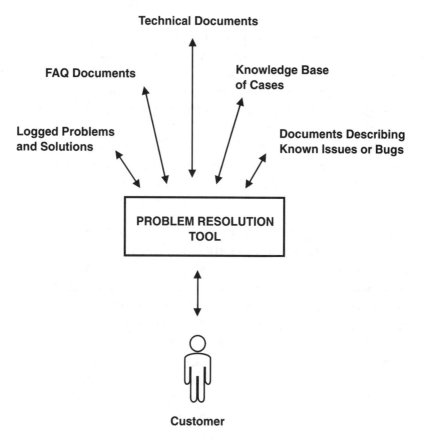

Figure 5.1 Information sources for problem-resolution functions.

the site. Some search engines accept only a phrase or keyword as input, while others ask for qualifying information such as which part of a document to search for (text, keywords, or titles), which products to include, and so on. For example, the search function of Dell Corporation's knowledge base, found at support.dell.com, enables customers to qualify the search by specifying words in the title of the document, the age of the document, or the document number. The search yields an immediate answer composed of documents from the site's Product Support Quick Notes, Technical Tips, Frequently Asked Questions, Technical Assistance Bulletins, Hot Topics, and so on.

One of the simplest problem-resolution implementations you can have is to ask the customer to select a product or topic and then present a list of issues and solutions. This list can draw information from all of the knowledge sources on your site, such as FAQs, known issues, knowledge base entries, and technical documents. You can see an example of this kind of implementation on the Service and Support option of Symantec Corporation's Web site at www.symantec.com. You select a product and a version number, and then click on the troubleshooting option. You are presented with a list of the latest issues for the product and version you selected. Each issue is a document that might be from the knowledge base, a news release, a download site, and so on. If you can't find what you need in the material presented, you are asked to do a keyword search.

Another immediate answer type of problem-resolution function is one based on a natural language search. You can find such an example at support.dell.com in the Ask Dudley support function. Dell gave its online problem-resolution function a user-friendly image by giving the function a character and a name. To use Ask Dudley, you simply key in a query in simple English, such as *My keyboard freezes up,* and Dudley responds by returning several documents from its knowledge base, which might include FAQs or Technical Tips, and from other knowledge sources on its support site such as technical specifications. Dell customers keep Dudley pretty busy. According to ASP's *The Year's Ten Best Support Sites, 1999 Edition,* Dudley answers over 75,000 questions per week.

As an interesting aside, if you go to the Microsoft support site at support.microsoft.com, choose Custom Support, and then choose Home Customers, you will see an Ask Maxwell function. Maxwell does not physically look like Dudley; Maxwell is human, while Dudley is a cartoon, but they act the same. Both Maxwell and Dudley are powered by a natural language search engine called Ask Jeeves.

Problem Qualification

Problem-resolution functions that attempt to qualify the problem by interacting with the customer are trying to increase the accuracy of the solution returned. The customer starts the process off by making an initial selection or by keying in an initial problem description. The function then continues through a series of steps presenting the customer with a series of symptoms or qualifications to select at each step until finally the function has enough information to select one or more solutions.

The first example of such a problem qualification system is one used by Intel Corporation's support site at www.intel.com/support. Intel calls this function the Troubleshooting Assistant. In the first step, the customer is asked to select a product category and then a specific product, such as Processors and then Pentium III Processors. In the next step, the customer is asked to select a statement that best describes the situation, such as *I need how-to information* or *I have a problem*. At this point, the Troubleshooting Assistant provides a list of documents, or common issues, that the customer can browse through to see if they solve the problem or provide the required information. If they don't, the customer is asked to narrow the search by selecting from a list of symptoms such as *System keeps locking up*. The tool then offers some of the most frequently used solutions based on what was asked. If none of the offered solutions apply, the customer is encouraged to try a search.

A second example of a problem qualification system is one that can be found on the support option of www.lucasarts.com, the Web site for the LucasArts Entertainment Company. The function is called Yoda's Help Desk and uses the *Star Wars* character Yoda to humanize the interaction (which interestingly it does even though the Yoda character is not human).

Yoda asks the customer to key in a question and select a product from a dropdown list. Based on the question entered and the product selected, Yoda then goes through a series of steps asking for a clarification of

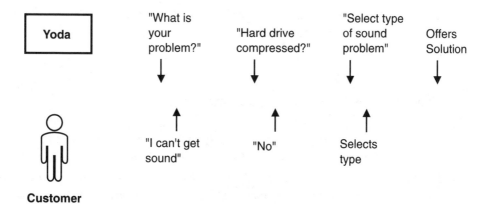

Figure 5.2 Problem qualification with Yoda.

symptoms. The clarification might take the form of a yes/no question such as *Is your hard drive compressed?* Yoda might ask the customer to select a product version, or he might ask the customer to select from a list of symptoms, such as specific types of sound problems being experienced. When he feels he has enough information to provide a correct answer, Yoda presents the customer with the response most likely to solve the customer's problem based on the question, product, and symptoms. Figure 5.2 describes the interaction between Yoda and the customer.

Immediate Fix

The Immediate Fix type of problem-resolution tool is taking us into the realm of what I introduced in Chapter 1 as a third-generation support site. The customer enters a problem, such as a problem with email. The problem-resolution tool has a remote control component that looks into the customer's PC, checks out the customer's email configuration against a stored checklist of what the configuration should be, and finds an incompatibility. The tool tells the customer that it would like to update the email software to the latest version and the customer gives permission. The customer's PC is updated and the software waits while the customer tries out the fix. If the fix was successful, the customer clicks on a button that says something like *Yes, this fix worked,* the statistics are captured, and the interaction ends. Note that the configuration checklist that the customer's PC is compared against could be a knowledge source such asa technical or standards document. You can see a demo of this kind of interaction if you go to support.com's Web site at www.support.com and select the products option within the solutions category.

The Value of Knowledge Sources

Whichever type of problem-resolution functions you choose to implement on your site, you should ensure that they use all the possible knowledge sources. You should also do what you can to keep the quality of knowledge sources high, and to tailor the information and organization to your customers. Offer them several ways of getting information and of resolving problems. You can offer them, as several support sites do, a searchable library of information and functions. The more successful your support site is at providing customers with correct answers quickly, the less they will go to their phones.

Online Training

Training is an excellent way to make customers more effective users and to eliminate calls to a support area. A support site can provide training through multimedia, text-based training modules, or sources such as tips and tricks or how-to documents. If you manufacture a product, such as software, you may want to create your own training modules or have training modules created for you. If you want to provide training for topics based on products that you do not create, you may want to find someone who has already created this kind of training and make it available on your site for a fee.

Corel Corporation is an example of a company that provides some online training modules for the products it creates. The online modules are multimedia tutorials illustrating specific concepts. The tutorials are very well done and the medium is appropriate for the topics. Watching someone work with a design is easier and more effective than reading about it. You can access the Corel training at www.corel.com/support. Select Support Services, Online Services and then Features in Action-Interactive Training.

Another example of Web-based training created by an organization for its own products can be found at Intuit's support site for its Quicken product. Long lists of multimedia Show Me video clips are available that demonstrate how to perform a specific task. Interactive video clips are also available, but a plug-in must be downloaded before the videos can be viewed. To see these videos, go to www.intuit.com/support and choose Quicken—All Versions and Support & Service Options from the drop-down boxes. This will bring up a new page. Click on the Free Support Options link to go to another page, and then click on the Online Training link.

Iomega Corporation offers short, focused training in the form of How Do I text tutorials that are offered for each product on Iomega's support site. To access the tutorials, go to www.iomega.com, select a product, and then click on the tutorials option. A list of available How Do I tutorials will then be displayed, each of which is a text document describing how to perform a specific task.

Trellix Corporation offers excellent online training for its Web development products. Their training is in the form of HTML documents that open in a separate window. Documents are textual and are very easy to navigate. To view Trellix's tutorials, go to www.trellix.com, choose the Support option, then the Reference Center, the How-to's, and then select Tutorials.

If you are a small business or simply don't want to be in the business of creating training modules, you have the option of partnering with a vendor of Web-based training. The training can be accessed from your site but actually originates and is purchased from the vendor's site. An example of this kind of partnership can be found on the support site of Echo Online, an Internet service provider. At www.echo-on.net/support, a Web-Based Training option displays the wide variety of training modules available from Web-based training vendors. Customers have the option of purchasing viewing options for a full year's training. Other forms of training include tips and tricks as well as What's New and What's Hot documents.

Downloads

Most support sites offer some form of download, which might include trial versions of products, product patches, updates, beta software, free viewers, plug-ins, or various types of documents. Downloads are fairly simple to implement. It is necessary to ensure, however, that the instructions for the downloads are clear and that you specify the product the download pertains to. Customers with slow connections become doubly upset if they discover they have downloaded the wrong software.

Discussion Groups

Discussion groups are a popular feature on support sites and contribute significantly to call elimination. They enable customers to share information about problems or different ways of applying a specific product.

Customers can contribute to discussions by posting a question, reply, or request, or they may choose to simply read through or search the postings. Discussion group forums can be public, open to anyone on the Web, or they can be private, open only to registered users. A forum can be moderated, which means a support practitioner reads the postings to make sure that forum guidelines are adhered to, and he or she responds to any unanswered questions. A forum can also be completely open, creating an environment in which anything goes. Discussion group postings are typically viewed via an HTML interface or a newsgroup interface. These postings can also provide useful information to the company, such as new product or service features that are most wanted by customers.

Intel Corporation offers a wide variety of moderated forums on its support site. Each forum focuses on a specific topic. Forums are moderated by support practitioners who try to respond to any unanswered or incorrectly answered questions within two days. Dell Computer Corporation also offers a variety of very specific forums on its support site via a support feature called Delltalk.

Rational, a company that provides modeling software that supports the Universal Modeling Language (UML), hosts a user forum called the UML Cafe. This forum is more of a user group than a support source and participants discuss UML issues, applications, and questions.

Some organizations offer live conferences. For example, Trellix Corporation hosts daily live conferences that use a Java-based chat tool to provide a one-to-many environment in which the support practitioner can respond to questions and problems from customers. Registered Trellix software users are also given access to search the online archives for the proceedings of each conference. Bentley Systems (www.bentley.com) hosts regularly scheduled moderated theater sessions on specific topics. Participants can view Web presentations for the theatre topic and participate in discussions by posting questions or comments that are screened and presented by the moderator.

If you are going to include some kind of discussion group as part of your support site offerings, you need to take some time to plan out the discussion topics carefully. You want to make them as focused as possible but wide enough to attract enough people to generate a useful discussion. You also need to decide whether or not the forums should be moderated and to what degree. Forums that are not moderated can be a disaster. They can turn into a flaming free-for-all or a whining session. If you don't moderate your forum, you might also miss out on what your customers are saying about your product and your support. Try participating in various discussion groups or at least reading through the postings to get a feel for what your customers may or may not want.

Email

I recently read an interesting article about email in the April 3, 2000, issue of the *Toronto Globe and Mail* newspaper. The article was titled "New E-slaves: People Who Handle Email Flood" and it exposed some statistics that were terrifying to me. It said that Chapters Online, an online retailer at www.chapters.ca, received more than 4,000 email messages from its customers daily. That's 4,000 messages every single day. Sixty-five Chapters employees, professional email responders, were employed in shifts covering 24 hours a day seven days a week to respond to the email load. The article also described how another organization, E*Trade Canada, handles its flood of email. The company holds after-hours email parties at which company employees, who are paid for the effort, compete for prizes to see who can answer the most email messages.

The article interested me because it brought home how quickly email can grow and get out of control. Just a few years ago, Chapters' email was being handled by one person. Email is scary because it is so easy to generate. You just key something in, press a button and presto . . . message sent. No effort is involved, no going to the post office, no buying stamps, nothing. Many support sites go live without giving a thought to how they are going to handle email and are totally unprepared to handle the amount of email they receive. The resulting unanswered email leads to irate customers, telephone calls to support areas, and worse.

On your support site, especially if you are not a large organization, you need to carefully consider what kind of email you want to receive, what kind you want to discourage, and how much you can actually handle. The two types of email you typically want to receive from a support site are customer feedback and support requests from customers who simply could not get help elsewhere on your site. The former will help ensure your site is useful to your customers. The latter type of email will help identify topics that need better coverage on your site so that you can eliminate future email on the same topics.

When you make email available on your site, you need to do the following:

- Target the email so they get to the right source as soon as possible. Some sites ask the customers to select from a dropdown list of email targets, such as Technical Support, Suggestions, and so on.

- Market the response times you can meet and then meet them. Make sure you have processes in place to ensure each email message is read and responded to.

- Ensure people answering the email have the skills necessary to do a good job: tact, good writing and grammar skills, and good overall customer skills.

- Use the information you get from the email to make improvements to your site, to your products and services, and to your processes.

You can help keep email at a manageable level by doing a good job of providing self-serve problem resolutions and by examining the email that you do get to continuously improve the problem-resolution capabilities of your site. Yes, email is easier to handle than calls but, just as with calls, if left unmanaged with no elimination initiatives, they will spiral out of control, and you may find yourself hosting email parties.

Customer Feedback

Email is very useful in gathering customer feedback, but you can try other methods. You can offer customer surveys, for example. You can have separate surveys or you can have questions placed at strategic intervals on your site. For example, if you want to know what other topics customers would like to see in a How Do I series of documents, include a question with a dropdown menu of possible responses on the page that lists the documents. Make it as easy as possible for your customers to respond. They should just have to select from the dropdown menu or click on some radial buttons and then click on a submit button.

Short, focused questions are used by many support sites to gauge the effectiveness of problem resolution methods. Customers are asked if a particular response solved the problem. The answers are then gathered by an automated process and they provide useful statistics on how effective each resolution is. Alternatively, after a customer has worked through several steps of a problem-solving process, the site might ask the customer to rate the usefulness of the process or of specific suggested improvements.

Another way of surveying is to include a question when you respond to an email from a customer. You have started a conversation; why not continue it and make it more valuable?

When you carry out a survey, be sure you understand exactly what information you are going after, what you're going to do with it, and how you are going to communicate the results to customers. If you don't plan to do anything with the information you gather, then don't make your customers provide it. Useless surveys are a waste of everyone's time and they sour your customers on future surveys and on your customer service.

E-Newsletters

E-newsletters are electronic newsletters that customers sign up for at a support site. A customer provides an email address and in return receives an e-newsletter at regular intervals. The content of the e-newsletter varies depending on the product and service involved.

E-newsletters that disseminate specific technical information can be very valuable to customers who need it. Customers may not visit the support site on a daily basis, but they do want to be informed when important information arises. On the other hand, e-newsletters that contain too much marketing information and not enough product support information end up in the trash bin and are an irritation to customers.

The best way to decide whether or not your customers want e-newsletters is to ask them. While you are asking them whether they want newsletters, ask them what they want in the newsletters. Use your existing sources of knowledge to provide newsletter content.

For an example of how this works, visit Symantec's support site. When you subscribe to a news bulletin, you are asked for a name and email address, and you are then asked to specify which products you are interested in. Unsubscribing is just as easy. In fact, I accidentally unsubscribed before I subscribed (I didn't have my glasses on). Each news bulletin that you receive could contain notification of product upgrades, tips and tricks, late breaking news on viruses, and so on.

Assisted Support with Online Chats

In the *Discussion Groups* section, we saw online chat services being used to promote user interaction or support practitioner interaction with users. In this section, we discuss online chat as a one-to-one support offering for customers who are at your support site and need more help than the site can give them. A one-to-one chat would be very inefficient if the support technician is handling just one customer at a time. The support industry standard (from data presented at the Spring 2000 CRM/SSCE) is that one analyst should be able to conduct up to four simultaneous chat sessions. This enables the technician to make productive use of the time when he or she would otherwise be waiting for a customer to try out a suggestion or type in further information. Chats are often fee-based services available only to specific customers who have registered for it as part of a support plan.

A customer initiates a chat session by clicking a button on the site. If a support practitioner is not available, the customer is put into a hold queue and can keep browsing on the site until notified that a practitioner is free.

Online chat capabilities are typically provided by a chat hosting service. Your organization pays a setup charge plus a monthly rate based on the number of support practitioners connected to the service. Services tailored for small businesses offer per-minute usage fees. Most services enable conversations with multiple customers at once and have the capability to push Web pages or other content to customers during the conversations. You can also use the chat medium in discussion groups if you want. Some services provide tools for archiving, searching, and reporting so you can see where to improve. An excellent article in the January 2000 issue of *PC Computing* discusses various chat services, pricing, advantages, and disadvantages. It is really two separate articles called "Make Your Customers Love You" and "Instant Contact," both by Bonny L. Georgia. To find the articles, go to www.zdnet.com and select PC Computing. You can search on either of the article names and then navigate your way through them. If your organization has its own servers and a dedicated high-speed line, then it is probably more economical to purchase chat software and host the chats yourself.

Assisted Support with Remote Control

An online chat is a useful form of assisted support, but it has the same limitations as a telephone conversation. The support practitioner can talk to the customer but must depend on the customer for information about the customer's problem. This can be a challenge if the customer does not understand the problem or is non-technical and does not understand the practitioner. Remote control tools address this challenge, however, and enable the practitioner to look at what the customer is experiencing. These tools, fortunately for smaller businesses, are available in a wide range of functionality and pricing. You can read some interesting remote control software reviews in *Network Computing* magazine at www.networkcomputing.com. Choose Technology Guides, Management, and under Features choose "Remote Control Saves Steps, February 7, 2000" by Sean Doherty. Check out the remote control software interactive report card. You can change the weight of the rating factors to tailor the report card to your environment.

I have divided remote control tools into two types to illustrate the range in functionality. I will discuss both the basic tools and those with expanded functionality.

Basic Remote Control

Basic remote control tools, which require software to be installed on both the customer and practitioner PCs, enable the practitioner to see what is on the customer's screen, to take over the PC in order to demonstrate a technique, to whiteboard a diagram (a valuable function since it is sometimes much easier to explain something with a drawing), to browse and update files, and to download files to the customer's PC. Let's look at an example.

A customer visits a support site and discovers that the problem cannot be solved; assisted support is required. The customer clicks on a button to indicate that support is needed and initiates a chat session. After discussion with the customer, the support practitioner realizes the problem needs further investigation. The practitioner must look at the customer's screen and perhaps some files. The customer may not have remote control software, so the practitioner asks the customer to download it from the Web site or perhaps emails it to the customer. Once the customer has the software, the remote control session is initiated. The practitioner can search the customer's PC and do whatever is necessary to fix the problem while the customer watches. The practitioner might carry out a short training session to show the customer how to perform a particular technique.

Extended Remote Control

Extended remote control tools expand the functionality of basic remote control functions and attempt to integrate all the aspects of remote customer interactions. A chat function is typically part of an extended remote control tool. Figure 5.3 illustrates the integrated process.

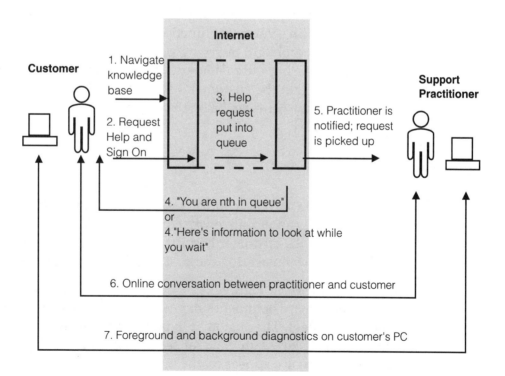

Figure 5.3   Extended remote control.

As shown in Figure 5.3, a customer tries to find help at the support site but cannot find the required resolution. The customer then clicks on a button to invoke an assisted support session. The customer is put into a queue and is given a message to this effect. The customer can either go back to searching while waiting or view files displayed by the remote control system. These might be FAQs or other support notes. When the support practitioner is free, a chat session is initiated. If this is the first time that the customer is calling, the customer will download a file to enable the remote control session. Once the file is downloaded, the practitioner communicates with the customer via the chat function while performing various diagnostics and making any required fixes. The diagnostics can be performed in the background, which is important for sensitive files such as system registries, while the customer is able to view a log of what is happening. The customer can chat with the practitioner or carry out other activities while the diagnostics are running. Once the cause of the problem is determined, the practitioner can make the fix using a variety of utilities and download information to the customer's PC as required.

Extended remote control tools typically have a toolkit of diagnostic programs that can perform a vareity of functions. These include finding the module causing the problem, querying peripherals, creating and executing macros, comparing the customer configuration against the standard configurations that the customer's should match, and so on. The required call router software can be on the organization's Web server or hosted by a third party.

Example

Let's walk through a remote control session, courtesy of Control-F1 software, so that you can visualize what an interaction might look like. We will assume that the customer has already initiated the session and the practitioner is now answering the customer's request for help.

The first screen, shown in Figure 5.4, is the practitioner's first interaction with the customer. The practitioner asks the customer for information about the problem. The customer explains that the system pauses when information is keyed in. Several seconds might pass before the keyed characters actually appear on the screen.

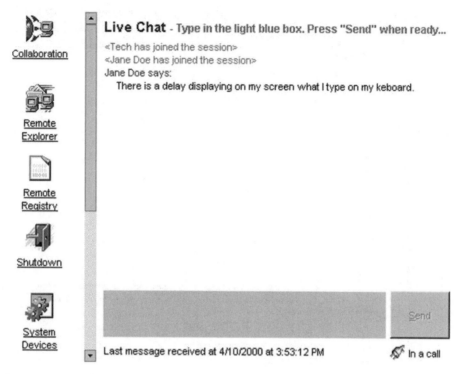

Collaboration

Remote Explorer

Remote Registry

Shutdown

System Devices

Live Chat - Type in the light blue box. Press "Send" when ready...

<Tech has joined the session>
<Jane Doe has joined the session>
Jane Doe says:
    There is a delay displaying on my screen what I type on my keboard.

Send

Last message received at 4/10/2000 at 3:53:12 PM   In a call

Figure 5.4 Starting a session.

The practitioner decides to check out the customer's PC configuration. First, the practitioner tells the customer what is being done and informs the customer that the system log, which will appear on the customer's screen, can be viewed during this process. The system log tells the customer which files are being accessed in the customer's system and which functions are being executed.

The practitioner uses standard reports accessed from a systems template window to view the customer's system configuration, as shown in Figure 5.5. The practitioner sees that the customer has a SCSI card driving a secondary storage device, a JAZ drive in this case.

The practitioner suspects a hardware interrupt conflict and proceeds to check this using the Properties function, shown in Figure 5.6. The practitioner discovers that indeed a conflict exists and then relays this information to the customer. The practitioner makes the required correction

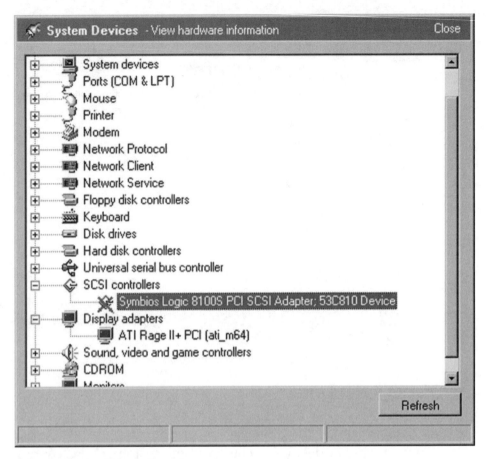

Figure 5.5 Checking configuration.

and does so in the background, just as he or she has done everything else; the customer sees only the chat interaction and the system log.

It is now necessary for the customer's PC to be restarted. The practitioner lets the customer know and initiates the shutdown, shown in Figure 5.7. The shutdown window appears on both the customer's and the practitioner's screens, and the shutdown will not take place until both customer and practitioner give permission.

When the customer's system restarts, the customer is automatically connected back into the session that was being carried out with the practitioner. The practitioner asks the customer to try to key something in and the customer goes into a word processing document and does so. The customer reports that the problem has been solved.

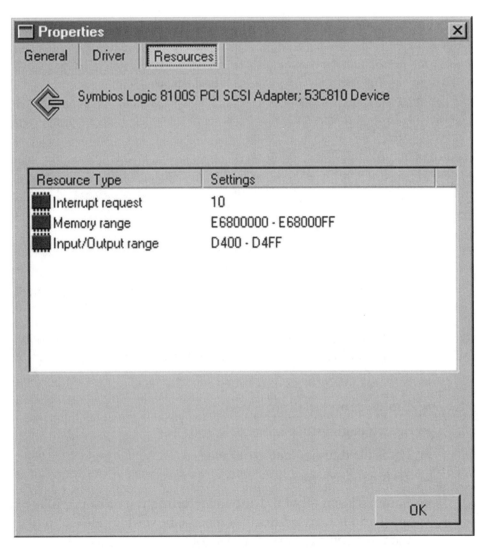

Figure 5.6 Identifying hardware conflicts.

Site Log Analysis

Web site management tools are really beyond the scope of this chapter, but I want to discuss one particular management tool: a site log analysis tool. Even if you are just a small business with a simple site, a log analyzer can provide you with a wealth of statistics that can show you how your site is used and provide clear directions for improvements.

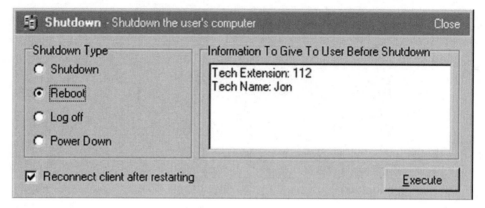

Figure 5.7 Restarting.

Log analyzers run across a huge range of pricing and functionality, from shareware to enterprise strength.

A log analyzer performs an analysis of the logs created from visits to your site. Some of the statistics the analyzer can show you are as follows:

- Site traffic volumes and times
- Browsers and platforms used to access your site
- Search engines used to access your site
- Paths used to navigate your site
- Traffic to each page or function
- Summaries of all of the above including the most popular path, the most and least used documents, the busiest and least busy times, the most common error, and so on

These represent just a small sample of the information a site analyzer can give you. It can tell you which problem resolution information is the most and least popular, which pages customers visit the most and least, and which features they use the most and least. Put this together with your customer feedback information and you get a very clear blueprint for improvement.

If you've never seen a log analyzer before, some very nice demos can be found on the Web. One set can be found at www.sane.com; just select the Online Demos option. One of the easiest ways to find log analysis tools on the Web is to simply use a search engine. Try entering the phrase *log analysis tools* or *Web site log analysis tools*. The technical online magazines listed in the *References and Resources* section in this chapter will also provide you with information on log analyzers.

Moving to Third Generation?

In Chapter 1, I talked about three generations of support sites. First-generation sites are informational, second-generation are conversational, and third-generation are decisional. Most of the tools and functions that I have described in this chapter would be found on a first- or second-generation site. I have described a third-generation site as one with a support engine that has the intelligence to make decisions and invoke functions based on customer activity. How close are we to this? We are already there. Consider the Immediate Fix problem resolution function that I described earlier. The customer keys in a problem description. Based on keywords in the description, such as "email," the support engine makes the decision to check some part of the customer's PC configuration against a template of what should be there. After checking out the customer's PC, the support engine decides that it needs to upgrade a specific piece of software and does so. It then asks the customer if the problem has been resolved. Here we have a support mechanism that is making decisions and implementing fixes on its own (with the customer's permission, of course).

Consider the problem-resolution application that, after a customer has tried unsuccessfully to navigate through to a resolution, decides to ask, "Would you like to chat with a support practitioner?" The software is making a decision, though at a simpler level than the previous example.

Moving a site to third generation involves integrating your support tools in such a way that they can watch what a customer is doing and analyze it against a predetermined set of criteria that is stored somewhere as a source of information. The tools would then make a decision to intervene based on the analysis, according to yet another knowledge source. The intervention could be a simple question, a suggestion, a system check and upgrade, or an automatic initiation of a chat session. You would, of course, have to closely examine the privacy issues involved in this kind of analysis.

The benefits of third-generation sites include faster problem resolutions for your customers and potentially fewer requirements for assisted support. The challenges include the work involved in collecting and maintaining the knowledge your tools need in order to make decisions and helping your customers feel comfortable with the support engine make decisions for them. I must admit that even as someone who has been comfortable with technology for almost 30 years, I am not completely at ease with live update functions when I don't understand exactly what they are doing and when they don't ask my permission before taking action.

If you are moving your site towards third generation, you should consider some simple things that will perhaps make the process easier and more successful for you. First, don't reinvent the wheel. Use all of the knowledge sources that you have to power your third-generation support engine. This means that existing technical or standards documents might provide the templates against which your support engine matches a customer's PC configuration. Second, build your third-generation support engine in iterations. Start with a few very simple scenarios, test these out on your customers, get feedback, and then continue to another iteration. Third, do everything you can to increase the comfort level of your customers with the support tool. Make sure the customer is told in simple terms exactly what the tool is doing at each point in time. Have the tool ask for the customer's permission at appropriate checkpoints.

References and Resources

The following is a set of references that will help further your own research into functions and tools.

www.asponline.com

I highly recommend this site for The Association of Support Professionals (ASP). In particular, check out their two publications entitled *The Year's Ten Best Web Support Sites, 1998 Edition* and the *1999 Edition*. The value in these publications is in the examples, ideas, and discussions that revolve around setting up support sites. You will get examples of things that did not work at all, things that worked very well, and the lessons learned. You can purchase these publications at their site. They are inexpensive. If you plan on ordering them, you should join the ASP first because the member discount means that you get the membership for free. ASP also has some other publications that you might be interested in, so check them all out while you're at the site.

www.zdnet.com

This is the home of Ziff-Davis' publications and is a good resource for articles and recommendations on support tools. It can be a bit overwhelming, but if you are looking for information on a specific product, you can find a lot of valuable information via the search function.

www.networkcomputing.com

Network Computing magazine contains product news and reviews for products such as remote control tools and Web site log analyzers. *Network Computing* also has an interactive report card feature that lets you change the weighting of rated factors in product reviews so that you get a rating that's tailored to your environment.

www.servicenews.com

This site is home to *IT Support News* and offers a buyer's guide that will show you some of the problem resolution tools available.

www.philverghis.com/helpdesk.html

The Help Desk FAQ published by Phil Verghis is a good starting point for lists of support tool vendors.

www.customersupportmgmt.com site

The site for *Customer Support Management* magazine has a good service and suppliers directory.

Finally, the Web itself is a wonderful resource. Spend a few hours checking out what other organizations are doing with their support sites. Often, the sites will tell you what technology was used. For example, you can see that Dell's Ask Dudley uses Ask Jeeves technology and Intuit's live chat function uses LivePerson.

Key Points

This section provides a summary of the key points covered in this chapter's discussion on support site functions, tools, and implementations.

Personalized support site interfaces can focus customers on information that is most relevant to them and get them to where they want to be more quickly, shortening their problem resolution experience.

Online problem reporting and tracking functions channel problems into a queue that can be managed more effectively than a *solve-me-right-now* phone call. Calls related to a problem status can thus be largely eliminated.

Self-service problem resolution involves creating and managing knowledge sources and then using them as input to problem resolution tools that customers interact with to solve their own problems. Knowledge sources include FAQs, logged problems and solutions, documents describing known issues or bugs, technical documents, product documentation, and archives of cases created for a specific organization.

Problem resolution functions have two goals: to provide a solution quickly and to provide the correct solution. The three types presented in this chapter are as follows: Immediate Answer, which presents a list of potential answers immediately based on the initial information provided; Problem Qualification, which tries to narrow down the problem by getting more information about it from the customer; and Immediate Fix, which looks into the customer's PC, compares what it finds with a checklist of what should be there, and then fixes what it can.

Training is an excellent way to make customers more effective users and to eliminate calls to a support area. A support site can provide training through multimedia, text-based training modules, sources such as tips and tricks or how-to documents. Training can also originate from a third-party training site.

Downloads are fairly simple to implement, but it is necessary to ensure that the instructions for the downloads are clear, so that customers get what they think they're getting.

Discussion groups can contribute significantly to call elimination. They enable customers to share information about problems or about different ways of applying a specific product. Discussion group postings are typically viewed via an HTML interface or a newsgroup interface.

The two types of email that most sites should be interested in site are customer feedback and support requests from customers who simply could not get help elsewhere on the site. The former will help ensure the site is useful to your customers. The latter type will help identify topics that need better coverage on the site so that future email on the same topics can be eliminated.

Customer surveys are a good way of gathering customer feedback. An effective means of surveying customers is to place questions at strategic intervals on the support site.

E-newsletters are electronic newsletters that customers sign up for at a support site. E-newsletter content varies depending on the product and service involved, but e-newsletters that disseminate specific technical information can be very valuable to customers who need that information.

Online chat services are assisted support functions that can be invoked by customers who cannot find the help they need on the support site. Chats are often fee-based services available only to specific customers who have registered for it as part of a support plan. Online chat capabilities are typically provided by a chat-hosting service that charges a setup fee and then a monthly rate based on the number of support practitioners connected to the service.

Remote control tools enhance an assisted support session by enabling a support practitioner to interact with the customer's PC to resolve problems directly. The practitioner can change files, update software, download files, and even reboot the customer's PC. Remote control tools are available in a wide range of functionality and pricing.

A log analyzer is a Web site management tool that provides a wealth of statistics showing how a site is being used. It also indicatesclear directions for improvements. Log analyzers have a huge range of prices and functionalities, from shareware to enterprise-strength.

If you are moving your site towards a third-generation setup, you can make the process more successful and less painful. First, don't reinvent the wheel. Use existing knowledge sources whenever possible. Second, build your third-generation support engine in iterations. Third, do everything you can to increase the comfort level of your customers with the support tool.

CHAPTER 6

Designing the Site

The topic of Web site design is a book in itself. In this chapter, I will not attempt to turn you into a Web site design expert but will present some basic design fundamentals for you to apply to your site or measure your site against. I will also review the tasks you need to carry out in order to ensure that your design meets all of your support site requirements.

I start this chapter off by describing the tasks that should be part of designing your Web-based support site. I will then cover design fundamentals and address each of the design tasks in more detail. The topics to be presented are as follows:

- The tasks involved in site design
- Design fundamentals
- Identifying factors that constrain site design
- Finalizing site functions
- Creating prototypes
- Researching and selecting tools

Tasks Involved in Site Design

Designing a support site involves translating the requirements and potential implementations that were identified in the scope summary in Chapter 3, "Establishing Scope," into a support site design that satisfies the organization's requirements. The tasks involved in design are shown in Table 6.1.

The first task in site design is identifying the factors that constrain site design. These factors typically fall into the categories of human factors: available skills, customer profiles, the business, and technology limitations. Once the constraints are identified, the impact on the design must be defined and then incorporated into the site as the design work progresses.

For the second task, site designers define the functions that are available on the site. This involves taking the work done in the scope summary and translating the requirements and suggested implementations into workable functions.

Tasks one and two can proceed in parallel to some degree. Once they are both completed, work can begin on site prototypes. *Prototypes* are typically iterative, starting very simply as design mock-ups and progressing to actual HTML shells. Prototypes facilitate the process of gathering feedback and getting a consensus on design.

Table 6.1   Tasks Involved in Site Design

TASKS	DETAILS
Identify the factors that constrain site design.	Identify the human, monetary, and technological factors that constrain site design decisions. Also define the affect of constraints on design.
Select the site functions.	Use the details of requirements and suggested implementations to select and design the site functions.
Create the site prototypes.	Using input from the previous two tasks, create the initial site layout and the navigation strategy. Get feedback from stakeholders and revise until an agreement is reached.
Research and select tools.	Work with analysts and developers to research tools required to satisfy the functions selected. Then integrate the tools into the site.

In the fourth task, site designers research various tools to find those that best fulfill the site's functional requirements. This work can occur while the prototypes are created. Once the initial tool selections have been made, designers must work with developers to check out the technical specifications and compatibility of the tools. They must also work with analysts to see how well the tools meet the various knowledge requirements that the site customers have. Designers must also decide how to integrate the tool into the site for optimal ease and speed of use.

I discuss each of these tasks in more detail, but before I start, I'd like to spend some time on design fundamentals, so that as your site is designed, you can test it out against some very basic design premises.

Design Fundamentals

The best way to start to think about the basic design of your site is to look at your site from a customer's perspective. Let's say that I'm your customer. Why do I visit your site? Do I go there to be entertained, amazed, and impressed by the incredible graphics, video clips, and sound that you offer? Probably not. I go there to get help. I have a problem or I need information. I want help, I want to find information easily and get it quickly, and I want to understand what I get. Too many distractions on your site will annoy me. Having to wait for things to load or to spend time figuring out how to do something will also annoy me. If you're thinking I'm an unusually impatient person, then think again. I've got work to do and if your site doesn't give me what I want quickly, then you are preventing me from doing it and I have a right to be annoyed.

Catering to Your Audience

The fact that your customers don't have a lot of time is a major factor in your design. Your site must load as quickly as possible. You cannot use complex graphics, photographs, or logos that take a long time to load. Any tools you employ should take into consideration the various types of Internet connections your customers might use. If some of your customers have slow connections, but you want to provide advanced functions for your customers with faster connections, then you may want to offer two different functions and warn customers that one may be slow in certain circumstances.

Avoid extra keystrokes. A keystroke may mean waiting for a page to load. For example, some sites require you to click on an entrance button or graphic to get into a site. Why? Why not just display the site? Customers, especially dial-up customers, will find the extra level of entry annoying and any of the marketing that the extra level is meant to get across will wind up being lost.

Your customers may have varying sizes of monitors and your site should work on all of them. If you design your site for a 17-inch monitor, then the people with 14-inch monitors, and a lot of them are still out there, may not see what you're seeing. They may have to navigate all kinds of scroll bars just to be able to display your main page.

When you design your site, put yourself into your customers' shoes. Think about the technology your customers might use to access the site and about the time constraints and pressures your customers are under and design accordingly.

Navigation

Site navigation is the process of moving from location to location on a site. Navigation tools are the methods employed to facilitate this process for site users. The navigation tools you employ can make the difference between your site being very easy to get around and your site being a very confusing place where everything is difficult to find. Never forget that your customers may only visit your site infrequently. You can't assume that they are familiar or will ever become familiar with the layout of your site.

The first rule of navigation is to ensure that your site itself is easy to find. If your site is a branch off of a main site, then is the option clearly indicated or is there a tiny "support" somewhere in a five-point font that is almost impossible to read? I hate to say it, but in my ongoing research of Help Desk tools and support sites, I am constantly running into sites in which I have to spend a fair bit of time figuring out where the support function is or the difference between various kinds of support. If I am a customer using a product and require technical support, do I click on Technical Support, Product Support, or Customer Support? You want your customers to visit the support site, and you want them to find support easily. Otherwise, you won't get the return on investment that you planned. That first navigational aid should shout out, "Support here! Come and get it!"

The second rule of navigation is to use navigation icons that are meaningful to the customer. The most meaningful icons, believe it or not, are words, but be careful not to use technical terms or acronyms that customers may not understand. I get very tired of trying to figure out what various icons on a site mean. Some display a description when you move your cursor over the icon, but that is just another unnecessary waste of time. Figure 6.1, a screen shot of an Internet service provider's home page at www.echo-on.net, illustrates a site with simple but effective navigation icons. The navigation icons are words, large enough for those of us who need reading glasses to see easily. The whole site is very easy to navigate.

The Internet is full of sites with terrible navigation icons. I won't point you toward any of them directly, but if you have time for a little amusement, you can visit a site that makes finding and identifying poor sites its business. Look at www.websitesthatsuck.com.

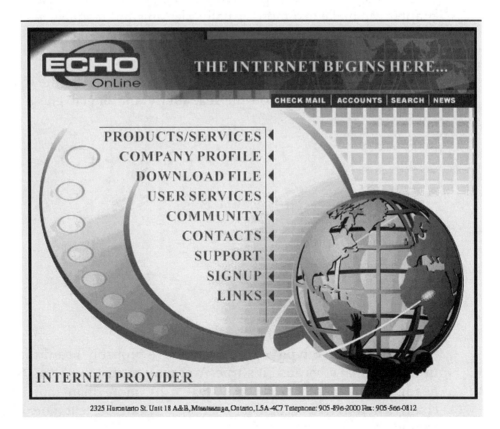

Figure 6.1 Good navigation icons.

The third rule of navigation is not to leave people stranded. I get very annoyed, and your customers will too, when I end up on a page where my back button doesn't work. That means I have to figure out where I was before I got to where I am and I have to start again.

Along these same lines, the fourth rule of navigation is don't keep opening new navigation windows at each step. You lose people, even patient people. Keep things simple to make navigation easy for your customers. A site map is also very useful, especially for sites that include many different sources of information. It can provide customers with a better understanding of the site layout and may help them find information more quickly.

Graphics, Text, and Background

I have grouped the topics of graphics, text, and background together because they have such a profound impact on each other. A well-placed graphic can make text more visually pleasing and readable. A choice of background can make text more readable or illegible and can make graphics stand out or be lost.

In planning how you will use text, you need to consider the following factors and their impact on the readability and effectiveness of your site:

- Font type
- Font size
- Font color
- Text structure
- Choice of graphics
- Choice of background

Font Type

Stick to one or two types of fonts. You have probably heard this many times, but that's because it's true. You may want to use one type for headings and another for body text. Any more than that and the changes in font will become distractions, making the text more difficult to read.

Your site will inevitably provide support to customers who have different font libraries. If you choose an unusual font, some of your customers might not have it and another font would be substituted. Your site may look totally different than you anticipated. Stick to common fonts such as Arial or Times New Roman.

Stay away from fonts that are elaborate or difficult to read. You can use these as adornments, but the body of your text should be in an unexciting but easy-to-read font such as the two mentioned previously.

Font Size

In terms of font size, most sites today tend to use fonts that are smaller rather than larger. Although fonts that are too large can be very distracting and difficult to read, fonts that are too small can simply be hard to see. Yes, you do get more words on a page when you use a smaller font size, but those words have a lot less impact when someone has to lean forward and squint to read them. Text that you want people to read shouldn't be smaller than 9 or 10 points. Also remember resolution. People will look at your site from a variety of monitor resolutions, so the text might appear even smaller on their monitors. Test your font size over a number of resolutions and pick one that works with all or most of them.

Font Color

Your video card may have 256 or more colors, but text on your support site is not the place to try them out. Dark text on a light background is the rule for easy reading, and black on white probably works best. Save your colors for headings or emphasis. Red makes a great contrast with black and white, which is why you will find many sites that use these three colors. Overusing of colors for emphasis results in a loss of emphasis.

Text Structure

Even if you choose good font types, sizes, and color combinations, you can still cause customer retention problems if you don't group the text into readable units. A page full of rambling text, unbroken by emphasis, white space, or some kind of grouping is text that won't be read. You need to break text up into readable units.

First, remove all unnecessary words. Make your text concise. Give your customers as few words to deal with as possible.

Second, use occasional emphasis such as bolding to accentuate words or points. The key word here is occasional. Too much emphasis removes the emphasis.

Third, break the text up visually by using tools such as bullets, graphics, tables, or white space. Text that comes in small packages is text more likely to be read.

Finally, refrain from using all caps. A mix of upper and lower case is much easier to read.

Choice of Graphics

I've already mentioned the importance of keeping graphics to a reasonable size. If a graphic takes too long to load not just on your machine, but on the PCs that your customers might use, get rid of it. Another consideration when choosing graphics is color. Some of your customers may not have 256 colors available on their monitors. Check out what your graphics look like on monitors of varying resolutions and with varying levels of color palettes. You may be surprised. Fortunately, fewer colors are not only safer in terms of what will appear on your customer's screen, but are often more effective.

When you add a graphic, ask yourself what purpose it serves. Is it illustrating a process or technical specification that will help your customer solve a problem? Is it breaking text up to make a page more readable? Does it portray an organizational image? These are all valid reasons for using graphics. If the graphic doesn't serve a purpose, don't use it.

Choice of Background

A background is just that, a background. It should not overshadow text or graphics, but rather provide a canvas for them. Text gets lost on busy backgrounds and becomes difficult to read. Graphics lose their impact. Support sites typically convey a significant amount of text to their customers, and text is easiest to read when it is dark and is presented on a light background. White, light gray, or light, mottled backgrounds may be boring in terms of artistic merit, but your customers will appreciate the simplicity when they are trying to read answers to their problems.

Photographs and Multimedia

The tools you use on your site may employ photographs or various forms of multimedia. For example, knowledge bases might show some photographs or run short film clips to illustrate a hardware fix. Online training may include some kind of sound and animation, and so on.

If your site uses photographs, take size, loading time, and resolution into consideration. If customers with less modern equipment won't see what you have designed, tell them so and offer alternatives. As with graphics, ensure each photograph has a purpose.

To make multimedia as effective as possible for your customers, test out all the uses of multimedia and any required plug-ins on a variety of platforms. Some multimedia presentations such as online training require that users set their monitors to a certain level of resolution. Make sure that you give customers all of the instructions they require for the multimedia to work effectively. Again, if customers with older equipment will have problems, put a caution on your site and offer them alternatives where possible.

Content

The golden rule for content is *if a particular page or piece of text does not provide the customer with something useful, then it shouldn't be there.* Don't waste customer time by providing irrelevant pages or sections of text. Everything you offer on your site should provide value to some segment of your customers.

I found a very interesting idea regarding Web site content in one of the sites I visited while researching design, www.grantasticdesigns.com. The idea is that people with a print design mentality put priority on the artistic elements of a site as well as features such as animation, sounds, and so on, while those with a Web design mentality put priority on the content. A print design mentality results in a site that focuses on the designer, a showcase for the designer's talent. A Web design mentality results in a site that focuses on the customer, a set of useful offerings to help the customer in some way.

Those designing support sites need to have a Web design mentality. They need to make it as easy as possible for people to get information and help. They need to resist the lure of interesting artistic effects and focus on giving the customer valuable content, however artistically uninteresting.

In terms of functions, one thing that your site should contain regardless of what you support is some way for the site user to contact a real person. This might be email, it might be an assisted support function, or it might be a list of phone numbers. Don't leave your customers without any kind of support in case the site fails to help them.

Layout

Layout refers to the arrangement of all elements on the pages of a site. All the topics I have covered so far in the discussion of design fundamentals apply to the layout. One thing I need to add is that the layout should be consistent from page to page. Navigational tools should be the same and should be in the same location on each page. Background, logos, and so on should all be the same, and the font, size, and color of text should remain consistent. The customer should know where things are on a page before that page is even displayed. Consistency in layout makes a site easier to navigate, easier to read, and gives it a more professional look.

Testing

Once you have put your site together, you should test it on a variety of equipment before you roll it out to the general public. Test your site on various screen resolutions, on dial-up Internet connections if your customers will use the site that way, and on various CPU speeds. Get feedback from people outside of the design team and from future site users if at all possible. This is very important because your design team is probably so well acquainted with the site that they may not be aware of usability problems. What is obvious or transparent to the team may be confusing to novice users.

Every time you run into technology that causes a problem with how your site is loaded or displayed, you must decide to either modify your site to accommodate the technology or to not support the technology.

You may have to make the latter decision for technologies that are out of date. You cannot let a few out-of-date customers hold you back from providing support to the rest of your customers. Of course, if a significant number of your customers still use technologies that are out of date, then you don't really have a choice; you have to support them. Any time your site does not support a certain technology, put a note on your Web site so that customers won't be unpleasantly surprised.

Back to Tasks

You now have a basic idea of the design fundamentals you need to keep in mind while designing your site. Now it's time to look at the tasks involved in site design.

Identifying Factors That Constrain Site Design

It doesn't do much good to design a fabulous site if you can't implement it. You should know what the requirements of the site are from the scope summary developed in Chapter 3. You must also consider the factors that constrain the design of your site. These are the factors that may force you to take that complex design you came up with that uses Java as well as direct customer interaction and database access and turn it into a basic HTML first-generation informational site.

Factors that can constrain your site fall into three categories: human, business, and technological. Your first task in the design process is to review these categories and identify the factors constraining your design. You'll then have to define how the factors impact your design. The rest of the design process must take this information into consideration.

Human Factors

The human factors that can limit your site design include both the skills of the staff who will develop and maintain the site and your customers, the people who will use the site. In Chapter 4, "Staff Selection," I talked about the skills required for the various work categories involved in building a support site. The people developing and maintaining the site require very specific technical skills. If your organization does not have those skills and is not willing or able to pay for them, then you will need to start off with a basic support site with no interactive functionality. For example, you may be constrained to a site that is built using HTML and that offers FAQs, downloads, email, and not much more. A simple site is better than nothing and it should reduce the workload of the support staff. They can then use this extra time to research the technologies and learn the skills needed to implement a more sophisticated site.

Similarly, if you outsource the building of the site, make sure you have the skills in place, either in-house or through an outsourcing contract, to keep the site up to date. If you do not have the skills to maintain a complex site, go with something much simpler.

Your customers can also constrain your site. How knowledgeable are they? Do they have the skills required to use the tools you are planning to provide? If you choose to make your navigational icons words, will your customers understand what they are? For example, if you have a section titled Knowledge Base, will your customers know what this means or do you need to title it something like Search For A Solution?

Business Factors

The strongest business factor that affects your site is budget. That fabulous site that you want to design may simply cost too much. If the cost of developing and maintaining a site is too high, then the site benefits are eaten away and the return on investment drops. If you do a cost-benefit analysis for your site, as discussed in Chapter 1, "Is Web-Based Support Worthwhile?," you can very easily see the impact that an increase in development and maintenance costs have on the time required for return and on the return on investment itself. Don't start design on your site until you know how much you can spend on it.

As an example, let's consider a company that has budgeted for a very simple site. The cost benefit analysis for the support site is shown in Table 6.2 under Scenario 1. The site will include some FAQs, various downloads, links, and an email option. The estimated creation time is 10 weeks. I will use the same figures for labor costs as in Chapter 1. Labor costs, including overhead, are $60 per hour, which translates into $420 per a seven-hour day, or $2,100 per a five-day work week.

Table 6.2 The Impact of Increased Development Costs on the Return on Investment and Payback

One-time costs	SCENARIO 1			SCENARIO 2		
		Year 1	Year 2		Year 1	Year 2
Site creation	$21,000			$25,200		
Ongoing costs						
Site maintenance		$10,080	$10,080		$12,600	$12,600
Total	**$21,000**	**$10,080**	**$10,080**	**$25,200**	**$12,600**	**$12,600**
Cumulative costs	**$21,000**	**$31,080**	**$41,160**	**$25,200**	**$37,800**	**$50,400**
Benefits						
Support calls eliminated		$18,000	$18,000		$18,000	$18,000
Publishing		$7,000	$7,000		$7,000	$7,000
Total		**$25,000**	**$25,000**		**$25,000**	**$25,000**
Cumulative benefits		**$25,000**	**$50,000**		**$25,000**	**$50,000**
Return on investment		**−20%**	**21%**		**−34%**	**−1%**

At $2,100 per week, the site creation cost is $21,000 in 10 weeks. Maintenance of the site will include updating the FAQs, checking and updating links, and updating downloads. Maintenance will take approximately two days per month for a total of 24 days per year. Twenty-four days at $420 per day translates into $10,080 for the year. Email support is absorbed into regular Help Desk support activity. It is estimated that the site will save approximately 150 10-minute calls per month, a savings in staff time of 1,500 minutes. At $60 per hour, this becomes $1,500 per month, or $18,000 over one year. An additional $7,000 per year can be saved in publication, mailing, and CD creation costs. As Table 6.2 shows, the site pays for itself in year two with a return on investment of 21 percent.

Now, let's consider a second scenario. The site developer has been playing with Java and wants to make the site more than just an informational site. The developer wants to add interaction with his newly gained programming skills. What impact might this have on the return on investment of the site? The rather inexperienced developer needs to create Java programs and test them out on various platforms and browsers. Let's be very conservative and say this takes two weeks longer than the original 10 weeks. This means an additional $4,200 in one-time development costs, bringing the total cost of site creation to $25,200.

The site in scenario 2 may also take a little longer to maintain, say, two and a half days each month instead of two days. At $420 per day over 30 days in one year, this pushes the ongoing maintenance costs to $12,600 per year.

We have not changed the functionality of the site; we've only increased the complexity of implementation, so the benefits have not changed. As you can see in Table 6.2, scenario 2 has increased costs without increasing benefits, resulting in no payback by year 2 and a negative return on investment. Looking at this project from a purely financial point of view, the site in scenario 2 is not worth building.

What other business factors might affect design? If your organization has a specific image it wants to promote, then your site must conform to that image. For example, if the site must portray a very serious, business-like image, then you might want to shelve the light-hearted set of navigational icons you were thinking of using. The business might also dictate that you include marketing information at strategic points and you would then incorporate this into your design.

Technological Factors

The design of your site may be constrained by the existing technology within your organization and by the technology your customers use. Any tool you choose has to be compatible with your organization's technological platform. If your organization already has a Web site and is hosting its own server, then your site must retain the look of the main site and must use compatible technology. If your design includes online access to a large knowledge base, before you finalize that design you need to make sure that the space you need is available either on your own server or on the server of the company that hosts your Web site.

Your design is also constrained by the technology that your customers use. How will they access your site? If any of your customers uses dial-up access, then you need to design your site so that these customers don't spend all of their time waiting for a response. Speed is one of your primary concerns and if you plan to implement any graphic-intensive functions, then you may want to include text-only options for those functions as well.

Finalizing Site Functions

The most significant input in the site design process includes the scope summary that we discussed in Chapter 3 and the information on functions, tools, and implementations presented in Chapter 5, "Functions, Tools, and Implementations." The scope summary describes which requirements the site must satisfy and it also makes some initial suggestions on implementations. In the design process, these must be translated into specific functions that are available on the site while keeping in mind any identified constraints and using information from Chapter 5 to see how the functions might be implemented.

To illustrate this process, let's go back to our two examples: Education Plus and Trace Software.

Education Plus

Table 6.3 shows the original Education Plus site requirements along with some potential implementations. The constraints on the new site come from customers and the budget.

Education Plus will outsource most of the development and maintenance work to experts so skills are not a constraint. Customers using the site may not be technically knowledgeable, so any terminology used should be business-oriented rather than technical. The budget will accommodate a moderately priced request management system with a Web interface, but not more than that. Management does require some site marketing, as specified in Table 6.3, so the site design must incorporate the marketing. Education Plus does not have a site currently; its customers are all organizations with high-speed Internet access, and it is planning to outsource the hosting of its Web site to an Internet Service Provider (ISP) so no significant technological constraints occur.

Table 6.3   The Original Education Plus Site Requirements

REQUIREMENT	POTENTIAL IMPLEMENTATIONS
Provide all customer support requirements.	FAQ, searchable knowledge base, and course download.
Promote professional image.	Hire a site designer.
Market new products.	Online ads in locations accessed by current customers.
Attract new business.	Separate products page with product descriptions, samples, and customer testimonials.
Respond quickly to email.	Implement a one-month pilot.
Download copies of courses.	A special customer-only function to access course downloads could be part of call or order management.
Provide high security.	A sign-in could be part of the call or order management system.
Request and track course changes online.	A Web interface to the call or order management system.

The site design for Education Plus is carried out by Kelly Rana, an Education Plus employee, and an outsourced resource from Gold Standard Sites. Together they review the requirements, constraints, and potential implementations and come up with two sets of functions: the public functions, which are available to all site users, and the private functions, which are available only to Education Plus customers. The public functions include product information, samples, customer testimonials, and email for sales-related questions.

To get to the private functions area, customers will have to enter a user ID and password. A FAQ is available to handle the most common customer issues and enables customers to receive responses to their most common questions very quickly. The private functions also include online access to a request management system that enables customers to log requests and problems as well as view any of their own logs. The database associated with the request management system could contain confidential data, so Kelly decides against making this data available online. Instead, she decides to put an update process into place that will involve scanning new logs and email to see if anything could be put into a FAQ. This will probably work for Education Plus because the questions tend to be procedural rather than technical and the volume is not high.

A course download function is also included as part of the private functions. Customers can view a list of courses that they have purchased and download any of their own courses. The user ID and password determine which courses can be viewed and downloaded so customers cannot access each other's courses.

You will also create a fast-response email function, as requested by the customers. The data from the email will be incorporated into the FAQs.

Table 6.4 shows the functions that Kelly and the site designer have settled on.

Trace Software

In Table 6.5, we can see the original requirements of the support site for Trace Software.

One of the biggest constraints on the design of the Trace Software site is its customers. The site will have both European and North American customers, and its design and content must be suitable to both audiences. Trace Software's customers have a wide range of technical knowledge so the site must cater to both novices and experts. It must incorporate several remote support options, and the budget for the site allows for the purchase of top of the line tools, so no significant budgetary constraints exist. Trace wants its customers to get the support they need and it firmly believes that tools are less costly in the long run than the equivalent in support staff.

Like Education Plus, Trace Software decides it needs both public and private sections on its support site. The public functions include product descriptions, downloads of trial software, and lists of customers showing how the software is implemented at specific customer sites

Table 6.4 The Education Plus Support Site Functions

PUBLIC FUNCTIONS	PRIVATE FUNCTIONS
Product information	FAQ
Downloads of course samples	Online logging of problems and requests, and online viewing of logs
Customer testimonials	Downloads of own courses
Email for product inquiries	Quick response email

Table 6.5 The Original Trace Software Site Requirements

REQUIREMENT	POTENTIAL IMPLEMENTATIONS
Reflect new international image	Create a site design committee including an international group to ensure acceptance.
Promote international business	A products page including descriptions, customer lists, and trial versions.
Remote support for European office	Have assisted support options on top of self-services and provide a support practitioner with adequate remote support tools.
Eliminate hiring necessity	See Offload support.
Offload support	FAQs, an interactive knowledge base, and improved processes for updating resolution information.
Customer training	Have Education Plus develop some training modules to be posted on a training page.
Online problem logging	Implement a Web interface.
Emergency support	A page can be initiated from the support site.
Improved email support	Have customers use an online call-tracking system for all communication as far as problems, requests, and questions.

and the resulting value. A FAQ is also required for questions that come up as potential customers evaluate trial software. This FAQ will probably be smaller than the one required for regular users of Trace Software products. The public functions will also include an email option for product and sales information.

The private functions of the site are accessed through a login screen. All registered users will have a valid user ID and password. These private functions include a weekly updated FAQ broken down by product and by major categories within the product category that are identified by the site analysts. The analysts are Help Desk practitioners in this case and will have a very good idea of the categories that need to be created.

The private functions also include online access to Trace Software's call logging system. Registered customers can use this function to log questions and problems as well as to view their own logs. An interactive knowledge base tool is available as a private function to enable customers to try to resolve their own problems. The tool will try to find a resolution by asking for symptoms, matching symptoms to potential resolutions, and collecting more data as required. An assisted support button is provided when two or more resolutions are recommended but do not solve the problem. The assisted support button will invoke interaction with a support practitioner. The support practitioner will have the tools required to carry on an online chat session with the customer, take over the customer's PC to illustrate a technique, and run an extensive set of utilities on the customer's PC in the background.

A training function will also be available to registered users. This function will initially offer three online training modules designed by Education Plus. One covers simple networking techniques, one covers how to implement and control security in an organization, and the final one deals with the installation and use of the home-based product. The courses can be taken online for those with a fast connection or be downloaded for viewing from a hard drive for those with a slow connection. Registered customers also have the ability to download fixes and patches for their specific version of software as well as all software documentation.

The private functions of the support site also include an emergency support function. During off-hours, this function invokes a page for a support practitioner who will have access to all assisted support tools. During regular hours, this function will page one of the on-duty practitioners who will then make that paged call a top priority. The site analysts and manager must define emergencies very clearly and must monitor use of this emergency support function so that it is not abused. Some further constraints may have to be placed on this function, so keeping it separate from the other private functions may make it easier

Table 6.6 The Trace Software Support Site Functions

PUBLIC FUNCTIONS	PRIVATE FUNCTIONS
Product information	FAQ
Software trial downloads	Online problem and question logging, and online viewing of logs
FAQ for trial software	Interactive knowledge base
Customer lists and implementations	Assisted support
E-mail for product inquiries	Online and downloadable training, downloadable software patches and documentation, and emergency support

to change in the future. Table 6.6 shows the functions that have been identified for the new Trace Software support site.

Creating Prototypes

Once the functions have been identified, the site designer can create a prototype of the site for feedback from all interested parties. People with an interest in the site need something to look at so that they can give feedback and offer suggestions for changes before the design is finalized and coded.

You will typically start with a very simple prototype showing the function layouts and perhaps some navigation. As feedback is received and applied, you will move on to a more detailed prototype that could include background colors, graphics, navigation icons, and so on. The more detailed prototype would convey the overall look and image of the final product.

Let's go back to our two examples to see what some initial simple site prototypes might look like.

Education Plus

Figures 6.2, 6.3, and 6.4 are early prototypes of the Education Plus site design. Education Plus doesn't currently have a site, so the main tab in the design shown in Figure 6.2 would be the home page of the Education Plus Web site. The designer has chosen a simple tab design for the functions and has penciled in a comment asking whether or not email should be available on the main page. Putting questions directly on any prototype drawings is a very simple way of ensuring they get resolved.

Figure 6.3 is a prototype for the Support tab. This is the entry into private support, and a user ID and password are required. Here it's important to bring up the issue of offering help to users if needed when logging in, and the designer has asked about this. What if a customer's user ID or password isn't working properly? How will this be handled? It is important to identify these kinds of decisions up front so that your customers aren't stopped dead by this problem if it occurs.

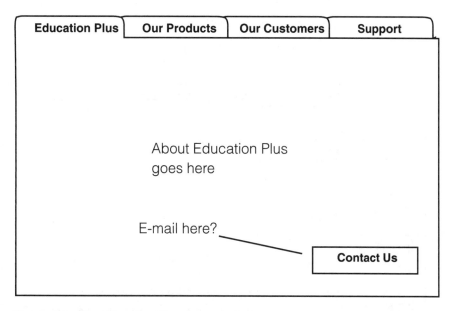

Figure 6.2   The Education Plus site prototype.

| Education Plus | Our Products | Our Customers | Support |

User ID [ ]
Password [ ]

If they can't sign on
they'll need some
kind of help

Help

Figure 6.3   The Support tab prototype.

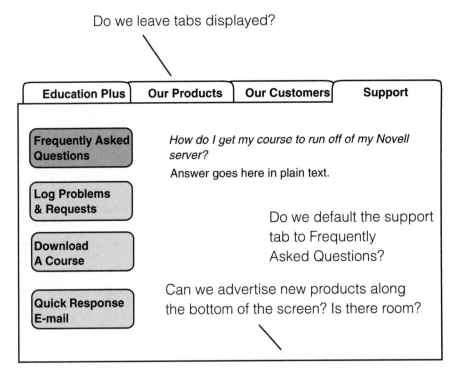

Figure 6.4 The FAQ option prototype.

Figure 6.4 suggests that when a customer logs into the support option, the main screen displayed is the FAQ. The rational for this might be that the FAQ is the most used function. The designer has asked for verification on this point. In Figure 6.4, we also see the basic layout that the designer has suggested, large print buttons on the side. The designer has asked if the original tabs should remain visible and has suggested a location for the marketing that will go on the site.

Laying out pages of a site in this way and getting feedback can save time in the site creation process. Important design decisions are made before anything is coded; nothing major has to be redone. At the next level of prototyping, colors and graphics can be added so that the image of the site can be established.

Trace Software

Figures 6.5, 6.6, and 6.7 are early prototypes of the design for the Trace Software support site. Figure 6.5 illustrates the main page of the business'

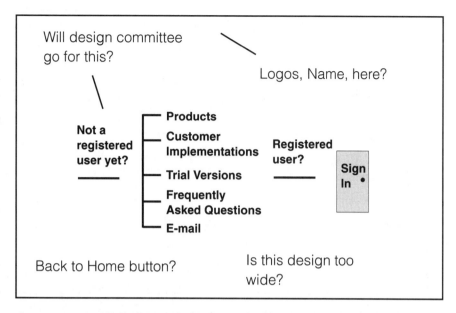

Figure 6.5 The Trace Software main support page prototype.

support site that is accessed from its main Web site. The public functions can be selected directly from a ladder-type structure, while the private functions require customers to sign in.

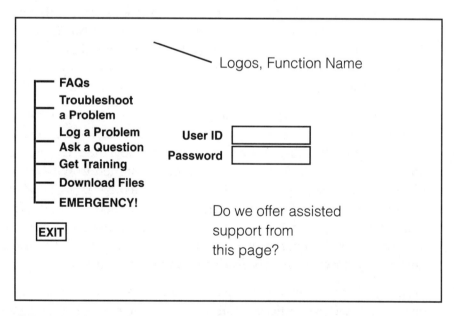

Figure 6.6 The prototype of the main page for registered users.

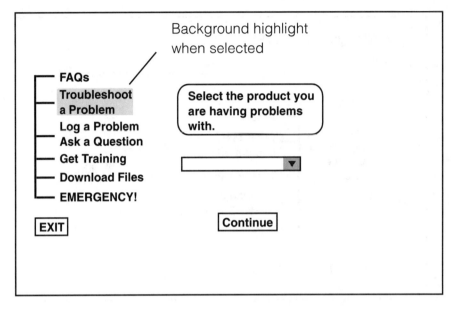

Figure 6.7 The Interactive Problem Resolution function prototype.

In Figure 6.5, we see a very early prototype that might be reviewed by two or more designers and analysts. The designer has penciled in questions asking how navigation back to the main site should be handled, if the top of the page is a good position for logos, and if the site might be too wide for customers with lower resolution monitors. The designer also has some doubts about this rather light-hearted design. Perhaps the design committee is looking for something more serious, more business-like.

Figure 6.6 is a prototype for the page displayed when customers have indicated that they are registered users of Trace Software products and want to sign into the private part of the support site. The functions on the left are not enabled until a customer has signed in with a valid user ID and password. The site designer has asked if assisted support should also be one of the functions available directly from the functions list. Up until now, the plan was that assisted support could only be invoked after the customer had tried to get help from the interactive knowledge base or directly from the Emergency function.

Figure 6.7 shows how the navigation will work. The selected option will be highlighted to indicate that it is the current selection. The page shown is from the interactive knowledge base. The designer has indicated how the interaction might work visually. At this point, the tool may have been selected already and the designer may know what it looks like or the designer may be suggesting a layout.

The previous figures should give you an idea of the amount of work involved in planning a site. Each page must be planned out, including the navigation, interaction, and information to be displayed. Colors, text, and graphics bring more complexity and demand more planning. Trace Software will probably create several prototypes before settling on a design. A committee of Trace Software employees from both Europe and North America are participating in the design approval, and getting a consensus may take some time. What the designers should do is get feedback from someone on the committee before formally presenting each design iteration to the committee. This will help ensure that each iteration presented is closer to what the committee will accept.

Researching and Selecting Tools

The task of researching and selecting specific tools can start once the functions have been identified. Chapter 5 will not only help with the function identification process, but will help you understand which-support site tools are available.

The process of researching and selecting tools can be time-consuming, but if not enough time and effort are allocated to it, the result is inappropriate tools that do not perform the required functions and yeild a poor return on the site investment.

Once you've purchased a tool, you're pretty much stuck with it. To help ensure that you buy what you need, I offer you the following four suggestions:

- Define exactly what you need and then see what type of software is available for your requirements. Use the references in Chapter 5 to look for sources of software.

- Try out the software before you buy it to make sure it meets all your requirements and is compatible with your technology configuration. If you are anticipating growth, the tool you buy should be able to handle it.

- Check out support for the tool. If the support doesn't look very good, choose another tool.
- Make sure that everyone who should be involved in tool-purchasing decisions actually takes part. Site designers need to work with site analysts and site developers to ensure that the tool's functionality and technological compatibility are what they need to be.

Let's go back to our previous examples to see what kind of tools Education Plus and Trace Software must search for. Earlier in Table 6.4, we see the functions that Education Plus is planning to implement on its site. The tools that are indicated should help format the FAQ and some kind of Web-enabled request-tracking system. Table 6.6 shows us the functions that Trace Software is planning to implement. The tools that Trace Software will require include a Web interface to its call-tracking system, an interactive problem-resolution tool, and a set of remote support tools. The remote support tools could include components for remote control, an online chat, and various remote utilities that will enable the practitioner to access and update all the files on the customer's PC.

Key Points

This section provides a summary of the key points in site design fundamentals and the tasks involved in site design.

The foundation for your support site design can be determined by answering the question, *Why do customers visit this site?* The answer will probably indicate that your customers want help, they want it fast, and they want it in a format that they can understand. This means anything that increases customer waiting time, such as extra keystrokes or loading complex graphics, should be avoided. Navigation should be simple and clear.

Another key aspect of site design is the combination of text, graphics, and background. Text should be limited to one or two fonts that everyone will have access to on their system, it should be of good reading size, and dark text on a light background works best. To make passages of text more readable, the text should be concise. All extraneous words should be eliminated, emphasis such as bolding should be used occasionally, and the text should be broken up into readable units through the use of bullets, graphics, tables, or white space.

Graphics should be quick to load and appropriate for their particular use. Backgrounds should be light and simple, allowing text to be read easily.

The final basic fundamental of site design is to test your design on all platforms that your customers might be using.

The first task involved in site design is to identify the factors constraining the design. These can be divided into three categories: human, business, and technological. The human factors that can limit some aspect of your site design include the skills of your staff who will develop and maintain the site and the knowledge of your customers. The strongest business factor affecting your site is budget. If the cost of developing and maintaining a site is too high, then the site benefits are eaten away and the return on investment drops. The technological factors that constrain your site include the existing technology within your organization and the technology your customers use. Any tool you choose has to be compatible with your organization's technological platform. If any of your customers use dial-up access, you are going to have to design your site so that these customers are not spending all of their time waiting for a response.

At the same time that you are identifying factors that constrain site design, you can start the process of finalizing the functions you want on the site. To do this, you will use the scope summary that was discussed in Chapter 3 along with the information on functions, tools, and implementations provided in Chapter 5. The scope summary describes the requirements the site must satisfy and suggests potential implementations. These can be translated into specific site functions.

Once the functions have been identified, the site designer can create a site prototype in order to receive feedback from all interested parties before the design is finalized and coded. A good idea is to start with a simple prototype showing the function layouts and perhaps some navigation. Then when feedback is received and applied, you can move on to a more detailed prototype that might include background colors, graphics, navigation icons, and so on.

The fourth task in creating a site design consists of researching and selecting the site tools. This task can go on while the prototyping is taking place. The importance of tool research and selection should not be underestimated. A poor tool choice leads to a poor return on investment for the support site.

PART FOUR

Implementation and Management

CHAPTER 7

Processes and Implementation

You have designed your support site and selected your tools. You know what your site will look like. You are now entering the build phase of your project. You need to design the processes required to run the site on a day-to-day basis and you need to build it. In the build phase, the design of your processes and the construction of your site can be carried out concurrently.

Process design is critical to the success of your site. The larger your site is, the more critical process design becomes. Processes define the workflow around your site, how you will handle email, and how you will keep your site up to date. Processes that are not clearly and formally defined are processes that are not followed. The time to define processes is before your site is completed. Once your site is up and running, the need for processes starts immediately and can escalate quickly. You might be swamped with email, for instance, or you might have all kinds of "hot tips" that need to be posted. If you don't have your processes in place, you could be facing disaster in the form of complaints from irate customers who are not getting responses to their email or who are not getting up-to-date information. Customers might not come back or they might turn to telephone support.

How you go about constructing your site is also critical to its success. You need to create a plan that lists all the tasks that need to be completed, the date that they need to be completed by, and who is doing them. In this way you can ensure that you have important procedures such as testing, quality reviews, and revision covered. You can monitor progress and manage risks to help ensure your site is on time, is within budget, and delivers the promised functionality. If your site is very simple, your plan might be a checklist, but if your site is more complex, you may want to use a project management tool to define your plan.

In this chapter, I will discuss how to identify the processes you require and how to go about defining them, including their format and responsibility. The chapter will also discuss creating a checklist or plan for the site's construction, tasks that need to be included to ensure quality, and establishing an initial support team for the site until you have some idea of the traffic volume. Specifically, the topics I will cover are as follows:

- The definitions of process and procedure
- Tasks involved in the build phase
- Identifying processes
- Defining processes and creating procedures
- Implementation and testing checklist
- Establishing initial support
- Implementing the site

A Definition: Process versus Procedure

For the purposes of this chapter, I will define a process as the series of actions that describe how a particular task is carried out from beginning to end. A procedure is the documented definition of the process.

Tasks Involved in the Build Phase

Table 7.1 shows the project tasks involved in the build phase of your Web-based support site, the phase in which you define processes and

Table 7.1 The Project Tasks Involved in the Build Phase

TASKS	DETAILS
Identify the processes required.	Identify the processes required for information maintenance, customer communication, and specific site functions.
Create a defined procedure for each process.	Assign responsibility for each process to a specific position. Also define and document (or automate) each process.
Create an implementation and testing checklist.	Create a list of tasks involved in completing the site. Also create test criteria and test plans.
Establish an initial site support team and procedures.	Assign a team to support the site in its early stages and create backup plans for identified risks.
Implement the site.	Carry out the implementation and testing. Make the site available to customers.

construct your site. The steps involved in defining the processes and in actually building the site can be carried out at the same time.

It is typically the responsibility of the site or project manager to identify which processes are required for maintaining and managing the site. The manager needs to look at all of the workflows involved with the site and pick out the processes that need to be identified.

Each process needs to be defined in detail to ensure its correct execution time after time. The person who actually performs the process should be the one to define it. This goes a long way towards establishing ownership and ensuring the definition is done correctly.

Before any site construction activities can be carried out, a plan or a checklist identifying all tasks and responsibilities needs to be put together. The manager needs to ensure that the tasks necessary to ensure quality are part of this plan or checklist.

When a support site is first put into place, it is a good idea to have an implementation support team behind it to quickly handle any unexpected problems or unanticipated traffic levels so that the site does not start off with any negative customer perceptions. The final step in the build site is to actually upload the site and make it accessible to customers.

Identifying Processes

Examining what it takes to maintain the information and functions on your site and to handle any communication will help you identify the processes you need to define. Processes will typically fall into the following categories:

- Maintaining site information
- Responding to email
- Handling online call tracking
- Gathering feedback
- Maintaining discussion groups
- Carrying out chat functions
- Using remote control tools

Tasks such as updating tools and functions would typically happen less often than the activities in the previously listed categories. They would also be handled as projects rather than as processes. Ongoing site evaluations and improvements are management issues and are discussed in Chapter 9, "Site Management."

Maintaining Site Information

Depending on how large your support site is and how many information sources you have, the amount of work involved in keeping the information on your site up to date can be very daunting indeed, as Figure 7.1 shows.

The information on your site probably consists of knowledge sources that provide solutions to problems and informational sources that provide general organizational or product information. Knowledge sources are used on their own or as part of a problem resolution tool. They include FAQs, logged problems and solutions, documents describing known issues or bugs, technical documents, product documentation, and knowledge bases of specific cases. Adjuncts to knowledge sources include links to other sites, training documents, e-newsletters, and downloads. Informational sources might include

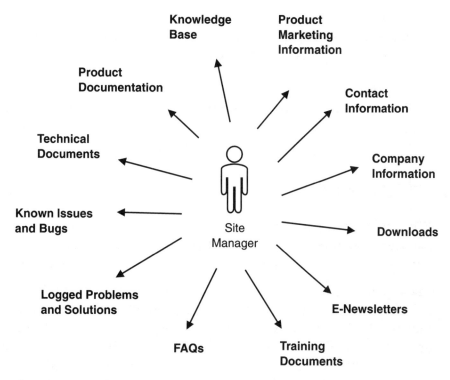

Figure 7.1 Keeping site information up-to-date.

company information, contact information such as who to contact for what, and product marketing information.

Each of these sources must be kept up-to-date. The challenges involved in updating this information include the following:

Volume. A great deal of information to keep up to date. If you have a large support site, you will need to consider automating your update processes as much as possible.

Managing update sources. Updates may come from a variety of sources and you need to ensure you understand all of the sources and collect all the updates.

Scheduling. Some sources such as FAQs may change on a regularly scheduled basis, such as daily or weekly. Sources such as a "Known Bugs" section may require changes infrequently, but the change itself has to be immediate. Other sources, such as product documentation, are more stable and require changes only when a correction is made or a new version or product is released. Keeping the various schedules straight can get hairy unless you define processes around each.

Your defined procedures must address these challenges. A good way to start is for each process to identify which specific sources you need to keep up to date, where the updates come from, who or what will work on them, and what the update schedule will look like.

Responding to Email

When identifying the processes necessary to respond to email, you need to look at the types of email you are receiving. Each needs to be handled differently, perhaps passed on to another group for handling.

The types of email you can expect are shown in Figure 7.2. Requests for information might include requests for product literature or pricing. You may need to pass these types of requests on to the sales department if you are large enough to have one. Complaints require their own handling process to ensure replies are tactful, customers are satisfied as much as possible, and that this data is included in ongoing evaluations and improvements of the support site. Suggestions for improvement need a process that will ensure that they are responded to and that the suggestion is considered in ongoing improvement initiatives. Email support requests need to follow a process similar to logged calls. Misdirected

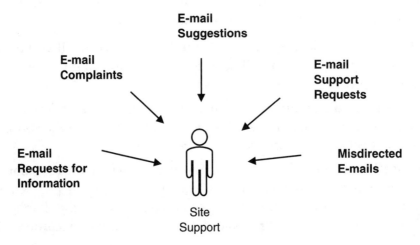

Figure 7.2 Email types.

email requires a process to ensure that customers sending the email can be put on track and will not get upset by false expectations.

Leaving any of these processes to chance can cause a breakdown of your support site, leading to customers that are dissatisfied and consequently turn elsewhere for help, such as telephone support.

Handling Online Call Tracking

If you are going to allow your customers to log calls directly into your call-tracking system via your support site, then you need processes in place to ensure that those calls are picked up and resolved within an appropriate timeframe. These logged calls might be the same as the processes for your regular logged calls, but you need to check this out to make sure things will work the way they should. If your customers can track the progress of their calls, you must have processes in place for updating the call problem progress. You cannot have customers looking at garbage text that was entered as an update.

Gathering Feedback

Gathering feedback might include collecting information from customer surveys, from Help Desk practitioners who may hear suggestions from customers, or from other areas within the organization. The marketing department, for instance, may suggest improvements or additions to the site. The processes involved in gathering feedback should specify how feedback is to be gathered and should define how it is input into the improvement process.

Once the processes have been identified and you start defining them, you will notice that it may make sense to combine processes that you first thought were separate and unrelated. For example, your process for handling email suggestions could be part of the feedback process because all of these are part of site evaluation and improvement. Figure 7.3 illustrates this structure.

Maintaining Discussion Groups

If your site hosts discussion groups, you must have processes in place for archiving and monitoring the groups. You will have to archive messages on an ongoing basis so that people aren't faced with prohibitive

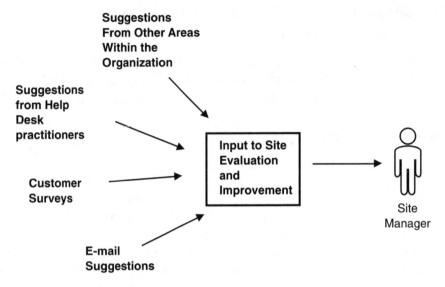

Figure 7.3 Processes feeding the same further process.

response times. If you are monitoring the groups, you will have to establish processes to handle any breach of discussion group policies, such as negative or abusive messages, and to correct false information. If you are moderating your discussion groups, you will also need processes for scanning the messages and answering any unresolved issues within a specific amount of time. You may also want processes in place for updating information sources and for site evaluations and improvements. Discussion groups can be a good source of ideas for improving the products or services that your company markets. You should have a process in place to ensure that these ideas are passed on to management as well.

Carrying Out Chat Functions

Aside from the task of picking up chat requests off of the queue, you need to set up a process for actually carrying the chat session out. You may have a series of diagnostics that you take the customer through, you may have some guidelines about how long each person can chat before being interrupted, or you may want to specify that after each chat session the customer gets a transcript with any supporting materials.

The more structure you put around your chat sessions, the more successful they will be. You will also want processes in place for making updates or corrections to information sources as well as for gathering suggestions for improvements that can be sent to management.

Using Remote Control Tools

If your site is to offer assisted support using remote control tools, you need to establish a method for using the tools and interacting with the customers. You will have steps to follow for taking over their PCs, getting the appropriate permission, and for informing the customer of what you are doing. You may want to specify a standard diagnostic sequence or a standard way to close a session, which could be done by emailing the customer a transcript and any supporting materials, such as specific documents. As with the chat function, you will probably want to set up a means of making updates and corrections as well as taking in ideas for possible improvements.

Putting Them All Together

When determining the processes that are required, list all of the processes you see a need for. You can pare the list later as you start to define your processes. Table 7.2 shows an example of a set of processes. If you have a task that you want to have happen the same way each time, you need to define a process around it. Without the process, you really have no control over how a particular workflow is executed each time it is carried out. The ultimate in process definition is automation.

Defining Processes and Creating Procedures

Once you have identified the processes you need, you are ready to start defining them, which means creating procedures for them. This is going to take some time. You're going to have to go through each process, identify the steps you want repeated each time that process is carried out, and then look at other processes that might be related to this one in some way. You then have to document this information and store it where it can be accessed by everyone who might be using it.

Table 7.2 Process Identification

CATEGORY	PROCESSES
Maintaining site information	Updating FAQs, solution logs, technical documents, product documentation, knowledge bases, links to other sites, training documents, e-newsletters, downloads, company information, contact information, and product marketing information.
Responding to email	Responding to requests for information, suggestions for improvement, support requests, and misdirected emails. Also identify and provide data for information source updates, evaluations, and improvements.
Handling online call tracking	Taking logged problems off the queue, resolving them, and updating their status.
Gathering feedback	Getting feedback from customer surveys, Help Desk practitioners, and other areas within the organization. Send this information to management for evaluation and improvement purposes.
Maintaining discussion groups	Archiving, monitoring, and moderating. Also includes identifying and providing data from discussion group messages for updates, evaluations, and improvements.
Carrying out chat functions	Handling chat queues for content, diagnostics, and closure. Also includes identifying and providing data from chat sessions for updates, evaluations, and improvements.
Using remote control tools	PC control, obtaining permission, keeping customers informed, and closing out sessions. Also includes identifying and providing data from remote control sessions for updates, evaluations, and improvements.

How to Create Effective Procedures

Procedures that work have the following attributes:

- Conciseness.
- Clarity (they use diagrams where possible).
- The people who use them create them.
- Everyone involved understands them.
- They are updated regularly.
- They are easily accessible.
- They are automated as much as possible.

Every extraneous phrase or piece of information you put into a procedure makes it more tedious to read. Put in only what is required for the procedure to be executed correctly. When you are creating a procedure, think of a scenario for the particular process you are documenting. This will help you define the steps in the procedure and will help you test it. For example, a scenario for handling email might revolve around getting a letter of complaint via email. Going through the scenario might help you define the whole procedure or at least a piece of it.

A diagram is often the easiest way to illustrate a process and is easier to follow than straight text. Figure 7.4 shows a diagram for a simplified procedure for handling complaints received via email. The support practitioner logs the complaint in the call-tracking system and then sends it to the site manager who responds to it and decides if the issue in the complaint letter signifies a required improvement or an update to a knowledge source. If the complaint does signal a required improvement, it is put into an improvement task list that the manager keeps. If the complaint signals a requirement for a knowledge source update, the update request is put into some kind of update engine that will perform the update. This might be a tool or another process. The manager then closes the complaint log to signify that handling the complaint has been completed. There is no need for any accompanying text around this procedure. The diagram is enough.

The people who can do the best job of describing procedures are the people who use them. If the people understand the procedure already, then they have expertise to develop it. If the people are developing the procedure from scratch, then they have a reason to get it right; they will be the ones depending on it.

All people involved in a procedure should be aware of and in agreement with their responsibilities in the procedure. This is particularly important if the procedure involves sending information to other departments, such as sending email messages to the sales department. You may need to develop some kind of agreement with all the departments you interact with.

If procedures are to be of any use, they need to be updated regularly. You're probably thinking, "Good heavens, a procedure for updating procedures . . . what next?" Well, you're partially right. The easiest way to make sure procedures are updated regularly is to assign the task to a specific position, perhaps on a rotating basis. The responsibility will then

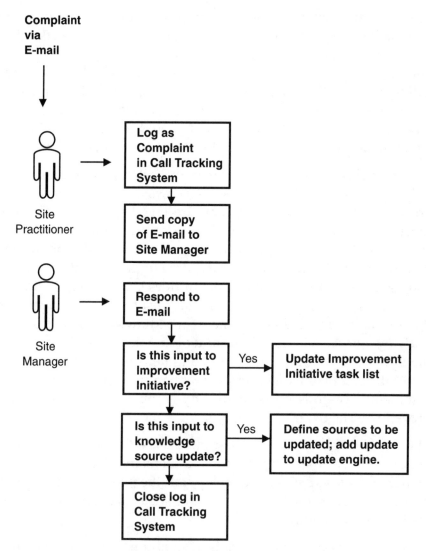

Figure 7.4 Process definition using a diagram.

need to be monitored and measured at performance review time. Practitioners need to know that procedure updates are an important part of the work they are responsible for and a component of their performance.

Procedures aren't much use if you can't find them. Put your procedures somewhere on the Web, either Intranet or Internet depending on your particular organization and its structure. If your Help Desk has a Web page that is accessible only to Help Desk practitioners, then you may want to put your procedures there behind a Support Site Procedures button. Figure 7.5 shows what an online procedure site might look like. Remember that the purpose of this site is not to win design awards, but simply to make your procedures easily accessible.

Support Site Procedures

Discussion Groups	Last Updated
Archiving	3/1/00
Posting General Notices	3/1/00
Monitoring	3/1/00
Responding to Message	3/1/00
Expelling Member	4/2/00
Adding New Group	4/2/00
E-mail	**Last Updated**
Complaints	4/2/00
Requests for Product Information	1/5/00
Suggestions for Improvement	4/2/00
Requests for Support	12/16/99

Figure 7.5 Storing procedures online.

Once you define a procedure, you may find you can automate all or part of it. The more automated a procedure is, the more consistently and correctly it will be applied. If you can't automate, you may be able to use existing tools to prompt the next step. For example, part of your procedure for using remote control tools might specify that the practitioner must send the customer a transcript of the remote control session with all the appropriate reference material, such as training documents. If possible, have the remote control tool pop up a reminder window when the practitioner tries to close the session. The reminder window can tell the practitioner exactly what should be sent to the customer. The following sections will look at how to define procedures for a specific category in more detail.

Creating Procedures for Maintaining Site Information

In a previous section, I stated that a good way to start defining a procedure is to identify the specific sources you need to keep updated, where the updates come from, who or what will do them, and what the update schedule will look like. Table 7.3 shows what this information might look like. Once you have this information, you can create a document in a table format or as a diagram to describe how it will happen.

Creating Procedures for Responding to Email

When defining procedures for responding to email, you must first determine which types of email you can expect to get. You can then decide who they will be sent to and what processing each will undergo. Table 7.4 shows this information for a support site in which all email goes to the site support practitioners. For each message received, the practitioners determine the type and create a log using the call-tracking system. If the email is a request for support, the practitioners will try to resolve it. Otherwise, the email will be forwarded to the next person or group in the process.

Table 7.4 also shows the time constraints on each process. The customer must receive a response within a specific number of hours. Since all instances of email are logged, the site manager can generate call-tracking reports that indicate any email processing that is still outstanding. The

Table 7.3 A Good Start to Defining a Procedure

INFORMATION TO BE UPDATED	WHERE DOES THE UPDATE COME FROM?	WHO OR WHAT DOES THE UPDATE?	WHAT IS THE UPDATE SCHEDULE?
FAQ	Call-tracking system (automatically generates top 10 calls), technical support team, Help Desk, and site staff (from email, online logs, chats, or remote control)	Site staff collects FAQ input from all areas and uses the site update manager software to update the FAQ.	End of day
Solution logs	Call-tracking system	Automatic database is online.	Immediate
Known issues and bugs	Technical support team, Help Desk, and site staff (from email, online logs, chats, or remote control)	Site staff via the site update manager.	Immediate
Technical documents	Technical support team, development team, Help Desk, and site staff	Technical support team via the site update manager.	As required. Corrections will be done immediately.
Product documentation	Technical support team, development team, Help Desk, and site staff	The development team makes changes and the site staff uploads them.	As required. Corrections will be done immediately.
Knowledge bases	Technical support team, development team, Help Desk, and site staff	User via knowledge base software.	As required. Corrections will be done immediately.
Links to other sites	Automatic log analyzer	Automatic-log analyzer.	End of day
Training documents	Technical support team, development team, Help Desk, and site staff	Site staff via site update manager.	As required. Corrections will be done immediately.
E-newsletters	Updates to FAQs, known issues, bugs, and technical documents for the last two weeks	The newsletter manager automatically pulls updates together and emails them out.	Every two weeks, if update material exists

(continues)

Table 7.3 (Continued)

INFORMATION TO BE UPDATED	WHERE DOES THE UPDATE COME FROM?	WHO OR WHAT DOES THE UPDATE?	WHAT IS THE UPDATE SCHEDULE?
Downloads	Technical support team, development team, Help Desk, and site staff	The technical support team provides updated materials, and the site staff updates the instructions or descriptions via the site update manager.	As required. Corrections will be done immediately.
Company information	Human resources	Web development team	On request
Contact information	Site manager	Site staff via site update manager	On request
Product marketing information	Marketing department	Web development team	On request

procedures generated from the table will show who is responsible for closing the logs and when. The manager will have no problem identifying where a procedure went wrong when a problem occurs.

As far as requests for support are concerned, it might be good idea to base response times on the critical nature of the problem. Email requests for help could range from minor to fairly urgent problems. It would not be good service to simply deal with all of them in the order in which they arrived. Priorities could be assigned by a technician with the responsibility of reviewing all the incoming email requests. A process could be put in place for responding to high-priority problems within three hours (during business hours) and to low-priority problems with 24 hours. This should result in high satisfaction ratings for email support, as customers with serious problems really appreciate prompt replies. It is probably not wise to advertise high-priority three-hour support because it could lead to complaints from customers expecting faster response times than their problems warrant. When you create procedures for email handling, use Table 7.4 as a measure of the absolute minimum of detail your procedures need to have. The more detailed they are, the easier it will be to measure their effectiveness. You will also want to make sure that all those involved in a procedure, such

Table 7.4 Creating Procedures for Email Handling

TYPE OF EMAIL	RECIPIENT	WHAT DOES THE INITIAL RECIPIENT DO?	FURTHER PROCESSING	TIME CONSTRAINTS
Complaints	Support staff	Create complaint log in call-tracking software and forward email to site manager.	Site manager responds to email, determines if a knowledge source update is required, determines if anything needs to be improved, and closes the log.	Respond to customer within 24 hours.
Request for product information	Support staff	Create sales information log in call-tracking software and forward email to sales department.	Sales department responds by emailing information to customer and copying the support staff who close the log.	Respond to customer within 24 hours.
Suggestions for improvement	Support staff	Create suggestion log in call-tracking software. Forward email to site manager.	The site manager responds to the email, determines if anything needs to be improved, and closes the log.	Respond to customer within 48 hours.
Requests for support	Support staff	Create problem log in call-tracking software and find resolution or get second-level support. If resolution is found, email the customer and close the log.	If escalated to second-level support, the second level will resolve the problem, close the call, and email the customer.	The high-priority standard is to respond to the customer within three hours. Low-priority is to respond within 24 hours.

as the Sales Department in Table 7.4, know what their responsibilities are and agree to carry them out.

Creating Procedures for Online Call Tracking

The procedures that you develop for handling problems logged by customers via an online call-tracking function on your support site will typically mimic the procedures you already have in place for telephone support. You will want to identify all the logs created online so that their response and resolution can be monitored and measured and so that, if necessary, they can be put into a separate support queue.

Creating Procedures for Gathering Feedback

When creating procedures for gathering feedback, you must first define all your sources of feedback, as shown in Table 7.5. For each source, you need to determine who the feedback will be sent to, what processing it will undergo, and how often the processing will take place. Again, as with email, if other departments are involved, this must be specified in the procedures and agreed upon with the departments in question.

If you look closely at Table 7.5, you will notice that the procedures for feedback coming from Help Desk practitioners, site staff, and other areas within the organization appear to be identical. This means you will only need one procedure to handle all of these sources of feedback. When you plan your procedures out in tabular format, you can easily see instances when you can create a single procedure to cover more than one scenario.

Creating Procedures for Maintaining Discussion Groups

The process of maintaining a discussion group tends to be task-driven rather than data-driven. You might want to start planning discussion group procedures by identifying the tasks that are part of maintaining such a group. Each task may turn into a procedure or be part of a shared procedure. Table 7.6 shows what some of these tasks might look like. For each task, you need to identify who is responsible for carrying out the

Table 7.5 Creating Procedures for Gathering Feedback

SOURCES OF FEEDBACK	RECIPIENT	PROCESSING	SCHEDULING
Customer surveys from support site (ongoing)	Designated site staff	Collect survey feedback and summarize. Then email it to site manager.	End of week
Help Desk staff (from interaction with customers)	Site manager	Send email to acknowledge the feedback, which is then analyzed. If viable, make improvements based on the feedback.	Ongoing, as feedback occurs
Support site staff (from support interactions)	Site manager	Send email to acknowledge the feedback, which is then analyzed. If viable, make improvements based on the feedback.	Ongoing, as feedback occurs
Discussion group monitor	Site manager	Analyze feedback. If viable, make improvements based on it.	Ongoing, as feedback occurs
Other areas within organization	Site manager	Send email to acknowledge the feedback, which is then analyzed. If viable, make improvements.	Ongoing, as feedback occurs

task, the steps involved, and the scheduling information. In your procedures, responsibility for a task should be defined at a generic level by position. The site manager can assign names to responsibilities as required.

Looking at Table 7.6, you can see quite clearly what the procedures for carrying out each of the listed tasks will look like. The table has also identified templates that you need to create. These include a template for posting general messages and for an email message that is sent to a discussion group member who has lost discussion privileges. If your procedures identify required templates, make sure you have the templates in place before the site is put into production.

Creating Procedures for Chat Functions

The purpose of having chat procedures is to create an environment in which customers can expect a consistently positive interaction with a support practitioner each time they participate in a chat session. Support

Table 7.6 Creating Procedures for Maintaining Discussion Groups

TASKS INVOLVED	RESPONSIBILITY	PROCESSING	SCHEDULING
Archiving	Selected site practitioner	Run the archive utility on all messages generated in the previous month to remove them from the current discussion area and make them accessible via the archives. Use site update manager software to make any changes to discussion group pages.	On the first day of the month, archive messages from the previous month
Posting general notices	Selected site staff	Use the message template to create a message that is posted to the notice board on the discussion group site using site update manager software.	As need arises
Monitoring groups	Selected site practitioner	Read through all the messages for the previous day. Identify any unresolved questions and post the solution or appropriate link. Update any information if required, pass on any product or service improvement suggestions, and identify any abusive behavior.	At the start of the day for the previous day
Expelling a group member	Selected site staff	Suspend the membership of the offending member immediately. Use the Expel Member template to send an email to the member, listing the policy violated and copying the site manager.	As need arises

TASKS INVOLVED	RESPONSIBILITY	PROCESSING	SCHEDULING
Adding a new group	Selected site staff	Clear a request with the site manager. Define a new group name as well as space on server and update the discussion group pages.	As need arises

practitioners need to start and end sessions in a consistent way, they need guidelines on which diagnostics to perform with the customers, and they need to know what to do with information they gather and how to ask for assistance when required.

Let's say Ben is one of your best support practitioners. His chat session might all start with, "Hi, you are chatting with Ben. How can I help you?" Ben then runs through a common list of diagnostics based on the customer's problem area. If Ben cannot resolve the problem, then he might log it to another level, initiate a site visit, or pass it directly to a specialist. At the end of the session, Ben types, "Is there anything else I can help you with?" If there isn't, he writes, "Thank you and let us know if any more problems occur. I'm emailing you out a transcript so you can refer to it if this happens again." Ben does a great job in this scenario and in all of his other customer interactions. If you want this scenario repeated for all of your other practitioners, specific customer chat procedures and canned chat templates, which are chat phrases and questions that you paste into your session, are a good start toward making this happen.

Table 7.7 displays some procedures you may want to set up to ensure your chat sessions follow the best practices. The standards and templates that are required for your procedures are also shown.

Creating Procedures for Using Remote Control Tools

If you offer assisted support options that involve the use of remote control tools, make sure that the tools are used correctly and consistently to maximize resolution success and minimize resolution time. It is also important to make sure that customer privacy is respected.

Table 7.7 Creating Procedures for Chat Sessions

STAGE	TASKS	STANDARDS/TEMPLATES
Opening	Insert template text to start a conversation.	A set of common opening templates that can be inserted directly into the session, such as "Hi, you are chatting with Ben. How can I help you?"
Diagnosing the problem	Run through diagnostic questions according to the problem area. Get the customer's permission before invoking remote control.	A separate set of diagnostic questions for each problem area can be set up as templates to insert into the chat session. A permission template for use with remote control software will request permission to access the customer's PC via a remote control.
Escalating the problem	If the problem requires a site visit, schedule this according to the standards. If the problem cannot be resolved after the time specified in the service template, it must be logged and escalated to the appropriate areas. For emergencies, receive help from a specific area for immediate resolution.	Standards for work order scheduling. A service document specifies the chat time limit and escalation areas as well as details on emergency escalation.
Communicating	Customer comments must be recorded and passed on to the manager. Problems encountered in a chat session or suggestions for improvements must also be recorded and passed on to the manager.	Practitioners can enter feedback into online forms that are emailed directly to the manager.
Carrying out a survey	Carry out a customer survey according to the template.	A library of short surveys to be used at the end of all or selected chat sessions can be inserted directly into the session or can be emailed to the customer.
Closing	Insert some template text to end the conversation and send customer backup reference material.	A set of common closing templates can be inserted directly into the end of the chat session, such as "Is there anything else I can help you with?" A standard list of reference material can also be selected and emailed to the customer.

To ensure correct and consistent tool usage, you may want to set up procedures that cover the use of standard tools in specific problem areas. For example, when dealing with printing problems, drivers can be scanned using predefined macros, and so on. Your procedures themselves might be macros that automatically run a series of diagnostics. If you name your macros so that their function is obvious, you may not need written procedures. Avoid using procedures to teach practitioners how to use tools. This practice could result in duplicate information, since the tools probably already have extensive documentation.

When using remote control tools, it is crucial that the customer's privacy be maintained. Ask the customer for permission each time you need to look at or modify the customer's data. You should also tell the customer what you are going to do and why.

A chat function is often integrated with extended remote control tools and, if this is the case in your environment, you will need procedures for using chat functions, as described in the previous section.

Table 7.8 lists certain tasks you may want procedures for when using extended remote control tools that have a chat component. The required standards and templates are also shown.

Table 7.8 Creating Procedures for Using Remote Control

STAGE	TASKS	STANDARDS/TEMPLATES
Opening	Insert the template text to start the conversation and request permission for initial PC access.	A set of common opening templates that can be inserted directly into the chat session or a permission template that can be inserted directly into the chat session.
Diagnosing the problem	Obtain the symptoms from the customer and run diagnostic macros based on the symptoms. To obtain the symptoms, use standard sets of diagnostic questions.	A series of macros can be run for specific problem symptoms and standard diagnostic questions can be used. Macro names should reflect their functions.
Resolving the problem	Update or download customer files or documents as required after getting the appropriate level of permission.	A text template describing what needs to be done and that asks for the necessary permission can be used. The text should be easy to understand and can be dragged and dropped right into the chat session.

(continues)

Table 7.8 (Continued)

STAGE	TASKS	STANDARDS/TEMPLATES
Escalating the problem	If the problem requires a site visit, schedule this according to the standards. If the problem cannot be resolved after the time specified in the service template, it must be logged and sent to the appropriate area. For emergencies, contact a specific area for immediate resolution.	The standards for work order scheduling can be used. A service document specifies assisted support time limits and help areas as well as details on emergency information.
Communicating feedback	Customer comments must be recorded and passed on to the manager. Problems encountered in assisted support sessions or suggestions for improving sessions must also be recorded and passed on to the manager.	Online templates for feedback entry can be used. Staff can capture customer input via logs or screen captures. This information, along with any other comments, can be entered into an online form that is emailed directly to the manager.
Carrying out a survey	Display a Web-based survey on the customer's PC and ask the customer to submit it before leaving the session.	A Web-based survey page that enables customers to enter and submit feedback is used here. Feedback goes directly to the manager. The page is displayed on the customer's PC by the practitioner at the close of a session.
Closing	Insert template text to end the conversation and send the customer a transcript of the remote control session or the reference material.	A set of common closing templates is used. These can be inserted directly into the end of the chat session. A standard list of reference material can then be emailed to the customer.

Creating Procedures: Final Words

As you saw in the previous sections, procedures can be data-driven or task-driven. A good way of developing a procedure is to create a table based on either data or tasks and list the actions required for each table entry. From these actions, you can determine which templates or standards are required for each procedure and if the procedure itself can be automated. The table then becomes your map for putting defined procedures in place. You might even find that the table itself becomes a set of procedures.

Implementation and Testing Checklist

While procedure definition is going on, you need to plan and carry out the actual construction and implementation of your site. You must define the tasks that are involved in setting up the communications environment, establishing the Web server or Web hosting, building the site code, using the applications for maintaining the site, installing purchased tools, creating and loading knowledge sources, and so on. If your support site is very small, your plan for these tasks might take the form of a checklist. The larger your site is, the more rigorous your project management must be. You may choose to use a project management tool to help you control the work that needs to be done. Figure 7.6 shows an example of task management using a project management tool. If you choose to use such a tool, you must start using it right at the beginning of your project so that all the work involved is planned, measured, and managed. The lines between tasks indicate dependencies and the diamonds are milestones.

Regardless of whether you are using a simple checklist or a formal project plan, each task you have identified should be assigned to one specific person wherever possible and should be of a short enough duration to be easily managed. If you have one person doing all of the coding for your site and you have one long coding task on your list or plan, you won't really know whether that task is on time or whether the code is accurate until the end of the coding process. Breaking the coding task into manageable units will allow you to monitor progress and measure quality.

The task of marketing your site may not be on your implementation checklist. Beware that many dangers are inherent in marketing a support site too early. Depending on your particular situation, it may be advantageous to do some marketing before you let your customers know your site is forthcoming, or it may be wiser to wait until your support site is actually completed and in place. Chapter 8, "Marketing,"

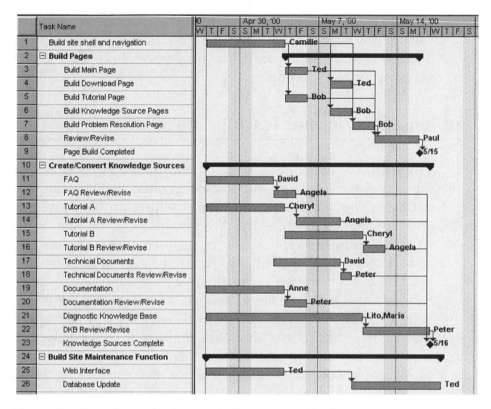

	Task Name		Apr 30, '00	May 7, '00	May 14, '00
1	Build site shell and navigation		Camille		
2	**Build Pages**				
3	Build Main Page		Ted		
4	Build Download Page			Ted	
5	Build Tutorial Page		Bob		
6	Build Knowledge Source Pages			Bob	
7	Build Problem Resolution Page			Bob	
8	Review/Revise				Paul
9	Page Build Completed				◆5/15
10	**Create/Convert Knowledge Sources**				
11	FAQ		David		
12	FAQ Review/Revise		Angela		
13	Tutorial A		Cheryl		
14	Tutorial A Review/Revise			Angela	
15	Tutorial B			Cheryl	
16	Tutorial B Review/Revise			Angela	
17	Technical Documents			David	
18	Technical Documents Review/Revise			Peter	
19	Documentation		Anne		
20	Documentation Review/Revise		Peter		
21	Diagnostic Knowledge Base			Lito,Maria	
22	DKB Review/Revise				Peter
23	Knowledge Sources Complete				◆5/16
24	**Build Site Maintenance Function**				
25	Web Interface		Ted		
26	Database Update				Ted

Figure 7.6 Managing work using a project management tool.

will help you decide which strategy to choose.

When putting your implementation task list together, you should not overlook three requirements: adequate testing, adequate reviews and revisions, and building in iterations.

Testing

No matter how small your site is, careful consideration needs to be given to testing in order to ensure that your site works the way you and all the site stakeholders expect it to. You need to identify what you need to test, how you can test it, when you should test it, and who should be involved.

Let's start with what you need to test. Your site scope summary, as described in Chapter 3, "Establishing Scope," can help you here. In your scope summary, you identify the requirements from all the site stakeholders, and for each requirement, you analyze the required data and processing, as well as the potential implementations of the requirement. When you develop site prototypes during the site design process, you need to check the prototypes against your scope summary to make sure that all the requirements have been taken into account. You need to do this check again when you develop your implementation plan or checklist. Have you included all the scope summary requirements? You may want to check again at selected points during the building process, and you certainly want to do a final check before you make your site available to customers. Other things you will want to test include the following:

- Do all the functions work as expected?
- Are the information sources easy to understand?
- Is the site easy to use?
- Is the site compatible with the technology the customers are using?
- What volume of traffic will the site handle?

Table 7.9 looks at all of these factors and describes how to test them, when to test them, and who should be involved in testing them.

Notice that in Table 7.9 most testing occurs throughout the site building. Very little is left to the end. There is an excellent reason for this. The sooner you can identify a problem area, the sooner you can fix it and the less expensive it will be to fix.

Table 7.9 Testing Your Site

WHAT TO TEST	HOW TO TEST	WHEN TO TEST	PEOPLE INVOLVED IN TESTING
That the site meets the stakeholders' requirements	Use the scope summary to check the requirements against what is actually being designed, planned, built, and implemented.	When a prototype is developed, when the implementation checklist is developed, at selected points throughout the implementation, or when the site is completed	Site manager or project manager

(continues)

Table 7.9 (Continued)

WHAT TO TEST	HOW TO TEST	WHEN TO TEST	PEOPLE INVOLVED IN TESTING
That each function works as expected	Define the test scripts that specify the expected outcomes from each function.	When the site skeleton and navigation is completed or as soon as each function is completed	Site analysts, designers, or developers develop test scripts or carry out testing
That information in knowledge sources is easy to understand	Take samples of each knowledge source to the people who will be using that source. Get feedback on its ease of understanding.	As soon as a sample for an information source is available	Site developers and analysts can do the initial review, and then information must be given to a sampling of site stakeholders
Its ease of use	Get feedback from site prototypes and from each iteration of site and function development.	As soon as prototypes are developed, when the site skeleton and navigation is built, or after each function is added	Site developers and analysts can do the initial review, and then a sampling of site stakeholders must provide feedback
Compatibility with customer technology	Duplicate various customer configurations.	When the site skeleton and navigation is built or after each function is added	Site developers
Usage volumes	For some functions, you might be able to use testing scripts to generate volumes. For other functions, you have to use may volunteers hitting specific functions at the same time.	As each function is completed or before the site is made available to customers	Site developers or any available staff or volunteers

Review and Revise

The purpose of review tasks is to review the test results or project deliverables at any stage to ensure that they meet the required standards, such as matching the expected test results or a scope summary's requirements. Project deliverables might be code or sources of information such as FAQs, procedures, and so on. Someone who is not involved in the work being reviewed typically carries out a review.

Time must be allowed for making any necessary revisions discovered in the review process. If you don't include a revision time in your project plan or checklist, you are assuming that every deliverable and every test result will be absolutely perfect, which is a highly unlikely scenario.

Reviews and revisions should appear at frequent intervals in your project plan or checklist (refer to Figure 7.6). This will help ensure that problems are found as early as possible and that they can be addressed immediately. Finding and resolving problems this way is much more cost-effective than waiting until the end of the project. By the end of the project, a problem or incorrect deliverable might be built into your entire site structure and could be very expensive to fix. Allowing time for the revisions that result from the reviews will help ensure that your project end date is realistic.

Built-In Iterations

If your site is very small, the coding and implementation process will typically take place in one pass. The site is created, it is tested against the requirements, the required revisions are made, and then the site is uploaded for access by customers. If your site is larger, the site creation process becomes more complex because you are dealing with several individual components that must work together. To ensure that your implementation is successful, you will want to build and implement your site in iterations. You can build the basic site structure as the first iteration of construction and then with each subsequent iteration you can add a function to the site.

As an example, you may first build your skeleton pages and navigation. Your next iteration might include adding the FAQ and product downloads. The third iteration might be adding the online call management software. Building in iterations will enable you to diagnose and resolve problems more easily and quickly as you are only adding one or two pieces of functionality at a time. If you subscribe to the big bang approach in which you build everything at once, you may find yourself fixing everything at once. Diagnosing problems will be more difficult because your problem domain is larger and resolving problems could be very expensive. If a problem involves something that runs through the whole site, then your resolution will involve significant work.

Establishing Initial Support

When your site is first made available to your customers, make sure you are prepared for the response your site generates. That means your site structure in terms of hardware, software, and staff must be able to handle the volume of site visitors. You need to have contingency plans and structures in place to handle unexpected volumes. For example, if your site generates an unexpectedly high volume of email, you need to be able to handle that email while you analyze it to determine if and how you can decrease the volume. If you don't handle the email in a timely manner, you will lose customers.

When establishing an initial support structure, you need to follow several steps. First, identify those areas of your site that you feel face some level of risk. These might include the following:

The volume of email. What if email volumes are much higher than expected?

Problem-logging functions. Will unexpectedly high traffic volumes cause problems? Will customer mistakes cause problems?

The volume of requests for assisted support. What if you offer assisted support and the number of customers requesting this service is much higher than expected? If this happens, your customers could be faced with long wait times in assisted support queues.

Complicated functions. Are any of your support functions, such as an interactive diagnostic knowledge base, difficult to use? Will your telephone support be flooded with calls asking for assistance in using the function?

New technology. Are there customers who may not be able to access your site because of an incompatibility in technology?

Once you have identified your major areas of risk, you need to determine the impact each will have on the success of your site and if the risk can be eliminated and how. If the risk cannot be eliminated, you need to examine how you can minimize the risk and which contingency plans you can put into place, should the risk occur. If a risk can be eliminated, such as if you are worried that some technology you are using is not quite stable, then eliminate it. Replace the technology in question with something more stable if you can. This is worth doing even at the cost of some decreased functionality.

If you have risks you cannot eliminate, do what you can to minimize them. For example, if you are worried about the volume of email, try to think about why your customers might want to email you. Are there functions that you don't offer on your site but should? Are some instructions difficult to understand? Do you offer email as a first choice rather than encouraging them to try self-service problem resolutions? Resolve all of these issues before you implement your site. Add the required functions if possible, make sure the instructions are easy to understand, and offer self-support alternatives before providing email. If you involve customers in site testing, they can identify many risks for you and tell you how to minimize them.

Once you have done all you can to minimize your risks, you need to decide what you must do to prevent a disaster if any of the risks actually happens. For each risk, you must define what your contingency plan will be: the resources you will require and the actions that must be taken. Take time to define these clearly. You don't want to be trying to work out a contingency plan while you are trying to handle the fallout from a risk that became reality. Table 7.10 illustrates the process of risk management: examining risks, minimizing them, and developing contingency plans.

The third step in establishing an initial support structure is to actually implement the contingency plans so that they are ready and waiting to be executed if necessary. This is your insurance policy for protection against your identified risks. You must also negotiate for the extra support staff you might need, give them clear instructions and procedures, and put them on standby. You may have to consider contracting for

Table 7.10 An Example of Risk Management in Establishing Initial Support

RISK	IMPACT	MINIMIZE/ ELIMINATE	CONTINGENCY PLAN
High volumes of email	Customers may wait days to get a response. You may then lose customers or they may resort to telephone support.	Do whatever possible to minimize the use of email. Add functionality, clarify instructions, or offer self-service options first.	Have staff on standby. This staff will respond to email per instructions and collect data on the reasons why email messages are sent.
High volumes of online problem logging via a call-tracking function	May lock up or bring down call-tracking functions. Customers may resort to telephone support or you could lose customers.	Do extensive online volume tests on the online problem-logging function. If a usability threshold is identified, then either remove the function until a resolution can be found or put some kind of lock into place that prevents more than a specified number of users from accessing the function at any one time. Denied users will receive an explanatory message.	Have extra telephone support staff on standby to take calls from those customers denied access to the online problem-logging function. Log these calls as a specific type so that their numbers can be tracked and a resolution can be found.
High volumes of requests for assisted support	Customers may wait hours to get support via chat sessions and remote control. They may resort to telephone support or you could lose their business.	Offer as much self-support as possible so that customers can get what they need without asking for help. Involve customers in this process so that you understand what customers can do on their own.	Have staff on standby to handle extra assisted support. Gathering data on the reasons why assisted support requests occur. This will identify the site's weak areas in self-support.
Functions are too complicated for customers	Customers won't use them and resort to telephone support. You could lose their business.	Test the functions out on customers. Simplify where possible and add instructions to aid understanding.	Have extra telephone support staff on standby to take calls from customers who feel that the functions are too complicated. Also collect feedback from customers on what would make these functions easier to use.

RISK	IMPACT	MINIMIZE/ ELIMINATE	CONTINGENCY PLAN
New technology	Some customers will be unable to access some or all of the site functions. Customers may resort to telephone support or you could lose their business.	Test the new technology with the typical browser, access speed, CPU speed, and operating system your customers use. Describe any identified incompatibilities on your site and offer alternatives where possible. If the technology you are using is compatible with only a small subset of your customers, you must abandon it.	Make all the support staff aware of the potential incompatibilities and alternatives so they can explain them to customers.

extra help for this period of time. You also need to negotiate for technical experts to be available, should any problem actually happen. If you've done a good job in eliminating and minimizing risks, then you most likely won't need your policy, but if even only one problem happens, you'll be very glad to have that policy.

Implementing the Site

The culmination of all your hard work is the implementation of your site. You are finally making your site available to your customers. Before you actually put your site into place, go over your implementation plan or checklist one more time. Have all the tasks been completed? Has all the testing been done and the results accepted? Have risks been identified and are contingency plans in place? If you've followed the suggestions in this book up to this point, then you are to be congratulated. Your site is truly ready for implementation.

If you haven't yet started marketing your site, you need to do this now. Chapter 8, "Marketing," will help you. As soon as your site is accessible to your customers, you need to start managing it. Be sure to measure the performance of your site, look for potential improvements, and monitor the processes you defined to make sure they are working. Chapter 9, "Site Management," will help you with all aspects of site management.

Key Points

This section provides a summary of the key points in support site processes and implementation.

As stated earlier in the book, if your site offers a function that operates the same way each time it is used, you must define a process of steps around it. Without such a process, you really have no control over how a particular function is executed each time it is carried out. Such a process can define the workflow around your site, how you will handle email, or how you will keep your site up to date. Processes that are not clearly and formally defined are processes that are not followed. In developing processes for your site, you need to first identify all of the functions you will require and then define them.

To identify the processes for maintaining site information such as product information, you need to identify which specific sources you need to keep up to date, where the updates will be coming from, who or what will be doing them, and what the update schedule will look like. To identify the processes around responding to email, you need to look at the types of email you are or will be getting. Each needs to be handled differently, perhaps passed on to different groups for handling. If you are going to allow your customers to log calls directly into your call-tracking system via your support site, then you need processes in place to ensure that those calls are picked up and resolved within an appropriate timeframe.

The process of gathering feedback might include collecting information from customer surveys, Help Desk practitioners, or other areas within the organization. If your site hosts discussion groups, processes should be in place for archiving and monitoring the groups. If you use some kind of assisted support, such as chat or remote control tools, you will need processes for each one. You may have a series of diagnostics that you take the customer through, you may have some guidelines about how long each side can chat before being interrupted, or you may want to specify that after each chat session the customer gets a transcript with any supporting materials. It is also important to have a process to follow for taking over a customer's PC, getting the appropriate permission, and for informing the customer of what you are doing. You may want to specify a standard way of closing a session, which could be done by emailing the customer a transcript and any supporting materials such as specific documents.

After determining a process needed for your support site, you can outline the steps of the process as a procedure. Once you have identified the processes that surround your support site, you must define and document them in some way. To do so, you'll have to go through each process, identify the steps you want repeated each time that process is carried out, and then look at other processes that might be related to this one. Then you must document this information and store it where it can be accessed by everyone who might use it. Procedures can be data-driven or task-driven. A good way of creating procedures is to create a table outlining the data or tasks by listing the required actions. From these actions, you can determine which templates or standards are needed for each procedure and if the procedure itself can be automated. The table then becomes your map for putting the defined procedures in place.

Effective procedures are concise, clear, created by those who will use them, understood by everyone involved, updated regularly, easily accessible, and automated as much as possible. Some suggestions for creating procedures include using diagrams and storing the procedures online.

While a procedure definition is going on, you need to plan and carry out the actual construction and implementation of your site. If your support site is very small, your plan for these tasks might take the form of a checklist. If it is larger, you may choose to use a project management tool to help you control the work that needs to be done. When putting your implementation task list together, you should not overlook three requirements: adequate testing, adequate reviews and revisions, and building in iterations.

No matter how small your site is, careful consideration needs to be given to testing in order to ensure that your site works the way you and all the site stakeholders expect it to. You must identify what you need to test, how you can test it, when you should test it, and who should be involved.

The purpose of a review is to examine test results or project deliverables at any stage to ensure they meet the required standards. A revision period allows time to be added to the process for making any necessary changes identified in the review. Reviews and revisions should appear at frequent intervals in your project plan or checklist. This will help ensure that problems are found as early on in the project as possible and that they can be addressed immediately. Finding and resolving problems this way is much more cost-effective than waiting until the end of the project.

If your site is very small, the coding and implementation process will typically take place in one pass. The site is created and tested against the requirements. The required revisions are made and then the site is uploaded for access by customers. If your site is larger, the site creation process becomes more complex because you are dealing with several individual components that must work together. To ensure that your implementation is successful, you will want to build and implement your site in iterations. You can build the basic site structure as the first iteration of construction and then with each subsequent iteration you can add a function to the site.

When your site is first made available to your customers, make sure you are prepared for the response your site generates. You need to have contingency plans and structures in place to handle the unexpected. In establishing an initial support structure, you must follow several steps. First, identify those areas of your site that you feel face some level of risk during implementation. Next, determine what impact each will have on the success of your site as well as if and how the risk can be eliminated. If the risk cannot be eliminated, examine how you can minimize the risk and any possible contingency plans you can put into place to handle the risk, should it occur. Finally, implement the contingency plans to the point that they are ready and waiting to be executed if necessary. This is your insurance policy for protection against your identified risks.

If you've followed the suggestions in this book up to this point, then your site will be ready for the culmination of all your hard work: implementation.

8

Marketing

You have invested a significant amount of money and effort into building a support site. You won't get any return on that site unless your customers use it. In order to use the site, your customers need to know that it exists and what it can do for them. You thus need to market your site. Marketing can do much more for you than just getting people to your site. Effective marketing can help your customers use your site as well as your products and services more effectively, it can promote your organization, and it can give you valuable feedback on how you can improve your site, and your products and services. Effective marketing takes some careful thought and planning, and in this chapter I will give you a structure to make the process easier. I will discuss segmenting your customers so that you can individualize marketing to different groups, how to build a marketing plan, and what you need to do when carrying out your marketing activities. In order to market effectively, you need to understand how effective your marketing actually is, so I will discuss how to measure the effectiveness of your marketing and how to identify any marketing adjustments or improvements that are required. I will include an example section to demonstrate what some marketing plans might look like for Education Plus and Trace Software. I have also set aside a section to talk about the specific issue of what kind of marketing you will want to do at site startup. I will finish the chapter off with selection of marketing ideas that you might find useful.

The topics that are covered in this chapter are as follows:

- Marketing tasks
- What is marketing and why is it important?
- Identifying customer segments
- Creating a marketing plan
- Carrying our marketing activities
- Measuring marketing effectiveness
- Identifying adjustments and improvements
- Marketing examples
- Ten suggestions for marketing at site startup
- Marketing ideas

Marketing Tasks

The tasks involved in marketing your site take the form of an ongoing cycle, as shown in Figure 8.1. The first task involves classifying your customers into segments so that you can customize the marketing required for each segment. Next is the creation of a marketing plan. You need to decide what your marketing objectives are. For each objective, you will define the marketing activities you will undertake to achieve the objective, which customer segment each activity will target, the timing of the activity, and who is responsible.

The third task involves carrying the activities out and gathering any data that the activities entail. In the fourth task, you measure how effective the marketing activity is. Does it achieve the objective you were hoping for? If not, why not? In the fifth task, you look at the results of your marketing and determine how you can adjust your activities to improve your results next time. You can also look at the data collected to examine the improvements suggested to your site, your products, or your services. At this point, you start the cycle again. You look at your customer segments and reclassify if necessary. You then update your

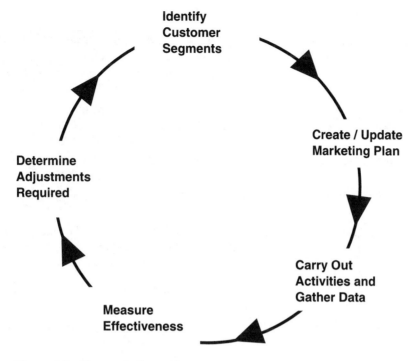

Figure 8.1 The marketing cycle.

marketing plan and so on. Table 8.1 lists and describes the five tasks involved in marketing.

I should note here that if you are just creating your site, you might have additional startup tasks. These are described in the section titled *Ten Suggestions for Marketing at Site Startup*.

What Is Marketing and Why Is It Important?

As I mentioned in the introduction to this chapter, marketing is much more than just letting people know that your site exists. Marketing includes all of the activities, from planning through to measurement, involved in accomplishing the following tasks:

- Attracting customers
- Helping customers use your site more effectively

Table 8.1 Marketing Tasks

TASKS	DETAILS
Identify or reclassify customer segments.	Divide your customers into segments that make sense for your product. These are customers that are using your site and that could use your site in the future.
Create or update your marketing plan.	Decide what you want to accomplish through marketing. For each goal, define the target audience, activities, schedule, and how the initiative is measured.
Carry out activities and gather data.	Perform each activity and collect the resulting data.
Measure effectiveness.	Analyze the results of the marketing activities to see which were successful.
Determine adjustments required.	Determine which adjustments should be made to your customer segmentation, your marketing activities, or your site. Then start again.

- Helping customers use your product or service more effectively via your site
- Promoting your organization and your product or service via your site
- Getting feedback for your site, product, or service

You can now see why marketing is so important. Not only can it bring customers to your site and get them away from telephone support, but it can tell you how your site and the products and services it supports can improve. Let's look at each of the five topics in the previous list in more detail.

Attracting Customers

If you support your own product or service, then you want to attract customers to your site so that they can get the help they need without resorting to telephone support wherever possible. For example, if you are an Internet service provider (ISP), you probably provide no-charge telephone support. You want to divert as much support as possible to your support site so that telephone support can be reserved for the more serious problems. You simply cannot afford to support an increasing number of customers and problems via the telephone.

The challenges you face in getting customers to your support site, whether you are an ISP or a software manufacturer or just about anything else, are based around two central questions: how do you let customers know that your support site exists and how do you get them to use it? Getting the word out to your customers about your site is a challenge because customers don't always read what you write and don't always hear what you say. You may email your customers a message or newsletter that tells them about the site, but they won't necessarily look at it. You can tell customers about the site when they call with a problem, but then they'll only know about it if they have a problem. So what do you do? First, make sure you understand the customer segment that you are marketing to. What do these customers read? What do they listen to? What sites do they visit? Then, depending on the specific customer segment, you can choose to do some or all of the following:

- If you know exactly who your customers are, you can email them weekly about four times. The message you send should be very short and can describe one of your site's features. Each week's email can describe a different feature.

- Advertise your site on other sites such as online magazines or discussion groups that your customers would likely visit. Which sites you choose depend on the specific customer segment you are after.

- Find out which paper-based magazines your customers read and advertise there.

- If you send customers newsletters, paper-based or electronic, write a headline story about your site. Again keep it very short and describe the site's main features.

- The telephone support staff should let all customers know about the site. After a few months, they might only mention the site if the problem being called in about is something that could be resolved from information on the site. You should probably have a greeting message that informs customers of the option of finding help on the support site.

- Include the site URL with all product and service literature and all software. If you manufacture software, you can have a help option in the software that takes the customer directly to the support site.

- If you support internal customers, put a link to your support site on the customer's desktop as an icon.

To be successful at reaching your customers, you must know them well and target the marketing specifically at them. You can't rely on only one of the methods described earlier; you will probably need to use several. If your customers cross several segments, you may have to employ an even wider variety of marketing activities to reach them all. The section titled *Identifying Customer Segments* can help you.

We've discussed letting customers know about your site. Now what about those customers that are unwilling to use it? Before you start deriding customers for not using the site, it's important to understand why they aren't using the site. It has been my experience that most customers will go to a support site for help if it is easy to use and if they believe it can help them. So if you have customers who know about the site but don't want to use it, the first thing you must do is find out why, and the easiest way to do so is to ask. You can have your telephone support practitioners ask customers if they've tried the site. If customers say no, the practitioners can then ask for reasons. The practitioners can also get contact information for customers so that once the problems are fixed, those customers can be notified. Sometimes all it takes, especially if the customer is new to the Internet, is for the support practitioner to walk the customer through the support site identifying where the answer to the problem is.

Once you fix any usability problems with your site, most of your customers will be willing to use it. For those who will not, you need to decide if you want to keep supporting them for free, in which case you are accepting their calls as the cost of doing business, or you can charge them for the call. You can let them know when they call that you will charge them if the problem or question they have could be resolved easily from the support site, and then make sure the charge covers the cost of the call. You will have to carefully define what you will actually charge for, but you will no longer be giving away a service you probably cannot afford.

Helping Customers Use Your Site More Effectively

Marketing includes the activity of helping your customers use your site more effectively. The more effectively customers use your site, the more help they can get from it, which means increased customer satisfaction and fewer calls to telephone support. Two of the ways in which you can help customers use your site more effectively are as follows:

Make all instructions clear and easy to understand. Even something as simple as a download can cause problems if it is not clear to the customer exactly what is being downloaded, where it is being downloaded to, or how it needs to be expanded once downloaded.

Give customers a map through your site. In other words, give them examples of how your site might be used in different situations. You may show them which information sources they might try for different types of problems. A map will show them not only what you have, but how and when to use it. Figure 8.2 shows what a site map that helps customers select specific paths might look like.

Helping Customers Use Your Product or Service More Effectively Via Your Site

One of the goals of your support site is to decrease the number of calls to telephone support. When customers understand how to use your products and services effectively, they will require less support. Marketing

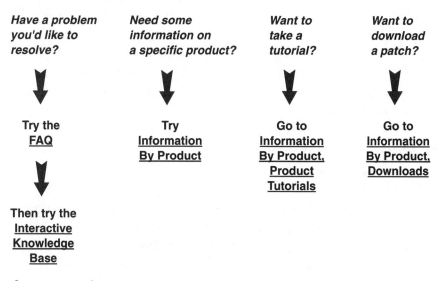

Figure 8.2 A site usage map.

includes anything you do on your site to give your customers a better understanding of the product they are using. This includes at least FAQs and online tutorials, but it could include several other knowledge sources depending on your site and your customers.

Promoting Your Organization, Product, or Service Via Your Site

Whether you intend it or not, your support site says something to your customers about your organization, product, or service. A poorly designed site implies a disorganized organization and an inferior product or service. A professional-looking, well-designed site that is easy to use and that yields positive results implies success, good organization, and a good product. If your support site is poor, it matters little if you have a great product or service. Anyone visiting it who may not know your product or service will get a negative impression. If you were hoping that your support site would promote sales, you would be disappointed.

When you have a site that implies success, you are ready to go further in promoting your organization, product, or service. You can use your support site to display ads, customer testimonials, case studies, commercial clips, and so on to promote what you support. This must be done be very carefully, however, or you will defeat the purpose of your support site. Customers seeking help are usually in a hurry and will not tolerate a lot of extraneous clutter. Don't forget that they have a problem with your product or service and having them wade through display ads or customer testimonials will only annoy them. They will very quickly pick up the phone if they can't find a direct route to the answers to their problems.

Getting Feedback for Your Site, Product, or Service

Marketing is not a one-way activity. It is a two-way interaction with the target customers. Marketing should be an ongoing conversation with your customers, and giving them opportunities to provide feedback is a good way to make them part of the conversation.

You can receive feedback on your site by collecting statistics from customers that call in to the telephone support staff. If you set up a process

```
┌────────────────────────────────────────┐
│                                          │
│   We need your feedback. Please select   │
│   the appropriate response and submit.   │
│                                          │
│   Were download instructions clear?      │
│                                          │
│       O  Yes      O  No                  │
│                                          │
│                                          │
│            ┌──────────┐                  │
│            │  Submit  │                  │
│            └──────────┘                  │
│                                          │
└────────────────────────────────────────┘
```

Figure 8.3   A customer survey.

for this, as described in Chapter 7, "Processes and Implementation," it becomes even easier to collect site or product feedback that customers are giving support practitioners. This may give you insights into why those customers aren't using your site to resolve problems. You can also collect feedback via more formal surveys that support practitioners deliver on the phone or via a chat session after a telephone support call or an online assisted support session.

For customers who don't use assisted support, your site should provide the opportunity to give feedback. This could be in a one- or two-question survey after a particular function is used, the more specific and simpler the better. Figure 8.3 shows an example of a simple but effective survey.

A byproduct of collecting and acting on feedback is an improved image in the eyes of your customers. Customers will perceive your organization as one that cares about its customers and is interested in making things better for them.

Identifying Customer Segments

Before you undertake any marketing initiatives, you may want to classify your customers into segments that you can market more specifically. This is especially true if you have a diverse customer base. In determining how to segment your customers, you need to think about the customer attributes that interest you the most. For example, if you manufacture and support software, you would be very interested in the computer platforms that your customers are running and what other software they have. You may choose to segment your customers by the type of operating system that they are running. If you offer a variety of software, you may choose to first segment your customers by the software products they are using. If you are an ISP, you may choose to segment your customers based on the type of services they have purchased from you. Targeting your marketing this way will help you make sure that the right message reaches the right customers and will help you select the appropriate marketing activities and vehicles.

Once you have defined your segments, you can decide how and what to market to each. If you manufacture several software products and you want to market a new function on the support site for one of those products, you can aim your marketing activities at the customers who actually use that product, rather than just sending the information out to everyone. Your customers will appreciate not being inundated with information that does not apply to them and will take the marketing they do get more seriously.

Table 8.2 shows some examples of segmentation that you might want to consider. You may use customer location to segment your customers if you are marketing activities such as onsite support, onsite seminars or services, conferences, or product showcases in specific locations. You might also want to market new services such as high-speed Internet access that is available or newly available only in specific geographical locations.

Segmenting customers by product allows you to target consumers of a specific product when a new support offering for that product becomes available, such as a software fix. If you segment by the number of software licenses, you can target those customers who might be interested in support offerings that involve license management. Segmenting by customer will allow you to target simpler support offerings at individual users and let you target fuller support offerings, such as fee-based assisted support via the Internet, for larger organizations.

If you segment by the type of customer business, you can market different support options, such as business-specific knowledge bases or pages, to customers that would be interested in them. Segmenting by the type of service that the customer uses will allow you to relay any support information, such as e-newsletters, about that service to those customers. If you support internal customers, then segmenting them by

Table 8.2 Customer Segmentation for Marketing

YOUR PROFILE	SAMPLE CUSTOMER SEGMENTS
Your site supports several software products that your organization manufactures.	By location (for marketing activities such as onsite support or live seminars), by product used, by product and operating system used, by the number of software licenses purchased, by how many customers, by the type of customer business, or any combination of the above
Your site supports one software product that your organization manufactures.	By location, by the operating system used, by the number of software licenses purchased, by how many customers, by the type of customer business, or any combination of the above
Your site supports several professional services.	By location, by the service used, by the frequency of service use, by the organization size, by the type of customer business, or any combination of the above
Your site supports one specific professional service.	By location, by the frequency of service use, by the organization size, by the type of customer business, or any combination of the above
You are an ISP.	By location; you may offer different services in different geographical locations based on area codes. By the service used, by the organization size, or any combination of the above
You provide internal support to an organization.	By the physical location, by the department or business area, by the software used, by the level of competency in the specific software (for example, you may have identified power users), or by any combination of the above
You are a small business that provides various consulting services.	By location, by the type of customer business, by the type of services used, or any combination of the above
Anything else.	Customers or potential customers use a specific function on the site

department or business area will allow you to market new business-specific support offerings, such as downloads of word processing templates for entry of particular data. If you know your customers well enough, you may even be able to target them by their level of competency in specific software so that you can market seminars or software downloads to the appropriate level of customers. The level of competency might be defined by training, by the customers themselves who specify what level of information they want to receive, or it may be used to identify specific power users who will disseminate information to others in their area.

You might also segment your customers or potential customers by the support site function used. For example, you may want to measure the effectiveness of a FAQ. You would target users of that FAQ for your marketing initiative, which might be a survey embedded in the FAQ. If you have product samples or trial versions, you might want to create a marketing initiative targeting the potential customers who downloaded the samples or trial versions. You might send them email asking for feedback or you might embed a survey in the samples.

Creating a Marketing Plan

Once you have identified your customer segments, you need to start thinking about what your marketing will achieve and how you will achieve it. Thus, you need to create a marketing plan. A marketing plan is not a static document. You will constantly be marketing your support site or the specific information it contains in some way. Your marketing plan needs to be a living document, one you are constantly changing and updating to improve marketing effectiveness. Keep it online where you can change it easily and where everyone who needs to can see what marketing needs to be done when.

Your marketing plan will consist of some or all of the following information for each marketing initiative that you plan to undertake:

Marketing objective. What you want the marketing to accomplish.

Customer segment(s) targeted by the marketing. Who you are aiming the marketing at.

Planned activities. The activities you carry out as part of the marketing initiative.

Data to be gathered. What information, if any, you want to collect as part of this initiative and what you will do with it when you collect it.

Timeframe. How long you will carry out the marketing activities.

Person responsible. Who is responsible for seeing that the marketing initiative is carried out.

Measurement. How you will measure the effectiveness of the marketing activity.

The way you would typically approach creating a plan is to first define what you need to accomplish through marketing over the next three to six months. Be very specific when describing each requirement. If you try to pack too much into one marketing initiative, you could end up inundating customers with too much information, some of which may not even be appropriate for them. In defining what you need to accomplish, you would be filling out the Purpose column shown in Table 8.3. The objectives might be as general as "Make all customers aware that the new site is in place" or as specific as "Let users of software X know that the knowledge base has been updated with more complex software X problems, so that telephone support for software X can be reduced."

Once you have determined all of your objectives, you can start to fill in the details of how you will achieve each objective. First, you need to consider which customers segment you need to target to achieve your objective. Does the objective require that you target all customers or do you only need to target a specific segment, such as home users?

Next, you need to select the specific marketing activities you will undertake to achieve each objective for the customer segment selected. You may be targeting more than one customer segment and each may require different marketing activities. The section titled *Marketing Ideas* might suggest some appropriate activities for you. If you are just starting your support site, you will want to see the section *Ten Suggestions for Marketing at Site Startup*. If your marketing activities include some kind of data gathering, such as a survey, you need to specify what data is to be gathered, how it is to be gathered, and what will be done with it.

Once you understand what your activities are, you need to define when or for how long you will carry them out and who is responsible for them. You also need to define how you will measure the effectiveness of the marketing. It doesn't make any sense to keep using the same marketing techniques if they aren't working. You'll want to know as soon as possible if a technique is ineffective so that you can stop harassing your customers with it and stop spending money on it. You'll also want to know which marketing techniques work so that you can make greater use of them.

Table 8.3 shows a sample of marketing plan entries for promoting a new fee-based assisted support function. We can assume that marketing activities to gauge customer interest in such a service have been carried

Table 8.3 Sample from a Marketing Plan

OBJECTIVE	TARGET CUSTOMER SEGMENT	PLANNED ACTIVITIES	DATA GATHERING	TIMING	RESPONDANT	MEASUREMENT
Promote a new fee-based assisted support function.	Corporate customers	A What's New for Corporate Customers button on the support site with a link to a description of the new function	Feedback is forwarded to the sales manager and site manager.	May to October	Site manager	See below
		Headline article in e-newsletter going to corporate customers	Feedback is forwarded to the sales manager and site manager.	May to June issues	Site manager	See below
		Email to specific corporate customer contacts describing the new service	Feedback is forwarded to the sales manager and site manager.	May	Sales manager with input from the site manager	See below
		Follow-up call from sales department	Feedback on proposed implementation to go to site manager.	Late May to August	Sales manager	All initiatives for this objective: the marketing initiative is considered successful if 20 percent of the corporate customers sign up by the end of August.

out and have concluded that a market for the service exists. The customer segment targeted for all activities is all the corporate customers. Small businesses or individual customers would most likely not be able to afford the service. The new service is planned for September and marketing starts with information posted to the support site. A prominent What's New for Corporate Customers button is linked to a page describing the new service. The button will reside there from May to October. The May through June issues of the corporate e-newsletter will contain headline articles about the new service. Any feedback generated by these two activities, either via email or to telephone support, is forwarded to both the site manager and the sales manager who each have a stake in the new function. The site manager is interested in feedback on the actual proposed implementation. The sales manager is interested in knowing who is interested in the new service, while the site manager is responsible for making sure these first two activities are carried out.

The next two activities are the responsibility of the sales manager. The sales manager sends out an email to corporate customers describing the new service and then instructs the sales staff to make follow-up calls to sell the service and collect feedback on the proposed implementation. Any feedback on the proposed implementation of the new function is sent to the site manager, who can use all the feedback to make adjustments to the implementation.

The success of all these initiatives is measured together and is based on the percentage of customers who actually decide to subscribe to the new service before September. If more than 20 percent of corporate customers sign up for the service, the marketing is considered a success and the same strategy is used again. If fewer than 20 percent of corporate customers sign up, then the marketing strategy needs to be examined and adjusted as necessary to be more successful. Further examples of marketing plans are shown in the *Examples* section.

Carrying Out Marketing Activities

Once your marketing plan has been completed, you are ready to start carrying the activities out and gathering any associated data. I'd like to make two main points about carrying out marketing activities. First, if solicited or unsolicited feedback generated by the activity is very negative, you should stop it before it runs its course. If you are annoying customers, then you are probably doing more damage than good and you need to reassess the activity. For example, if you are sending email to customers about a new service and the first batch of customers respond back with "Stop sending me this junk email!," you need to stop sending them and find another way to get this information across to your customers.

Second, make sure each person participating in the activity understands the responsibilities involved, but these may not always be obvious. For example, if the telephone support staff receives unsolicited feedback concerning a specific marketing initiative, they should be sending that feedback to the site manager and not just shrugging it off. You may want to define some procedures for handling all unsolicited feedback so that it does not get lost. If you are having trouble selecting marketing activities, see the *Marketing Ideas* section.

Measuring Marketing Effectiveness

When you carry out your marketing activities, you need to know whether or not they were successful. In your marketing plan, you identified how you would measure effectiveness, and at the completion of the activity, or even during the activity, you need to take this measurement. You'll want to know if a particular activity was successful in achieving the objective it set out to achieve. If it was, you can use this activity again in the future with some confidence of success. If no, you'll want to look at why the activity didn't work and either scrap it forever or make adjustments and try it again in a future initiative. Carrying out the same marketing activities over and over without even knowing how successful they are makes no sense. It is a waste of time and money. Some marketing measurements that you might want to use are shown in Table 8.4.

Identifying Adjustments and Improvements

This section describes the step that completes the marketing cycle. After you have measured the effectiveness of your marketing activities, you need to analyze how you might adjust the activities to make them more

Table 8.4 Measuring Marketing Activities

MEASURE	USE	DESCRIPTION
The number of responses versus the number of customers in a specific segment	As a survey or any kind of feedback	This tells you what percentage of your target customer segment actually responded. If this is too low, your target segment may not like giving feedback or the survey might have been too cumbersome to fill out. If the percentage responding is acceptable, you can consider the survey or feedback mechanism a success.
The number of customers using a specific function	To communicate information in some way, such as an email or a message on the site, about a new site function	If few customers are using a function that you have been marketing, and you know the function is sound, you can assume that your marketing activity was a failure. You need to find out if you may have used an inappropriate medium, if your message was perhaps unclear, or if your timing was poor.
The number of site visitors	To increase site traffic	You can use your site log analyzer to compare the number of visitors to your site before, during, and after your marketing initiative. If the number increased by at least a defined target percentage, you can assume your activity was successful.
Sales of a fee-based service	To market fee-based services	The number of sales is a fairly straightforward measure. If your site is involved in marketing a fee-based service, then sales of the service will reflect how successful the marketing is. This is assuming that the service has proven to have a demand and be a viable implementation. If other marketing activities for the service are taking place at the same time, you may not be able to get a true measure of your site-based marketing. You probably won't know which marketing activity generated the sales.
Unsolicited feedback	As any activity	It is important to consider unsolicited feedback when measuring the success of your marketing activities. The feedback carries a much greater weight than solicited feedback because someone felt so strongly about something they did not wait to be asked. A significant amount of unsolicited negative feedback is a sure sign that your marketing activity is a failure, while positive feedback indicates an excellent chance of success. Be sure to set up processes to capture as much unsolicited feedback as possible.

successful. You may need to adjust the target customer segments that you used, you may have timed the activity incorrectly, or perhaps the implementation of the activity on your site was poor. You must make these adjustments so that in your next marketing cycle you will increase your marketing success. When identifying required adjustments and improvements, you may find the following checklist helpful:

- Is the target customer segment you selected appropriate? Are you perhaps targeting customers who are not interested in what you are marketing?

- Do you know your customers well enough? Have you put them into the appropriate segments? You may be targeting the correct segment, but the customers in that segment might be incorrectly classified.

- Is the timing of your activity appropriate? Is it too early or too late to achieve the objective you are looking for? What else is going on for your customers at the same time? Are they simply overloaded?

- Is the marketing media you used appropriate for the message relayed and the customer segment targeted? Did you perhaps send out long emails or emails with large attachments? Could the information have been communicated more effectively with a short email indicating where the rest of the information could be accessed on your support site?

- Is the content of your marketing material clear? Is it understandable by your target customer segment? Do you perhaps need someone to proofread your marketing material before it goes out?

- If the marketing activity is based on your support site, is the implementation good? Is it easy to find and easy to execute or respond to? If it is a download, does it work? If it involves instructions, are they clear? If it involves a survey or feedback form, is the amount of information requested reasonable and is it easy to respond to?

Examples

In this section, the concept of the marketing cycle is illustrated through two examples of marketing plans. We will go back to Education Plus and Trace Software to have a look at the marketing plans they create as they work to complete their support sites.

Education Plus

Education Plus is building a support site with both public and private areas to support its custom course offerings. The support site will go live in mid-March. Johnston Reeves has put together a marketing plan, shown in Table 8.5, for the first few months of the new site's life. The first two marketing initiatives have the objective of letting all customers know that the site is coming. All customers calling in to Education Plus are told about the site and in the first week in February Johnston will send an email to all customers letting them know about the site.

In mid-March, once the site is up, customers will receive another email letting them know that the site is available. All customers who call in with a request that could be serviced by the site are to be told about the site. Johnston will measure the effectiveness of all of these initiatives by checking the site logs to see how many customers are using the site and by looking at the number of calls coming in for functions that could have been handled by the site. Notice that Johnston has planned ahead of time how he will measure the effectiveness of these initiatives so he knows that he needs to analyze the site logs and that he needs to track specific types of calls.

Johnston has also looked past startup to gathering feedback on the site's effectiveness. He wants to know how effective the FAQ is, so from May to August a short online survey is to be added to the FAQ with results sent to Kelly Rana who will analyze them and make any indicated changes. Kelly will measure the success of the survey by comparing the number of surveys returned with the number of customers visiting the FAQ, a statistic available from the log analysis tool. Johnston also wants to know what prospective customers think of the course samples that are available for download. From May to August, he will include a short feedback form with the course downloads. When the customer fills out the form, it is emailed to Johnston and will help him plan future course development directions. Again, success of the feedback form is measured by the number of returned feedback forms versus the number of potential customers downloading sample courses.

Johnston's plan illustrates the cyclic nature of marketing. He decides which customers to target, he plans the activities, he measures them, and he uses the information gathered to plan improvements to the site and to the business. The collected information is also used to help plan the next few months of marketing activities.

Table 8.5 Site Marketing Plan for Education Plus

OBJECTIVE	TARGET CUSTOMER SEGMENT	PLANNED ACTIVITIES	DATA GATHERING	TIMING	RESPONDANT	MEASUREMENT
To let customers know that the new site is coming in mid-March	All customers, including those calling in	Inform customers through email and during telephone conversations that a new site is coming.	N/A	The first week in February for email, and all February for customers calling in	Johnston for email, all for calls	Look at the number of customers visiting the site each month versus the number of customers calling.
To let customers know that the new site is available	All customers, including those calling in	Send email to all customers as well as inform customers who call in that problems can be handled by the site. Also track the number of these calls.	N/A	Mid-March, once site is up. Again later, if necessary, based on success	Johnston for email, all for calls	Look at the number of customers visiting the site each month versus the number of customers calling.
To collect information on how effective the FAQ is	Customers who use the FAQ	Short survey with each FAQ category.	Survey data is submitted to Kelly. Changes are made by end of May.	May to August	Kelly R.	Check the number of customers using the FAQ against the number of customers responding to the survey.
To collect feedback from potential customers about the course samples, they download to get input on directions for future development	Potential customers who download the course sample	Short email survey to go along with the download. The survey is actually part of the course sample.	Email responses to be sent to Johnston	May to August	Johnston	Number of surveys sent out versus number returned.

Trace Software

Trace Software is planning the release of their revised site in April. Trace Software has a site currently but is making extensive changes and improvements. Jesse Kim is heading up the site improvement project and has worked with the new site manager to come up with a marketing plan for site startup and the few months after that. Jesse's plan is focused on four main issues. Table 8.6 shows what this marketing plan looks like. First and foremost, Jesse wants to let customers know about the improved site. Once the site is up and running, Jesse wants feedback on how easy the interactive knowledge base is to use and whether customers taking tutorials would be interested in advanced topics. Jesse will also want feedback from European customers on potential new assisted support functions.

The first objective of Jesse's marketing plan is to let customers know that the improved site is coming so that customers are not surprised by the change. Jesse will put a notice on the main page of the support site in March telling customers that the new site is coming. The notice will offer them a link to a page that describes the new site and includes screenshots of key features. Any comments that customers send in are to be collected and reviewed.

The next four activities have been directed at specific customer segments. Corporate customers are going to be targeted with activities that are different from small business or home customers, and marketing activities for European customers are going to be different than those for North American customers. A Trace Software representative will explain the changes to large European customers and then mail out an information package describing the revised site that is different from the North American package. It focuses on the functions that would appeal most to European customers. Large North American customers will receive an information package first and will then be called by a Trace Software representative. Cultural preferences identified by the European Trace Software staff have dictated the difference in activity order. It is felt that European customers would prefer to be called before receiving the package, while small European and North American customers will receive an email notification about the site. The email messages for the two different customers segments are also different; each focuses on those features most important to each segment.

Table 8.6 The Site Marketing Plan for Trace Software

OBJECTIVE	TARGET CUSTOMER SEGMENT	PLANNED ACTIVITIES	DATA GATHERING	TIMING	RESPONDANT	MEASUREMENT
To let customers know that the upgraded site is coming in April	All customers	Set up a page off of the current site that describes the new site and includes some screenshots of new features. Also keep a reminder on the main support page.	Collect any comments from phone or email.	All of March	Site manager	Any email or phone feedback
	All large (corporate) European customers	European representatives will call large European customers to tell them about the site and will follow up with a hard copy marketing package describing the features.	Collect comments from customers.	Last two weeks in March	Jesse Kim	Direct feedback from customers when talking to representatives
	All small European customers	An email that describes the key features of the new site for European users and refers to information on the main site page.	Collect any email or phone feedback.	Last week in March	Site manager	Any email or phone feedback
	All small North American customers	An email that describes the key features of new site and refers to information on main site page.	Collect any email or phone feedback.	Last week in March	Site manager	Any email or phone feedback
	All large (corporate) North American customers	The key contacts at the corporations will receive a hard copy marketing package describing the new site features. A sales representative will make a follow up call.	Collect comments from customers.		Jesse Kim	Direct feedback from customers when talking to representatives.

Table 8.6 (Continued)

OBJECTIVE	TARGET CUSTOMER SEGMENT	PLANNED ACTIVITIES	DATA GATHERING	TIMING	RESPONDANT	MEASUREMENT
To let all customers know the revised site is available	All customers	An email reminder. The email going to all large (corporate) customers will include a reference to the marketing package.			Jesse Kim	Measurements should be taken on the number of customer complaints, the kudos from call tracking, the number of customers using each function on the site, and any decrease in calls to telephone support.
To measure the ease of use of the interactive knowledge base tool	Users of the interactive knowledge base tool	Customers will receive a short online survey at the end of each session with the interactive knowledge base.	Responses are directed to the site manager.	July to October	Site manager	If at least 30 percent of the target segment respond, it will be considered a success.
To gauge interest in advanced courses	People taking online training	At the end of each online training session, customers will be presented with a short online survey.	Responses are directed to site manager.	July to October	Site manager	Will be considered successful if at least 30 percent of the target segment responds.
To get feedback about a new assisted support function for European customers	Assisted support European customers	The support practitioner will discuss and get feedback on the proposed function with all European customers using assisted support.	Responses are written up and sent to the site manager.	August and September	Site manager	The willingness of the customers to respond and the quality of information received.

The fifth and sixth activities will take place once the site is actually up and running. Customers have been segmented into large and small customers. Large customers will receive short email reminders that refer to the information packages received, while small customers will receive short email reminders without the references. During the marketing initiatives, all customer comments are collected. These will help determine how successful the marketing initiatives are. Success will also be measured by complaints or comments after the revised site is in place, by the number of customers using each function, and by any decreases in the number of specific types of calls coming into telephone support. The site manager will then plan improvements based on the measurement information gathered.

Once the new site has been up and running for two months, other marketing initiatives will start. Jesse is interested in measuring how easy to use the interactive knowledge base function is. From July to October, the site will present an interactive tool to customers along with a short online survey when they exit from the function. The site manager will automatically receive the results of the survey and use the comments to make improvements. The marketing initiative is considered successful if at least 30 percent of the customers from the targeted segment (users of the interactive knowledge base) respond to the survey. If this initiative is successful, Jesse and the site manager will use it again in the future. If it is not, they need to find out why and change something they are doing or try something different.

The next marketing initiative to get feedback on whether customers would be interested in advanced online training has the same measurement criteria and the same timing as the initiative around the interactive knowledge base function. All customers taking online training are given a short online survey upon completion. The results of the survey are sent to the site manager who then decides whether creating more advanced training modules is worthwhile. If advanced training is created, the site manager can target announcements about the training to those customers who have indicated an interest.

The final initiative in Trace Software's marketing plan is targeted at European customers using assisted support. The objective of the initiative is to find out if they would use a new assisted support function to replace the chat component with two-way audio. The data gathered would be sent to the site manager who could then work with Jesse Kim to make the decision on whether or not to put the function in place. The success of this marketing activity would be determined by the quality of feedback from the customers and their willingness to give it.

Ten Suggestions for Marketing at Site Startup

Marketing a site at startup can be a tricky proposition. You want to let people know the site is coming so that they can flock to your support site in droves, driving down the number of support calls you receive. However, you want to be very sure that your site is working properly before the masses descend upon it. It might be a good idea to have a rather quiet implementation and then start the traffic-generating marketing activities once you have a good handle on how things are working. It is easier and much, much less stressful to adjust your site when traffic volumes are relatively low than when you are swamped.

I have noticed that many large retail outlets follow this same pattern when they are about to open. They open quietly and operate for a few days without fanfare getting the kinks out of their equipment and processes. Then they have the grand opening with the incredible sales and door-crasher specials. If equipment malfunctioned or the staff didn't know what to do during a grand opening with hordes of people waiting for service, the grand opening would be a disaster for all.

In this section, I present 10 suggestions to help make your marketing at site startup successful:

Realistic Availability Date. Can you really get the site up and running completely with all the processes in place and tested by the date you plan to advertise? Before you market a site's availability date, go back to your project plan or checklist, look at your estimates, and decide if you believe in the end date is a realistic one. If not, adjust it as required.

Test the site, then market it. Hold off on mass marketing until your site is up and running and you know the processes work. You can save your customers and your support team much stress if you do this and you can improve the image of your site, your organization, and your products and services. Put the site into place and test everything out. You can either password-protect the site and open it up for a few customers who have agreed to do some beta testing or you can put it up but hold off on marketing it.

Send out announcements about the site before you go live. If you allow ample time to test the site out and are very confident of the implementation date, you may want to try some iterative, appetite-whetting marketing. I must emphasize that you should be very sure of your date before you do this; otherwise, you could be shooting yourself in the foot. About four weeks before your site goes live, start sending out very short weekly emails to your customers. The last email should arrive at the time the site goes live. Each email should be no more than one or two sentences, and one of which should describe a feature on your site that is very attractive to customers. For example "Coming July 2: You can download all plug-ins and updates directly from our site with no waiting." This would work well in an environment in which the site is ready and waiting with final process tests and adjustments in progress. The email could start while the adjustments were being completed.

Keep email announcements short and sweet. If you are sending an email to your customers to market the site, make it a short email and include a link to your site address so they can access it directly.

Don't put a sign up on your site that says "Under Construction" or "Coming Soon." This tells your customers nothing except that you're working on something, but you don't know when it will be finished. If you want to put something at your site's URL, include a description of the functions available on the future site and the date it will be available. Again, make sure the date is reasonable. If you're early, great, but if you're late, your customers will be annoyed and your image will suffer.

Don't rely on one marketing activity. For example, don't depend solely on email to spread the word about your site. You can market your site in discussion groups, with ads in online or paper-based magazines, in any e-newsletters you put out, or with any product or service literature you produce.

Ensure that all of your telephone support practitioners tell everyone who calls in about the site. You might want to do this for a specific period at startup and then limit this to those customers who could have found the information or resolution they required on the site.

Provide one-click access to the site for internal customers. If your customers are internal to your organization, then give them a direct link via an icon on their desktops to your site, be it Internet or Intranet.

Collect as much customer feedback as you can at startup. This is when customers will see your site or your improved functions for the first time, and it's when you can get some of the most valuable feedback in terms of clarity and usability. Identify all the areas where feedback might be channeled and put processes in place to capture that feedback.

Think about improvements even before your site is up. Your marketing plan should have not only startup activities, but also the next set of marketing activities to increase traffic, market new functions, get feedback on proposed functions, and so on. You can see examples of this in the marketing plans in Tables 8.5 and 8.6.

Marketing Ideas

In this section you will find a collection of suggestions for various marketing activities that will hopefully give you some ideas for your own site marketing.

Email that works. Email is a very powerful tool that can reap great rewards when used correctly. You can use email to make announcements about your site or specific functions. In order to ensure that your email is actually read, it needs to be very concise. Your message should never cover more than a few lines. Include the address of your site or the specific location of what you are marketing so that the customer can click on it and access at the location immediately. Thus, your message can be acted on right away. Figure 8.4 shows an example.

Telemarketing. If you are creating a support site from scratch or even if you are upgrading an existing site, you may not have email addresses for many of your customers. You probably have phone numbers, however, so give them a call and let them know about your online support site. You may be unaware that many of these customers already have email, so don't forget to ask for their email addresses as well.

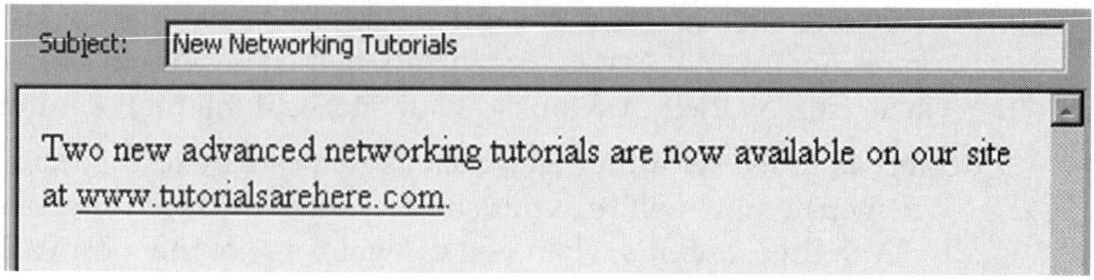

Subject: New Networking Tutorials

Two new advanced networking tutorials are now available on our site at www.tutorialsarehere.com.

Figure 8.4 Email that works.

E-newsletters. E-newsletters are very effective at disseminating technical or business information and updates. Make your e-newsletters as focused as possible so that customers are only given what they are interested in. You may want to give customers the option of subscribing to a number of e-newsletter topics, develop an automated process that will select the appropriate topics for each subscribed customer, and then email them out as one e-newsletter.

Targeted surveys. Put your online surveys where your intended audience is most likely to be on your site. Avoid having a separate survey button. Put the survey right in front of the customers. For example, if you want feedback on your download function, display a survey when the customer leaves the download page or as soon as the download is finished. Surveys should be short, no more than one or two questions, and should not require text entry, only mouse clicks. Target your questions very carefully so that you get useful data. Consider the responses that you might get and then adjust accordingly. For example, if you ask, "Was this function useful?," and if your customer answers No, then you really haven't learned anything. If instead you ask, "Were the download instructions clear?," you will find out if you need to change your instructions or not. You can give surveys at regular intervals and change your specific questions to get the information you need and to test out your improvements.

Ads in the right places. Look at the customer segment you want to market to and think about sites or online magazines that itwould visit. Visit each site and see if the information there is what you would expect that customer segment to be interested in. Once you're satisfied that you've identified the places your target customer segment is likely to visit, you can place ads for your site there.

Go to the telephone. Your telephone support practitioners should always be encouraging customers to use your support site. Make sure this is happening. Each time a customer has a request that could have been serviced by the site, the support practitioner should suggest using the site or could even walk the customer through the site.

Links to valuable stuff. If you want to promote the products or services your site supports, you can include links on your site to articles that mention these products or services positively. If you want to help customers use your product or service more effectively, give them links to sites that can help them do things that are perhaps not within the domain you support. For example, an ISP might offer a link to instructions on how to set up password protection for a site.

Go to your customers. If you attend conferences or meetings that your customers also attend, use the opportunity to promote your site. If it's appropriate, talk about your site to the group or otherwise mention your site at the end of your presentation. Make sure your business card has the address of your support site on it.

Package your site with products. Include the address of your site with all the promotional materials for the products or services you support. Where possible, have your site directly linked to the product or service. For example, if you manufacture a software product, have a link to your support site from your help function. You might even go so far as to have a list of problem symptoms as part of your help function. Each problem could have a direct link to a specific entry in a FAQ on your site that contains the solution to the problem.

Give customers a map. You can help customers use your site more effectively by offering them several paths through it. You might do this with a site usage map, as shown in Figure 8.2.

Offer case studies for your site. You can help corporate customers make better use of your site by offering them examples or case studies of how other organizations have used your site effectively. This is particularly useful if you are offering free telephone support and want to either reduce the number of calls you are getting or if you want to discourage telephone support by charging for it.

Provide commercials on your site for your site. To help customers use your site more effectively or to encourage them to have a look at what is on it, you could offer video clips that are short, interesting commercials that describe what is on your site or what your customers can accomplish using your site. You can change these commercials on an ongoing basis to profile different aspects of your site. If you make them focused, interesting, and useful, they will likely become very popular with your customers. If you plan to use commercials, put together a group of customer volunteers to give you feedback. This will help you ensure that the commercials offer something of interest.

Offer freebies to entice. If you want something from your customers that they might be reluctant to give you, such as a response to a lengthy survey, offer them something in return. Similarly, if you want to entice customers to use your site, offer them a freebie to get them there. This might be a useful piece of software that they can download, a complimentary online tutorial, a set of graphics, a spreadsheet that carries out calculations they are interested in, business articles, and so on. You probably already have many of these things within your organization. You can offer these to everyone who visits your site or you can give the freebie to only those customers who specify a password you give them when they provide you with the information you are looking for.

Key Points

Marketing is a cyclic process. The first task in the cycle involves classifying your customers into segments so that you can customize the marketing required for each segment. Targeting your marketing this way will help you make sure that the right message reaches the right customers and it will also help you select the appropriate marketing activities and vehicles. Next is the creation of a marketing plan that defines objectives and activities for specific customer segments. Then the activities are carried out and data is gathered. The fourth task involves measuring results and the final task involves determining how to adjust activities to improve the results for next time. Then the cycle starts again.

Marketing is not only for letting people know your site exists. As well as attracting customers, marketing can be used to help customers use your site more effectively; help customers use your product or service more effectively via your site; promote the organization, product, or service you support via your site; and get feedback for your site, product, or service.

A marketing plan needs to be a living document, one that is constantly changing to improve marketing effectiveness and meet organizational needs. A marketing plan will consist of your marketing objectives as well as, for each objective, the customer segments being targeted; the planned activities; the data to be gathered; the timeframe for the activity, person, or people responsible; and how the activity is measured.

When you are carrying out marketing activities, you should keep two points in mind. First, if you are getting solicited or unsolicited feedback that is very negative, you should stop the activity before it runs its course. You are probably doing more damage than good, and you need to reassess the activity. Second, make sure each person participating in the activity understands the responsibilities involved so that all tasks are completed and all required data is gathered.

You can save time and money by avoiding marketing activities that don't work. This means you need to understand whether or not your marketing activities are successful. In your marketing plan, you identified how you would measure effectiveness and at the completion of the activity, or even during the activity, you need to take the measurement. Some suggested measures are shown in Table 8.4.

Once you have measured the effectiveness of your marketing activities, you are ready for the step that completes the marketing cycle. You'll need to analyze the activities to see how you could make them more effective. You may need to adjust the target customer segments that you used, you may have timed the activity incorrectly, or perhaps the implementation of the activity on your site was poor. These adjustments can increase the success of your next marketing cycle.

Site Management

M anaging a support site involves measuring the site's performance, monitoring all the processes of running the site (we looked at many of these in Chapter 7, "Processes and Implementation"), evaluating and analyzing various aspects of processes and performances, and making improvements. Site management is a cycle, as shown in Figure 9.1, and it never ends. A site manager is constantly measuring, monitoring, evaluating, and improving.

Customer needs are constantly changing as technology evolves and as market trends and business environments change. A site manager needs to be aware of these changing needs and must respond to them quickly. For example, as your customers move toward powerful technology, they may want direct online access to functions such as multimedia training modules that they may have previously found too slow for online access. A site manager must also keep a close eye on the processes that keep the site running smoothly. Not all of these processes are automated, so they are subject to human errors and omissions and they must be managed. For example, if one person does not carry out a process correctly, such as not responding to email in a timely fashion, the performance and image of the site will suffer. Without effective site

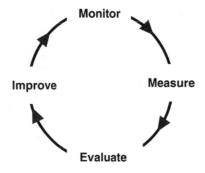

Figure 9.1 The site management cycle.

management, processes can break down and negative trends can become disasters.

In order to carry out this monitoring, evaluation, and improvement, a site manager must have thresholds to measure against so that potential trouble or improvements can be identified. The site manager can establish this threshold by defining measures of performance and carrying out these measures on a regular basis. Measuring performance also proves the worth of the site, which may be a requirement in some organizations and shows whether or not improvements being considered are financially justified.

In this chapter, I discuss how to set up effective performance measures for your support site. These include what to monitor and for how long. They also include how to evaluate performance, how to identify areas for improvement, and how to implement the needed improvements. I supply various templates and specific suggestions that you may be able to use for your support site.

The topics I cover in this chapter are as follows:

- Tasks in establishing site management process
- Defining measures of performance
- Reporting on performance
- Monitoring performance, traffic, and processes
- Evaluating performance and processes
- Making improvements

Establishing Site Management Processes

Before a site manager can measure site performance, the measures or threshold must first be defined. The site manager needs to define any financial criteria that must be met, such as a return on investment or an objective that must be satisfied, which could be a reduction in calls to telephone support. The site manager must also define which factors must be taken into consideration when measuring how effectively the site delivers solutions and other services. He or she must also determine whether the responsiveness to market and customers is a performance factor.

Once performance criteria have been set up, the site manager must set up the cycle of ongoing management, as illustrated previously in Figure 9.1: measurement, monitoring, evaluation, and improvement. In defining measures of performance, the manager also must define how performance is to be reported on and when. This is the measuring segment of the management cycle. Next, the site manager needs to set up processes to monitor day-to-day site activity and overall performance so that trends can be identified and analyzed. This defines the monitoring segment of the management cycle. The evaluation segment of the cycle is addressed by the third management task. The third task involves setting up processes to analyze trends and evaluate what needs to be done to improve the site. The final task required to complete the structure of the management cycle is setting up improvement processes. The manager must set up processes that will ensure that the results of the evaluation phase of the cycle will not be lost but will be turned into site improvements. (See Table 9.1.)

The more rigorously this management cycle is defined, the greater the chances are that it will become a continuous cycle and result in a site that is constantly improving.

Defining Measures of Performance

Your definition of support site performance is based on how you define success for your support site. This would include any specific objectives you have for the site. If you created a scope summary for your site when

Table 9.1 Tasks Involved in Establishing Site Management Processes

TASKS	DETAILS
Define measures of performance.	Define the site objectives and service levels as well as the most critical functions. Determine all the components of site performance.
Set up site-monitoring processes.	Decide which statistics or processes need to be monitored, how frequently, and who should monitor them.
Set up evaluation processes.	Create forums to evaluate the ongoing performance and decide who should participate.
Set up improvement processes.	Define how the evaluation results are turned into site improvements.

you were planning it, as described in Chapter 3, "Establishing Scope," going back to it and looking at your requirements will give you a starting point for determining what defines success for your site. Let's look at an example. We'll use our Chapter 3 example of Education Plus. The requirements are as follows:

- Provide all customer support requirements
- Promote professional image
- Market new products
- Attract new business
- Provide quick responses to email
- Download copies of courses
- Offer high security
- Request and track course changes online

The first requirement, *provide all customer support requirements*, indicates that the site must channel all or most support away from other areas. It must reduce the support workload in other areas, which can be used as a measure of performance if the support workload can be quantified. *Attract new business* can be used as a measure, again if it can be quantified; we can look at sales before and after the site was in place and at sales trends. *Provide quick responses to email* is another measure of performance that can be used. A target response time for email can be set and actual times can be measured against the target. The other requirements in the list are geared more towards the design of the site and the functions it needs to contain.

To obtain additional performance measures, you need to answer some questions. What would you require of your support site to consider it a success? What factors are important to you or to your organization? You will find that the responses to these questions along with the performance measures you gathered from your scope summary can fit into five categories, as shown in Figure 9.2. These categories are as follows:

- Specific objectives
- Return on investment (ROI)
- Reduction of workload in other areas
- Effectiveness of solution and service delivery
- Responsiveness and proaction

Going back to the Education Plus example, a reduction in the support workload would fall into the *reduction of workload in other areas* category, quick responses to email would fall into the *effectiveness of solution and service delivery* category, and the attract-new-business measure would fall into the *ROI* category. Any or all of the measures could be put into the *specific objectives* category. The site manager would then

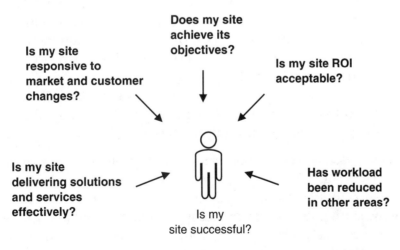

Figure 9.2 Categories of performance.

decide if the measures could be quantified and which category makes the most sense for the performance measurement requirements of that specific organization.

You should constantly set objectives for your site in terms of improvements that must be made or business thresholds that must be met. You may have an objective to increase the number of times that visits to your FAQ result in successful resolutions for your customer. If you don't specifically measure the objective, then you won't know whether or not you have achieved it. Measuring the ROI will show you the dollar return that you achieve based on what your site costs. Even if you accept the fact that the site is an expense, you need to be aware of what the ROI percentage is so that the expense doesn't get out of hand.

One of your site's objectives might be to reduce the calls to your support area or to other areas involving human intervention. Your site might provide self-service options so that customers don't have to call other areas. If this is the case, you need to know how well your site is achieving this objective. If your site is not reducing the workload to other areas, it is failing. Every support site is interested in the third category listed, the effectiveness of solution and delivery. If your site is successful, every knowledge source is up to date and gives the customer the required information, all functions work perfectly, the customers get exactly what they need every time they visit, and so on. You must measure this effectiveness so that you can ensure that you see how far from success you are and what you need to do to get there. Responsiveness refers to how quickly your site responds to changing market and customer needs. Proaction means anticipating and making changes to your site as or before the market or customer requirements change. Responsiveness and proaction are especially important to you if the domain you support is volatile. Being successful in the responsiveness and proaction category means having the processes in place to monitor changes and trends, identify the required changes, make the required site modifications, and communicate the changes.

Before we discuss each of these categories in more detail, I would like to clarify the relationship between performance and time. Performance is measured across time. When you are measuring performance, you are really measuring how performance is changing. If you don't know how performance was yesterday, then your performance measures for today are meaningless. You have no idea if your site is improving or getting worse. When measuring performance, you always need to show performance over time, as Figure 9.3 illustrates. Performance without a time component is meaningless, as the figure illustrates. If you just looked at point A, you would not see that performance is positive, improving continuously. If you just looked at point B, you would not see that performance is rapidly deteriorating; you would only see excellence.

The next sections will cover how to set up your own measures of performance within each of the five categories. We'll also discuss how to put all of the measures together.

Specific Objectives

Objectives give you goals that describe specific thresholds that you want your site to meet. Describing a goal as increasing traffic to the site does not give you a useful measure since you don't know how much you need to increase traffic by or for what time interval. Would an increase of one customer per month be acceptable? Probably not. Would

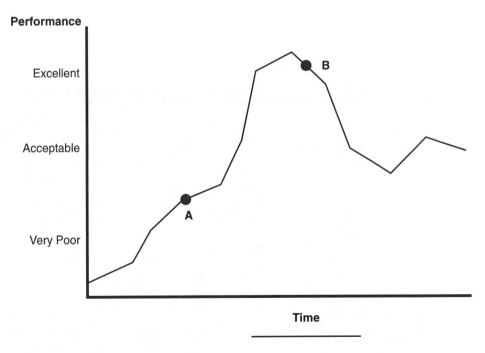

Figure 9.3 Performance across time.

an increase of one thousand customers per month be acceptable? Maybe you would be quite satisfied with an increase of one thousand customers, but your management might be looking for an increase of a minimum of four thousand customers in one month. Your objectives are performance measures, so they need to be specific with a defined timeframe; there should be no doubt about whether or not you achieved them. Your goal of increasing traffic to the site needs to be changed to be more specific, such as to "increase traffic to the site by at least four thousand customers monthly from May through August." If you need to ask questions about your objective, it is not specific enough.

Objectives typically come from two sources: from management and from your own evaluation and improvement processes. Objectives define the improvements you are working to make. This includes the specific level you are aiming at and the timeframe in which you plan to achieve it. If you don't measure yourself against specific objectives, then your improvements are in danger of not getting done. Behind each objective you create should be a plan to reach that objective and a structure to measure it. Consider the example of two objectives in Table 9.2.

Table 9.2 Creating Objectives as Performance Measures

OBJECTIVE	PLAN	HOW TO MEASURE
Decrease Help Desk calls by 20 percent of March's call volume. The deadline is September 1.	Update all knowledge sources to make information easier to understand by the end of April. Reorganize the site so that information sources are organized by product by April 30. Market these changes on the site starting April 30 and via the telephone support staff starting April 30.	Measure changes in the number of calls per customer to calculate the decrease in the number of calls to the Help Desk. Measure this monthly starting in June to ensure that the changes are working.
Decrease the email response time to a maximum of 24 hours by June 1.	Add two new FAQs to cover the gap that currently exists in the information sources for home users by May 3.	Use the email management tool to monitor and report on email queues.

Each objective is very clearly defined with specific thresholds and time-frames specified. The site manager knows what has to be done to achieve these objectives and has described the necessary work in the Plan column. The manager has also thought about how to measure whether or not these objectives have been achieved.

Consider the first objective in which the manager wants to decrease the calls to the Help Desk by 20 percent by September 1. In order to achieve those changes, the information sources need to be easier to understand and reorganized. The manager has planned for this work. The manager has also realized that customers aren't necessarily going to know about the changes, so they need to be marketed. Marketing has also been included in the plan. Although the decrease of 20 percent is not expected until the end of August, this wise site manager wants to start measuring this objective earlier, in June, to make sure that the changes made are having the desired impact on the Help Desk call volume. If the call volume is not decreasing, the manager will have a bit of time to make further changes or carry out additional tasks. Notice that a decrease in calls will be measured based on the calls per customer—the average number of calls each customer makes—rather than just the overall volume of calls. This choice is necessary since an increase in customers will cause an increase in calls and if only the call volume is looked at, it might be difficult to see if any calls had been eliminated and if the support site was responsible. To illustrate this, let's look at Figure 9.4 to see what the site manager might be measuring at the end of August.

Since we are using March's volume to measure against, we look at the calls per customer in March. The 2.6 calls per customer is what we will measure our performance against to see if we reach the 20 percent decrease in calls. If we look at Figure 9.4, we can see that the number of customers increases by 200 between March and July. These customers will be generating more calls, but this won't affect our measurement since we are working with calls per customer. For June, July, and August, we use the number of customers to calculate what our call volume would be for each month at 2.6 calls per customer. We then compare these values to the actual call volume for these months and calculate the difference. The difference is 321 in June, 408 in July, and 589 in August. These differences are the reduction in calls. To calculate a percent reduction, we take these differences as a percentage of the call volume calculated at 2.6 calls per customer. June's difference of 321 is 11 percent of 2,811 calls, July's difference of 408 is 14 percent of 2,658, and

		March	April	May	June	July	August
1							
2	# Calls	2,300	2,175	2,490	2,490	2,250	2,150
3	# Customers	900	900	1,000	1,100	1,100	1,100
4	Calls/Customer	2.6	2.4	2.5	2.3	2.0	2.0
5							
6		Target To					
7		Measure Against					
8							
9							
10	Threshold: # Calls if calls/customer stayed at 2.6				2,811	2,658	2,739
11	Difference between threshold and actual calls				321	408	589
12	**% Difference**				**11%**	**15%**	**22%**
13							
14							

Figure 9.4 Measuring objectives.

August's difference of 589 is 22 percent of 2,739. We surpassed our objective of 20 percent.

Note that if we had not used calls per customer but only considered total calls, we would be looking at the difference between 2,300 calls in March and 2,150 calls in August, which works out to only seven percent. This would not be an accurate reflection of the true situation.

As you can see in the preceding example, setting an objective is not simply a matter of writing the objective down. You want to make sure you can meet the objectives you set, and to do so, you need to plan how you will achieve the objectives. Thus, you must have a strong understanding of how you will measure whether or not you have achieved the objective.

Return on Investment (ROI)

In this section, we are going to examine two types of ROI measures. The first involves measuring the actual ROI of your site against the ROI you projected when you did your cost-benefit analysis justifying the site. You may or may not use this as a performance measure, but even if you don't, it is an excellent lesson in understanding the factors that impact the return your site generates. The second ROI measure does not take any cost benefit into account. It is simply the net sales or savings your site generates, that is, sales or savings minus operating costs over a given period of time expressed as a percentage.

Actual ROI Versus Projected ROI

When you were first determining how much money you could spend on your site while still generating some return for the business, you came up with a cost-benefit analysis to show the projected site return. To measure yourself against this, you need to calculate the actual startup and ongoing costs of your site and the value of the benefits that were actually realized. You also need to add in any costs or benefits that affect your ROI but that your original analysis did not take into account. As an example, consider Figure 9.5. This is a spreadsheet showing the original cost-benefit analysis that was used in Chapter 1, "Is Web-Based Support Worthwhile?," for SGS, Inc. as well as the actual values. You will notice a significant difference between what was projected and what actually happened, and it is not good news.

SGS, Inc.'s problems started slowly in site creation. SGS was $13,500 over budget, probably because someone underestimated the work involved in getting the site up and running. After the first year, SGS found that it had underestimated the work involved in site maintenance by $8,000 and had overvalued the savings in support calls and in onsite visits. SGS saved a total of $28,000 less than planned in its support area: $6,000 less than planned in support calls and $22,200 less than planned in onsite calls. Perhaps the original estimate was correct, but the site was not designed effectively as it could have been, so customers called in to the telephone support area, rather than visiting the site. As a result, the first year's ROI was negative, not a good performance against the projected first-year ROI of 64 percent. In year two, the trend continued. Site maintenance costs were $10,000 more than planned and

		Startup Planned	Startup Actual	Year 1 Planned	Year 1 Actual	Year 2 Planned	Year 2 Actual
1	**One time costs**						
2	Software (2 seats)	$10,000	$10,000				
3	Installation & Training	$3,000	$3,000				
4	Software Selection	$6,300	$6,300				
5	Site Creation	$31,500	$45,000				
6							
7	**Ongoing costs**						
8	Software Maintenance			$1,200	$1,200	$1,200	$1,200
9	Site Maintenance			$21,000	$29,000	$21,000	$31,000
10							
11	Total	$50,800	$64,300	$22,200	$30,200	$22,200	$32,200
12	**Cumulative Costs**	$50,800	**$64,300**	$73,000	**$94,500**	$95,200	**$126,700**
13							
14	**Benefits**						
15	Support Calls			$18,000	$12,000	$18,000	$14,000
16	Onsite calls saved			$43,200	$21,000	$43,200	$22,000
17	Publishing			$6,000	$6,000	$6,000	$6,000
18	Put off hiring			$52,500	$52,500		
19							
20							
21	Total			$119,700	$91,500	$67,200	$42,000
22	**Cumulative Benefits**			$119,700	**$91,500**	$186,900	**$133,500**
23							
24	**ROI**			64%	**-3%**	96%	**5%**
25							

Figure 9.5 Measuring the ROI against the original cost-benefit analysis.

the savings in support calls and onsite visits were $25,200 less than planned. This planned ROI of 96 percent turned into an actual ROI of five percent. I can hear some of you saying, "At least it was positive," but that might not be what the rest of your organization is saying since you came in at 95 percent under plan.

If you did not perform well against the ROI you projected in your cost-benefit analysis, you need to look at the reasons and correct them so that your next year's ROI will be more on track. Is your site poorly designed, do you need more and better processes, are you marketing effectively, or did you simply make very poor estimates? I will look at identifying the reasons for poor performance in the *Evaluating Performance and Processes* section.

ROI as Costs versus Sales and Savings

Even if you did not do a cost-benefit analysis when you set your site up, you still need to understand how profitable your site is and, in fact, management may be pressuring you for this statistic. Knowing your site's ROI will help you decide whether certain expenditures are justified or if you should hold off. For example, if you have found a direct correlation between how many customers visit your product information page and the number of sales that your site generates, you may decide that an expenditure for developing product commercial clips is worthwhile. Similarly, if the site is bringing a return in terms of staff that does not have to be hired, then spending a certain amount of money to improve self-serve functions will be justified. In fact, you will know exactly how much money you can spend before the endeavor ceases to be worthwhile.

The ROI is calculated by first determining the sales or savings your site generates in a given period of time: the return and the operating cost of the site during that time, known as the investment. You then calculate net return by subtracting investment from return. To express this as a percentage, you divide by investment and multiply by 100.

Determining Return

What goes into return? Any sales or savings your site generated. If your site is not directly involved with or linked to sales of your products, you could make an assumption that the more people that visit your site, the more exposure there is to the organization, products, and services you support. This means that as traffic to your site increases, your site's positive impact on sales also increases. If you think conservatively, you can assign the impact a value. This will be easier if you can compare sales numbers before the site to sales numbers after the site and extrapolate a dollar value as the impact.

Savings that your site generates could come from the following areas:

- Calls no longer going to a telephone support area such as a Help Desk
- Publishing costs lowered or eliminated by posting information to your support site
- Remote sites might no longer require onsite support or may require reduced onsite support

Determining Investment

Investment is typically much easier to calculate than return; you just add up what the site is costing you. In the interests of simplicity, I will not differentiate between capital costs and expenses. Your costs might include the following:

- Salaries and overhead costs for all staff supporting or maintaining the site. If some or all of these people only work on the site part time, you would only calculate costs for the time they spend supporting the site.

- Ongoing maintenance costs for software or hardware that the site uses

- New software or hardware costs

- Communication and server hosting costs

Calculating the ROI

Let's look at an example to see what a ROI analysis might look like. Figure 9.6 shows a very simple ROI analysis for this year as compared to last year. Remember that performance is measured across time. An investment consists of staff salaries, maintenance costs for hardware and software, costs for new hardware and communications equipment, and new software costs. The return is generated by a reduction in calls to telephone support, a reduction in onsite customer visits, a savings in publishing costs of documentation, and an increase in sales generated by the site.

Last year, the investment was significantly more than the return. The ROI was a negative 20 percent. This year saw a terrific improvement with a return of 11 percent. Perhaps the new software purchased last year made the difference in increased savings generated by a reduction in support calls and fewer visits to the remote site. It may have also contributed to the higher sales.

Reduction of Workload in Other Areas

Even if the ROI is not one of your measures of performance, you still may be measured on what your site returns, which includes the workload

	Investment	Last Year	This Year
1	Investment	Last Year	This Year
2	Salaries plus Overhead	$160,000	$160,000
3	Software Maintenance	$6,500	$6,500
4	Hardware Maintenance	$22,000	$13,000
5	New Hardware/Comm.	$6,000	$15,000
6	New Software	$22,000	$0
7	**Total Investment**	$216,500	$194,500
8			
9	**Return**		
10	Savings in Support Calls	$22,000	$40,000
11	Remote Site Savings	$42,000	$54,000
12	Publishing Savings	$12,000	$12,000
13	Increase in Sales	$98,000	$110,000
14	**Total Return**	$174,000	$216,000
15			
16	ROI	-20%	11%
17			

Figure 9.6   The ROI this year versus last year.

your site reduces in other areas. Your site may be keeping calls to the Help Desk to a manageable level. If you can calculate how many calls your site is eliminating, you can use this as a measure of your site's performance. The sales department might be another area affected by your site. If your support site offers information on your organization's products and services, customers may be going to the site and perhaps even downloading brochures, samples, or trial versions, instead of calling the sales department. Again, if you can calculate or estimate with some degree of confidence how many calls or how much work your site is eliminating, you can use this as a performance measure.

If you want, you can measure workload reduction to a finer granularity: by site function. You would use statistics from your site log analyzer to analyze traffic to specific functions. You would also need data that tells you what percentage of function visits customers considered successful. You could gather this data with a one-question survey that customers fill out on exiting a function. You would then extrapolate the number of successful site visits by applying the percentage to the number of hits. This would give you an estimate of the number of calls that customers did not have to make to other areas; they got what they wanted from your site. This process is similar to the one I use later on in this section to illustrate measuring the workload reduction without the benefit of call-tracking statistics.

I will illustrate the process of measuring the workload reduction by using the Help Desk example. If you have a good idea of your Help Desk call profile before you put your site up, then measuring the impact of your site on the Help Desk workload will be fairly straightforward. If you do not know what the call profile of your Help Desk was before you put your site up, then measuring the impact of your site is going to be somewhat more challenging. Let's take the easier path first and illustrate it with an example, shown in Figure 9.7.

Let's say that for the three months preceding your support site implementation, your Help Desk, which supports external customers, has been fielding an average of about 2,000 calls per month. Calls dropped to 1,500 per month for the first two months after the site implementation and to 1,200 in the third month. The number of calls cannot be looked at on its own because it depends on the number of customers. If the number of customers goes up, calls will go up, so any decrease in

	Help Desk Statistics	Month 1	Month 2	Month 3	Month 4	Month 5	Month 6
2	# Calls	2,000	2,000	2,200	1,500	1,500	1,200
3	# Customers	900	900	1,000	1,100	1,100	1,100
4	Calls/Customer	2.2	2.2	2.2	1.4	1.4	1.1
5							
6	Calculated Savings			Site Implementation			
7	Calls/Customer						1.1
8	Calls saved						1,220
9	Minutes / call						7
10	Total time (min.)						8,540
11	Total Time (hr.)						142.3
12	Wage / hr.						$60
13	Monthly Savings						$8,540

Figure 9.7 Measuring workload reduction with call-tracking statistics.

calls could be negated by an increase in customers. The number of calls per customer will give you a more accurate picture of the impact of any changes. If we look at Figure 9.7, we will see that the number of customers has been increasing, while our calls have decreased, so the benefit is greater than we could see by just looking at call volume. The calls per customer have dropped from 2.2 to 1.1, a significant change.

You can assign a dollar figure to the workload reduction by estimating the cost of each call in terms of employee time and then calculating the total. Let's assume each call averages seven minutes and we'll use an employee wage of $60 per hour. First, we calculate the difference in calls per customer since we implemented the site. The calls per customer fell from 2.2 to 1.1 so the difference is 1.1 calls per customer. We are now in month six of the chart in Figure 9.7, the third month after the site was implemented. Our customer count is 1,100. At 1.1 calls per customer, we are saving 1,100 x 1.1, or 1,220 calls per month. At seven minutes for each call, we have a total of 8,540 minutes, which is 142.3 hours, which translates further into 142.3 x $60, or $8,540 per month. This becomes a significant $102,480 over one year

How you use this information depends on your specific environment. You may choose to just report on the calls per customer or you may use the dollar value.

Now let's consider a not-so-easy example, illustrated in Figure 9.8. For whatever reason, you don't have any Help Desk statistics to go on. You do, however, have a site log analyzer. You have no excuse for not having one because you can download one for free, and you are capturing success rates on your knowledge sources with short surveys that customers fill out when exiting the knowledge source.

In month 1, whenever that happens to be, your site log analyzer tells you that your FAQ had 3,000 hits and your interactive knowledge base had 2,500 hits. I am assuming that the hits measure entries into the FAQ and interactive knowledge base functions, not hits on individual pages within these functions. Your survey statistics tell you that your FAQ is successful in solving your customers' informational requirements 29 percent of the time. Not all customers will respond to the FAQ survey, but you should have enough responses that you are confident that 29 percent is fairly accurate. You determine the total number of hits on your FAQ by taking 29 percent of 3,000. What you get is an estimate of

	Log Analysis Statistics	# Hits Month 1	# Hits Month 2	# Hits Month 3
1				
2	FAQ page	3,000	3,300	3,100
3	Interactive Knowledge Base	2,500	2,200	2,400
4				
5	Survey Statistics			
6	FAQ positive	29%	32%	31%
7	IKB positive	30%	31%	30%
8				
9	Extrapolated Savings			
10	FAQ calls saved	870	1,056	961
11	IKB calls saved	750	682	720
12	Total calls saved	**1,620**	**1,738**	**1,681**
13				
14	At 7 min. / call	11,340	12,166	11,767
15	Hours	189.0	202.8	196.1
16	$ at 60$ / hr.	**$11,340**	**$12,166**	**$11,767**
17				

Figure 9.8 Measuring workload reduction with log analysis statistics.

the number of visits to the FAQ in which customers got the information they needed and did not have to call the Help Desk. Twenty-nine percent of 3,000 is 870 calls to the Help Desk eliminated by the FAQ. You can apply the same logic to the interactive knowledge base and you end up with 30 percent of 2,500 hits, which is 750 calls saved. The total calls saved in month 1 is the sum of 870 and 750, which is 1,620. At seven minutes per call, this is 11,340 minutes or 189 hours. That's $11,340 at $60 per hour. If the savings continue at approximately this rate, which they do in months 2 and 3, as Figure 9.8 shows, the savings in one year will be approximately $136,080.

Again, how you present this information depends on your environment. You might be satisfied with looking at the number of hits to a specific function and the number of positive responses to surveys measuring the usefulness of the data retrieved.

The Effectiveness of Solution and Service Delivery

Is your site meeting all the promised response or delivery times? Are reported problems resolved quickly? Is your site giving your customers accurate answers in a timely manner for all or most of what they need? These are the questions that you are trying to answer when you measuring the effectiveness of solution and service delivery. Let's look at how to answer these questions so that we can come up with some measures you might want to use.

Service Levels

You may want to define the specific levels of service that your site needs to meet. Customers and management should contribute to decisions on these levels. For example, you may have a service level that specifies all email must be responded to within 24 hours. You may have another service level that specifies that customers should be able to get where they want to be within a function with three or less mouse clicks. You must be able to measure any promised service levels; otherwise, it's not worth setting them.

Service levels are often related to objectives. Once your original objective has been achieved, you may want it to continue. For example, in Table 9.2, we saw the objective *Decrease email response time to a maximum of 24 hours by June 1.* This objective is necessary in order to get the response time down to 24 hours. Once the 24-hour response time is achieved, it could be established and measured as a service level and marketed as such to customers.

Assisted Problem Resolution

If your site offers functions that enable customers to log their own problems, or functions that offer assisted support, you need to measure how well these are meeting the needs of your customers. If customers are logging their own problems, then you need to make sure that the priorities and resolution times you agreed on with the Help Desk manager are being met. You will need the call-tracking system to give you details on calls that were logged by customers from your site. Alternately, this may be the responsibility of the Help Desk manager. You'll have to work this out with that person. If you are both the Help Desk manager and the site manager, great. You'll already have the processes you need in place to look for logged calls.

If you offer assisted support, you will want to know how successful those calls were. The easiest way to do this is to have the support practitioners log all assisted support interactions to the Help Desk call-tracking tool. This will ensure those calls are handled by the processes already in place for the Help Desk.

Data Accuracy

You can measure the accuracy of data by using surveys, looking at the number of complaints, and reviewing processes. Surveys will tell you how accurate your customers think your data is. Short, one-question surveys in strategic locations on your site (when they are exiting a knowledge source, for example) will give you an idea of how accurate your customers feel your data is. From your survey results, you can determine the percentage of customers that felt your data was accurate or up to date. You can validate this percentage by using your site log analysis tool to determine how many people visited the knowledge source and then calculating what percentage of customers answered the survey.

If you put processes in place to gather feedback, as suggested in Chapter 7, you will be able to capture any complaints about data being out of date or inaccurate. If you do get complaints, you need to make note of these as part of your measurement.

Another measure of accuracy is the processes that you have in place to maintain your site. Do these processes exist? Are they being followed? Are they correct? If the answer to all of these questions is yes, your site data very likely has an excellent degree of accuracy. If the answer to any of these questions is no, then you have some work to do before you can have any degree of confidence in your knowledge sources and other site data.

Your site log analyzer can tell you much about how accurate your navigation is. It will show you the most common navigational paths and you can see if those paths make sense, if they are the ones intended. A navigational path consists of the site pages a customer must go through to get to a specific destination. You can use this data to optimize the most commonly used paths to shorten the time customers spend getting to where they want to be.

Timeliness

Measuring timeliness involves answering the question, "How quickly are your customers getting the answers or information they need?" Timeliness might include the following factors:

- The site response or loading time, or how long customers have to wait for a page to load or to get a response from the site
- The lengths of the paths that customers need to follow to get to a solution
- The length of time customers must wait to get a response to email
- The length of time that customers must wait to get online assisted support

Ideally, when you first designed your site, you designed it to minimize loading and response times. Loading and response times can be affected by numerous factors, so you must constantly monitor these times to be aware of any negative trends. You will need site management software to be able to measure these numbers.

If your customers have to rifle through 20 different pages to get the information they want, then they would probably not consider that they are getting the information in a timely fashion. You may want to set a limit to the number of pages your customers must navigate or the mouse clicks your customers must use to get to information within a specific function. Your site log analysis tool will give you information on paths that customers are following. You will need to identify which paths you want to monitor and then use your log analysis tool to get the numbers you need.

You probably have already set up a service level to define the acceptable email response times for your site. Email management tools are available that can monitor and report on email queues for you so that you can measure your email response times and identify any problems before they become serious.

When customers make a request for assisted support, they are typically put into a holding queue until a support practitioner becomes free to establish a chat and remote control session. You need to measure customer hold times so that you can identify negative trends and take measures to prevent high wait times and irate customers. Chat services typically provide wait time reporting that you can use to measure how long your customers are waiting to get assisted support.

The Breadth and Depth of a Domain

Finally, let's consider the domain of your customers' problems and requirements. Does your site cover them? You can answer this question by using surveys, looking at the number of complaints, and analyzing the number of Help Desk calls that your site eliminates.

Short, one-question surveys will tell you whether or not a specific function has satisfied a customer's requirement. From your survey results, you can determine the percentage of customers that felt your data met their needs and gave them the information they required. You can validate this percentage by using your site log analysis tool to determine how many people visited the knowledge source and then by calculating the percentage of customers that answered the survey.

If you put processes in place to gather feedback, as suggested in Chapter 7, you can capture any complaints about data being inadequate for customer requirements. You will need to include any complaints as part of your measurement.

If your site is meeting the objectives or service levels for eliminating Help Desk calls, then it is probably doing a good job at providing information aimed at the customers' problem domains. Any negative trends in this area might indicate inadequate domain coverage. You would have to perform a further analysis to ascertain the causes of the trend.

Responsiveness and Proaction

Responsiveness and proaction are really the result of all of your other measures of performance. You would notice negative trends in other measures if your site is not responsive or proactive. If your site has these characteristics, however, then your other measures of performance will remain positive, even when the domain within which your site operates changes. If the domain you support is volatile, you need to be concerned about keeping up with it, responding to it, and preparing for changes before they happen. You might even be initiating changes.

An important indication of how responsive and proactive your site can be is whether or not you have processes in place to measure, monitor, evaluate, and improve. It is within these processes that you determine how responsive and proactive you can be.

To measure how responsive and proactive your site is, review your management processes to make sure that you are constantly looking for improvements. Also look at how your site performs against your other measures during times of change.

Putting Your Measures Together

I have given you an assortment of suggested measures that you might want to define and use in managing your site. You might also want to add measures that I may not have discussed. You then need to make the following decisions:

- Which measures are you going to report on, how you will report on them, and for what time frames.
- Which measures you are going to watch on an ongoing basis to monitor trends. You also need to define what an ongoing basis means.

The following section titled *Reporting on Performance* will help you decide how to report performances and for how long. The section titled *Monitoring Performance and Processes* will help you define what you want to monitor as well as how and when to monitor it.

Reporting on Performance

Reporting on performance involves defining the audience for the report, identifying the performance measures that the audience is interested in, and then taking the measures and creating the report at suitable intervals. The audience for your reports include management, yourself as the site manager, and any other stakeholders within the organization who are affected in some way by the site, such as the Help Desk and marketing department, for example.

Management will most likely be interested in the impact your site is having on the business versus what it costs. Reporting to management will typically be carried out on a quarterly basis. Your management report will include all or some of the following information:

Changes in overall site traffic. Management will want to know what kind of traffic the site is generating.

Performance against service levels.

Performance against objectives. Management will specifically want to see what you are doing about any problem areas.

Operating costs. Management wants to know that you are within budget and where your budget is going. A good idea is to show the return as well so that management can see what is generated by the expenditure. In effect, you're justifying your budget.

ROI. How you show the ROI will depend on your organization and how quickly the return changes. Your choices include the ROI this quarter compared to the last quarter or the same quarter last year, the ROI for a rolling 12 months compared to the ROI for the previous entire year, the year-to-date ROI for the current year compared to the year-to-date ROI for the previous year, and so on.

Figure 9.9 shows an example of a quarterly performance report for management. The report includes site traffic information, the performance against service levels and objectives, the operating cost, the return, and the ROI. The ROI is shown for this quarter, for last quarter, year to date for this year, and for the entire previous year. Notice that in every measure the report shows the change over time, which is a critical dimension of performance. The example is a good overall indication of quarterly performance, but your management may want more detail or a different focus. You would have to add the measures that make sense for your particular organization.

The reporting that you as site manager want to see will be more frequent than quarterly. You will want to look at some statistics daily and weekly. This will be part of your monitoring process, which I will discuss in the section on monitoring processes and statistics, and you will probably want to look at the overall performance monthly. You will

Quarterly Support Site Performance Report			
1. Site Traffic	**Current Qtr**	**Previous Qtr**	**Change**
No. Site Visitors	82,000	75,000	9%
2. Service Levels	**Current Qtr**	**PreviousQtr**	**Change**
Success at meeting 24 hour E-mail response	95%	89%	6%
3. Objectives	**Actual**	**Planned**	**Difference**
Help Desk call reductions	22%	20%	2%
4. Operating Cost	**Current Qtr**	**Previous Qtr**	**Change**
Salaries plus Overhead	$40,000	$40,000	$0
Software Maintenance	$1,625	$1,625	$0
Hardware Maintenance	$3,250	$5,500	-$2,250
New Hardware/Comm.	$3,750	$1,500	$2,250
New Software	$0	$5,500	-$5,500
Total	$48,625	$54,125	**-$5,500**
Return			
Savings in Support Calls	$10,000	$5,500	$4,500
Remote Site Savings	$13,500	$10,500	$3,000
Publishing Savings	$3,000	$3,000	$0
Increase in Sales	$27,500	$24,500	$3,000
Total	$54,000	$43,500	**$10,500**
5. ROI	**Current Qtr**	**Previous Qtr**	**Change**
Quarterly ROI	11%	-20%	31%
	YTD	**Previous Year**	
Comparisons	11%	-21%	

Figure 9.9 Quarterly Management Report.

want to see selected log site analysis statistics showing traffic trends, the performance of meeting any objectives, or the service levels you need to meet. You may also want to look at your operating costs and return so that the quarterly report is not a surprise for you.

For reporting on other areas within the organization that are affected by support site performance, you will first have to find out what these areas need. You might start off by showing each area your personal reports as support site manager and the quarterly reports you produce for management. Sales departments might also want to know about traffic to product information pages. Help Desks might want to know about traffic to various knowledge sources. Your log analysis tool could provide you with much of the information that you need to satisfy their reporting requirements.

Monitoring Performance, Traffic, and Processes

Monitoring performance involves looking at various key statistics on a day-to-day basis to keep on top of trends. You will want to know about any potential problems at the first indication or even before. Monitoring traffic can be part of monitoring performance, but you need to look at traffic that is not directly related to your performance measures, such as which operating systems your customers are using. Monitoring processes involves reviewing processes and the people involved in them frequently to make sure that what should be happening is happening.

As site manager, you have a lot of measures and statistics to choose from. Your site log analysis tool is probably your most valuable ally in your monitoring activity, but you need to focus yourself or you will get lost in the deluge of statistics. You can't possibly follow them all on a day-to-day basis, so you must choose those measures and statistics that you are most interested in for both performance and traffic monitoring. For example, if you have made improvements to one of your functions, you should look at the traffic to that function and any survey results from that function to see if the improvements have accomplished what you hoped for. Once you are pleased with the way that function is performing, your focus will probably change to something else. The following suggestions may help you decide what you should be monitoring on a day-to-day basis:

- If you are changing specific functions or areas of your site, you will want to keep an eye on them to see how they are performing. You will want to monitor changes in traffic volumes or patterns, or in survey return trends. You will want to know as soon as possible the impact that the change has on your site.

- If you have identified problems or suspected problems in specific areas of your site, you need to monitor the information and traffic around that area. Perhaps download times have been increasing and you aren't sure why. You will want to monitor the traffic and download times to see if the increase is an anomaly, if it is the start of a trend, or if it is being caused by other trends.

- If you are considering changes that may affect customers with specific operating systems, you should monitor the variety of operating systems of the customers coming to your site.

- If you want to understand how to improve a specific function, you will want to monitor traffic to that function. You will want to monitor paths that customers use to get there and any feedback that the function generates.

- If you want to know how people are using your site so that you can understand what changes the next iteration of your site should incorporate, you need to look at traffic statistics that identify the most frequently used paths and the lengths of the paths.

Let's turn now to process monitoring, which I will work through using an example. In Chapter 7, we examined the various processes required for running a support site. For each process, I reviewed how to go about defining procedures. Some of the procedures identified can be automated, but many require users to do specific things at specific times. You, as site manager, need to check that these tasks are actually begin performed.

Consider the procedures you have defined around maintaining site information; this will be our example. Table 9.3 shows what some of these might look like. You might recognize this table as part of Table 7.3 from Chapter 7. Note how easy it is to convert the table into procedures. The first entry in the table is the procedure for keeping the FAQ up to date. At the end of each day, the site practitioner should be collecting FAQ input from all areas and using the site update manager software to update the FAQ directly. To monitor that this is happening, you may want to occasionally, say, weekly or biweekly, check the logs from the update software to see what updates have been made to the FAQ in the

Table 9.3 Procedures for Maintaining Site Information

PROCEDURE	WHERE WILL THE UPDATE INFORMATION BE COMING FROM?	WHO OR WHAT WILL BE DOING THE UPDATE?	WHAT IS THE UPDATE SCHEDULE?
Keeping the FAQ up-to-date	The call-tracking system (automatically generates top 10 calls), technical support team, Help Desk, site staff (from site email, online logs, chats, or remote control)	The site staff will collect FAQ input from all areas and use the site update manager software to update the FAQ.	At the end of the day
Updating information on known issues or bugs	The technical support team, Help Desk, site staff (from site email, online logs, chats, or remote control)	The site staff via site update manager software.	Immediate
Creating e-newsletters	Updates to FAQs, known issues, bugs, and technical documents for the last two weeks	The newsletter manager automatically pulls updates together and emails them out.	Every two weeks, if update material exists

last few days. If the answer is none, you may have to have a chat with the site practitioner and perhaps some of the parties who should be providing information. If you find that you are consistently satisfied with the way the FAQ update procedure is being carried out, you may decide to monitor it less frequently.

The next entry in the table is the procedure that updates information on known issues or bugs. You can monitor this the same way you monitored the FAQ update procedure, or you can ask the site practitioner to send you a copy of any updates to this information so that you can check their frequency and that they were actually made. Again, you would adjust how often you checked this procedure based on your level of confidence in its accurate execution.

The third and final entry in the table is the procedure that creates the e-newsletter. An easy way to ensure that this procedure is working is to make sure you are on the mailing list for the e-newsletter you want to monitor. Make a note in your schedule telling you when you can expect to receive it. If you receive it, check the material that it contains to ensure that it is appropriate. Once you are satisfied with the e-newsletter, take yourself off the list.

When monitoring processes, you choose the procedures that you are most interested in, monitor them until you are satisfied that they are working properly, and then move on to other procedures. You should be constantly cycling through your procedures in such a manner that you hit them all within a reasonable timeframe. The actual timeframe will depend on the size of your support site. You don't want to make that timeframe too large; otherwise, procedures might get out of control and cause problems before you can get around to monitoring them.

Evaluating Performance and Processes

As you monitor performance, traffic, and processes, you need to be evaluating each to determine the improvements that are required, the functions that should be added, and even which functions should be eliminated. A good idea might be to create an online evaluation sheet that you fill out while you are carrying out your monitoring activities. Table 9.4 shows an example of a simple evaluation sheet. For each item, you indicate the status (active or inactive), any concerns you have, any notes about causes or results, and any recommended actions. The recommended actions might include notes on how long you want to keep monitoring a particular item. The status of an item would remain open until the site manager feels confident that no further concerns exist or until the item is picked up by the improvement process in the site management cycle.

You might want to incorporate a evaluation sheet into your desktop management, scheduling, or organization software so that you can be reminded of any recommendations you need to act on at the appropriate time. How complex you make your evaluation sheet will depend on how large your site is and how much monitoring you have to do.

The important concept in this discussion is not the evaluation sheet itself, but the fact that you need to be tracking what you find during

Table 9.4   An Evaluation Sheet

ITEM	STATUS	POINTS OF INTEREST OR CONCERN	NOTES	RECOMMENDED ACTIONS
Download function	Active	Download times are increasing.	March 3–12 times are normal; March 12–14 times are approximately double the norm.	Talk to technical support to see what else was going on March 12–14.
An update to the online training videos is being considered	Active	Windows 3.1 will not handle these videos.	March 1–15: 15 percent of the online training users are on Windows 3.1.	Talk to sales and customer service: can we go ahead with the new software?
FAQ update procedure	Active	No updates made in the last week.	Looks like the site staff has not been entering the updates.	Review procedure with site staff and keep monitoring for next month.
Email response	Active	Five percent of customers are waiting longer than 24 hours for a response to email sent to Sales.	Sales hired a new person and neglected to train that person in email response procedures.	Monitor for two weeks and then close.

your monitoring process and evaluating each item so that you can decide which items should be fed into the improvement process.

Making Improvements

Improvements are the culmination of all of your support site management activities. The improvement stage is where you want to be all of the time. You want to constantly be in the midst of one or more improvement initiatives. In this chapter, you have set up the processes that will funnel all potential improvements to you via one of two sources. You need to review these on a regular basis.

The first source of improvements to consider is your monthly performance reporting. In these reports, you are measuring the performance of those areas that are most important to your support site and your organization. If you notice any negative trends or results, these become candidates for generating improvement initiatives. The second source of improvements is the set of evaluation sheets generated by your monitoring and evaluation processes. Each active entry in these sheets is a potential improvement initiative.

As site manger, you want to establish a routine in which you are constantly looking at these two sources, picking out and prioritizing the improvements that need to be made, and then carrying them out. If your measuring, monitoring, and evaluating activities are working as they should, you will most likely never run out of improvements to make.

Key Points

Managing a support site is a cycle that involves measuring the site's performance; monitoring all the processes that are involved in running the site; evaluating the various aspects of processes, traffic, and performances; and making improvements.

Establishing the site management processes consists of four main tasks. The first of these involves defining the measures of performance that will be used and how they will be reported. The second task involves setting up the monitoring processes. The site manager must decide which statistics, measures, and processes should be monitored and how frequently. In the third task, the site manager sets up a process to evaluate what is being monitored and decides what must go into the improvement process. The final task is to set up a routine for identifying, prioritizing, and carrying out the improvements.

The performance measures that are appropriate for your site can be determined in two different ways. The first is to examine the requirements portion of the scope summary you created in Chapter 3. The second is to answer the questions, "What does your support site need to accomplish for you to consider it a success?" and "Which factors are important to you or to your organization?" Performance measurements fall into five categories: specific objectives, the ROI, the reduction of workload in other areas, the effectiveness of solution and service delivery, and responsiveness and proaction.

Objectives give you specific goals you want your site to meet. They typically come from two sources: from management and from your own evaluation and improvement processes.

You need to consider two types of ROI measures. The first involves measuring the actual ROI of your site against the ROI you projected when you did your cost-benefit analysis justifying the site. You may or may not use this as a performance measure, but even if you don't, it is an excellent lesson in understanding the factors that impact the return your site generates. The second ROI measure does not take any cost benefit into account. It is simply the net sales or savings your site generates, that is, sales or savings minus operating costs, over a given period of time expressed as a percentage.

Even if the ROI is not one of your measures of performance, you can still measure what your site returns, which includes the workload your site reduces in other areas. In order to measure workload reduction, you need to use data from other areas, such as sales data or Help Desk call-tracking data and data from your site log analysis software.

Measuring the effectiveness of solution and service delivery involves measurements in five main areas: service levels, assisted problem resolution, data accuracy, timeliness, the breadth and depth of the problem domain, and responsiveness and proaction. You may want to define specific levels of service that your site needs to meet, such as all email must be responded to within 24 hours. Once you develop service levels, they become measures of performance. If your site offers functions that enable customers to log their own problems or if it provides functions that offer assisted support, you need to measure how well these meet the needs of your customers. If customers are logging their own problems, then you need to make sure that the priorities and resolution times you agreed on with the Help Desk manager are being met. If you offer assisted support, you will want to know how successful those calls are.

The third area within the effectiveness of solution and service delivery that needs to be measured is the accuracy of data. You can measure accuracy by using surveys, looking at the number of complaints, and reviewing processes. You should also optimize the most commonly used paths to shorten the time customers spend getting where they want to be. Measuring timeliness involves looking at the site response or loading time, the lengths of the paths that customers need to follow to get to a solution, the length of time customers must wait to get a response to email, and the length of time that customers must wait to get online assisted support.

The fifth area that needs to be measured is the breadth and depth of the problem domain. You need to measure if your site covers the domain of your customers' problems and requirements. You can answer this question by using surveys, looking at the number of complaints, and analyzing the number of Help Desk calls that your site eliminated. Responsiveness and proaction are really functions of all your other measures of performance. An important indication of how responsive and proactive your site can be is whether or not you have processes in place to measure, monitor, evaluate, and improve. It is within these processes that you determine how responsive and proactive you can be.

Once you have decided on the performance measures you will use, you need to decide which measures you will report on, how you will report on them, for what time frames, and which measures you are going to watch on an ongoing basis in order to monitor trends.

Reporting on performance involves defining the audience for the report, identifying the performance measures that the audience is interested in, and then taking the measures and creating the report at suitable intervals. The audience for your reports includes management, yourself as the site manager, and any other stakeholders within the organization who are affected in some way by the site. Management reporting is typically carried out on a quarterly basis. Site management reporting is typically monthly and other reporting will depend on the stakeholders involved.

Monitoring your site includes monitoring performance, traffic, and processes. Monitoring performance involves looking at various key statistics on a day-to-day basis to keep on top of trends. You will want to know about any potential problems at the first indication or even before. Monitoring traffic can be part of monitoring performance, but you need to look at traffic that is not directly related to your performance measures, such as which operating systems your customers are using. Monitoring processes involves frequently reviewing processes and the people involved in them to make sure that everything is going the way it should be.

As you monitor performance, traffic, and processes, you need to determine if any improvements are required, which functions should be added, and even which functions need to be eliminated. You need to document and track your evaluations so that they can be fed into the improvement process.

Improvements are the culmination of all of your support site management activities. You have two sources of improvements: your monthly performance reporting and the set of evaluation sheets generated by your monitoring and evaluation processes. As site manger, you want to establish a routine in which you are constantly looking at these two sources, picking out and prioritizing the improvements that need to be made, and then carrying them out.

CHAPTER 10

Problem Prevention and Troubleshooting

During the process of creating and managing a support site, you may allow certain undesirable events to occur. These are your support site mistakes. These events will produce various troublesome symptoms that, if left unchecked, could lead to disaster: the failure of your site. In this chapter, I will look at 20 symptoms you may see in various stages of building and managing your Web-based support site. For each symptom, I will identify the events that may have caused it, what you can do about the symptom to prevent or minimize the negative impact on your support site and the organization it supports, and how you can prevent any recurrences in the future. I take this approach of presenting problems by their symptoms since symptoms are often the first indication that problems exist. My goal is to help you avoid support site problems or solve ones that have already occurred. The topics I will cover are as follows:

- Earliest problem symptoms
- Problem symptoms during the scope definition
- Problem symptoms during the staff selection and design
- Problem symptoms involving the functions and tools

- Problem symptoms involving the processes and implementation
- Problem symptoms during site operation

For each of the symptoms I present, I use the same template of information. First, I will describe the symptom, the potential negative results, and what the prognosis is for recovery: good, fair, or poor. Good means that a full recovery from the problem can be realized if suggested actions are taken. Fair means that some negative impact will occur in terms of site success, but recovery is assured if suggested actions are taken. Poor means that the support site manager must change the ingrained processes, create new processes, or undertake significant other changes. A prognosis of poor means that correcting the problem may take a significant amount of time and effort. Recovery will be lengthy.

I will suggest some steps that may be taken to recover from the problem and will offer suggestions to prevent recurrences. At the end of each discussion of a specific symptom, I will summarize the results in a table.

Earliest Problem Symptoms

The earliest symptoms around site creation and management become visible at the time that the support site is just an idea. No analysis of requirements has been undertaken and no formal proposal has been made.

"For heaven's sake, everyone knows we need a support site. Let's just do it."

This phrase is an indication that people want to avoid doing the work of justifying a site and perhaps even determining scope. They don't want to have to think about the costs involved in getting the site up and they don't want to have to figure out what the return will be. They want to hurry and get the site up.

The impact of this symptom will vary. In the worst case, this symptom leads to little or no thought being given to gathering site requirements or determining scope. The resulting site could have functions that do not meet the needs of the customers and other stakeholders. The return of such site will be negative, a loss. It will cost more to run the site than the sum of the benefits it generates. Customers may even decide to take their business elsewhere, which would generate an even greater loss to future business.

If no cost justification is performed, no thought will be given to the return that each specific function could bring or the amount of money that could be spent on tools without driving the site into a loss situation. The resulting site might not pay for itself and may not be focused on the functions that give the customers the most value and generate the highest return. A support site project that has no cost justification behind it also risks having its budget taken away by management. In other words, if you decide to go ahead without a cost justification, you need to go as fast as you can before someone hauls you back to explain your expenditures or decides to replace your project with another justified one. Your support site project could be cancelled or you may be forced to backtrack and perform the processes you tried to avoid. The work you have done will have been wasted.

Why do people want to avoid cost justification and perhaps scope definition? This could happen if the environment is one in which no formal process is in place for the justification of initiatives and budgeting based on justification. Perhaps the process is in place, but it is poor. An interesting note is that this is less likely to happen in a small business because typically little money can be spent and the business owner needs to justify every dollar spent. The avoidance of cost justification could also happen if the person spearheading the initiative is more of a technologist than a business-oriented manager. Ex-programmers have a terrible reputation for leaping into things without worrying about the financial impact, but speaking as an ex-programmer I can tell you that this is only the case when ex-programmers haven't learned business skills.

The prognosis for recovery here is good. If you are the person who is refusing to do the cost justification, then the prognosis becomes excellent if I have convinced you of the need. Read Chapter 1, "Is Web-Based Support Worthwhile?," use the template provided, and start hammering out a cost justification. By taking the time to do so, your take will be rewarded with a greater understanding of how much your site will cost and what benefits it will generate. This will help you see where you should be spending the most money. You will have proof of your project's benefits, should your project ever come up for financial review. If you do the cost-benefit analysis and you realize that a support site would generate little or no return, then you have to make some decisions before you go ahead. Your organization may create the site at the cost of doing business, but you may have to reduce some of your projected costs. Once you've done the cost-benefit analysis, you must be sure to do a proper scope definition. Chapter 3, "Establishing Scope," will make it easier for you. Include the scope in your project plan. You may choose to develop some or all of the scope definition before you do your cost justification to get a more accurate idea of the size, costs, and benefits of your site.

If you are in a position where you can force the cost-benefit analysis and scope definition to happen (for example, the person who is refusing to do the analysis works for you), then the prognosis for recovery is good if you manage the work carefully. If you do not have the authority to influence whether or not the cost justification takes place, you can still do a cost justification and take it to the people that do have that authority. Seeing it may convince them to pay attention to what it shows, especially if you have done an accurate job. If that doesn't work, you will have to live with the results of the prognosis of possible failure, especially if no scope definition is undertaken.

You won't be building support sites on a day-to-day basis, but you will need to go through the project initiation process again when the site evolves to its next iteration. You want to take steps to ensure that any future initiatives will get a cost justification. Measure the return on investment (ROI) of the site against what was proposed in the cost justification. This will give the cost justification more credibility. It becomes a quality or process measurement. Train at least your senior staff in the basics of business, including cost justification. If possible, get them involved in more business aspects of the department or organization. Make cost justification and scope definition part of every project of a certain size. People will become used to carrying out these processes and will get practice in them as the processes become routine. Table 10.1 gives a summary of how to deal with the symptom of people not wanting to do a cost justification.

Problem Symptoms during Scope Definition

Most of the problems that crop up around the scope definition revolve around staff not being willing to do the work to get the information, site stakeholders not willing to give the information or unable to give the

Table 10.1 "For heaven's sake, everyone knows we need a support site. Let's just do it."

Symptom	People want to avoid doing the work of justifying a site and gathering requirements. They want to start building the site without any planning.
Eventual Results	A negative support site return if no requirements are gathered, cancellation of the project or parts of the project if no cost justification is undertaken, or overspending on the project
Possible Causes	No formal justification and budgeting processes, or the project initiator is a technologist without any business skills
Prognosis and Suggestions for Recovery	Good if you have authority over the cost justification and scope definition processes. Do a cost justification and schedule a scope definition into your project plan.
Prevention	Measure the actual costs and return against the projected values. Train senior staff in business concepts. Also make the cost justification and scope definition part of every sizable project.

information, and a scope that just keeps growing and growing. This section will examine some of the most common symptoms of things going wrong in the scope definition phase of your support site project.

"We want the site to eliminate all other support, triple sales, bring world peace, and so on."

What this phrase is trying to illustrate in its exaggeration is the situation in which site stakeholders are asking for too much from the support site. They are trying to expand the scope to unreasonable limits or have completely unrealistic ideas about what a support site can do. This may occur at the beginning of the project or it may happen as the project progresses. As site stakeholders start to think about the functions they want on the site, they get carried away. If the site can reduce telephone support, why can't it eliminate all support? If the site provides problem resolution tools for the less knowledgeable customer, why not also provide more powerful and complex resolution tools for the more sophisticated user?

When site stakeholders start expanding a site's scope to unreasonable limits, usually one of four causes is the reason. First, the site stakeholders have unrealistic expectations of what a support site can deliver. They may be basing their expectations on something they heard or read. Second, the project or site manager may have poor project management processes in place and is allowing the site stakeholders to bully their way into an increased scope as they think of things. Third, no cost justification has been done, so people have little idea of what the site will cost and what return each function will generate. Fourth, a cost justification has been done, but unrealistic estimates for savings are used to present a false picture of what the proposed site could return.

If the scope is allowed to expand, the project will take longer than planned, so the support site will be late and will be over budget. The people working on the project may try to do too many things at once and end up doing everything poorly, rather than focusing on the most important functions and doing a good job. If expectations are not brought into line with reality, then, in the eyes of the stakeholders, the site will be a failure. The fact that the expectations are impossible to satisfy would not matter. In all of these situations, the most likely result is a site that is not as useful as it could be and that does not generate the return that it could.

If you catch this problem early enough before you have agreed upon any unreasonable results with the stakeholders, then the prognosis for recovery is good. Two things can also help you: a realistic cost justification and a project plan. A project plan is your proof of how much work is involved in the project and how long it will take. Much more credence is given to a project plan than to verbal claims that specific tasks will take a certain length of time. If project stakeholders try to increase the scope, you can show them the plan and ask them what they are willing to give up for the extra functionality they are asking for. Chances are they will back down because they aren't willing to give anything up. For unreasonable site expectations, an accurate cost justification will show the calculations that go into determining how many calls can be eliminated from a support area, what publication costs can be saved, and so on. Your calculations will help bring management and other stakeholders back to reality.

To prevent this situation from recurring or from happening in the first place, you need to employ tight project management, negotiating with stakeholders for any increase in functionality, or, in other words, what functionality they would be willing to give up for the new functionality. You need to make sure you have a solid cost justification in place that

Table 10.2 "We want the site to eliminate all other support, triple sales, bring world peace, and so on."

Symptom	The scope for the site is unrealistic.
Eventual Results	The site is late, over budget, and poorly implemented. It does not meet the expectations of the stakeholders and has a poor return.
Possible Causes	Site stakeholders have unrealistic expectations, there is little or poor project management, or no cost justification exists or it is inaccurate.
Prognosis and Suggestions for Recovery	The prognosis is good, if problems are caught early enough. Negotiate with clients against a project plan and use an accurate cost justification to show the benefits versus the costs.
Prevention	Put good project management practices into place. Make cost justifications mandatory and review for accuracy.

presents a realistic picture of what benefits the site can bring versus what they will cost to implement. Table 10.2 summarizes how to handle the problem of unrealistic scope.

"I know what all the stakeholders need. There's no need to bother anyone else."

This phrase is a warning sign that someone, probably the project manager, is trying to build a site based on perceived requirements rather than real requirements. If the project manager is allowed to continue, then the delivered site may have little bearing on what customers and other site stakeholders need. The site will bring little or no return. The site stakeholders will not be happy and customers may not use the site and may go elsewhere to get what they need.

The problem may or may not be related to the skills of the person involved. If the time given for completion of the project is too short, perhaps dictated by management, then the project manager may feel pressured into cutting corners. Gathering requirements and defining scope takes time. The project manager may not be adequately trained in project management and may not understand the importance of the scope definition. The project manager may also simply not have a very high opinion of project stakeholders.

If you have control over project management, whether you manage the project manager or you are the project manager, and you catch this problem before any serious design is started, then the prognosis for recovery is good. Identify the stakeholders and schedule some meetings with them and the project manager, letting the stakeholders describe their requirements and the reasons for them. It should become obvious fairly quickly that without the stakeholders' input the site would probably fail. Assign the project manager a coach for some project management skills training. If a short deadline is the issue, review the project plan with the project manager to adjust the schedule to allow some time for a scope definition that includes gathering requirements. Also suggest alternate ways to shorten the schedule. This might mean some rapid application development (RAD) techniques or postponing some functionality to the next iteration of the site.

To prevent this problem of presuming what the stakeholders need, have all the appropriate staff trained in effective analysis and project management techniques. Where possible, get these people more involved with stakeholders so that they can understand the requirements of the stakeholders and their importance to the organization. Table 10.3 gives a summary of how to address the problem of a project manager who refuses to gather information from stakeholders.

Table 10.3   "I know what all the stakeholders need. There's no need to bother anyone else."

Symptom	The project manager does not want to gather requirements from stakeholders.
Eventual Results	The site will not meet stakeholder requirements. Customers may not use the site and may go elsewhere.
Possible Causes	The deadline is too short, the project manager is untrained, or the project manager has no confidence in stakeholders' input.
Prognosis and Suggestions for Recovery	The prognosis is good if caught before the design is done. Schedule meetings with stakeholders to get input and coach the project manager. Also adjust the schedule to allow for gathering requirements.
Prevention	Train all appropriate staff in analysis and project management techniques. Also get staff involved in stakeholder interactions.

"We're very busy right now. We don't have time to talk to you about the support site."

Sometimes project stakeholders are their own worst enemies and this phrase is an indication of that. If, as project manager of the support site project, you accept the statement that the stakeholders don't have time and proceed with the project, you will end up in the situation described in the previous section. You will be building the site based on perceived requirements, rather than real requirements, and the site may not generate its expected return.

Stakeholders may not want to talk to you for a number of reasons. First, you may be asking for too much of their time or perhaps you have not been very effective at gathering requirements. You may have been unprepared for meetings, stretching them longer than necessary. Second, site stakeholders may not understand the importance of their input into the project. They may not realize that without their input the site could fail.

If you react the first time you hear this statement, the prognosis for recovery is good. First, plan out what information you need from each stakeholder. Create a prototype of what the specific functions might look like. This will help ensure that the stakeholder gets interested and provides some input. The visual model will give the stakeholder something to criticize and will illustrate what the site might look like without stakeholder input. Ask the stakeholders for a specific, short amount of time (say 20 to 30 minutes), tell them exactly what you will cover in that time, and explain why you need their input. You could email them your list of questions and the prototype. This strategy should get you time with every stakeholder you need to talk to.

To prevent this problem from happening in the future, get the stakeholders involved as early on in the project as possible. Make them part of the cost justification so that they can see the return expected and understand their role in building a site that gives that return. Make the most of every minute with stakeholders. Make question templates and prototypes part of every stakeholder interaction. Table 10.4 summarizes how to address the issue of stakeholders who don't have time to give requirements.

Table 10.4   "We're very busy right now. We don't have time to talk to you about the support site."'

Symptom	Stakeholders don't have time to give requirements.
Eventual Results	The site will not meet stakeholder requirements. Customers may not use the site and may go elsewhere.
Possible Causes	The project manager is asking for too much time or is ineffective at gathering requirements. Stakeholders don't realize the importance of their input.
Prognosis and Suggestions for Recovery	The prognosis is good if this problem is caught early. Prepare questions and prototypes for stakeholders. Ask for a specific short amount of time.
Prevention	Get stakeholders involved early on in the project and in cost justification. Make question templates and prototypes part of every customer interaction.

"We don't know what we want on the support site. Just do what you think is best."

That statement is an indication that the site stakeholders don't know what they want. They may not know what functions a support site could offer or how it could help them. They may not be familiar with the concept of Web-based support or they may not believe in it. If you take their advice, you'll end up with a site that does not meet their real requirements and does not generate a strong return. Customers may not find the site useful and be forced to go elsewhere for help.

If you decide not to take the stakeholders' advice, then the prognosis for avoiding the problem is good. What you need to do immediately is to help the site stakeholders figure out what they want. The best way to do this is by giving them examples of what they could have on the site. Show them other support sites. Create very simple prototypes of your support site. When they have something to look at, they will very quickly understand what they don't want and will get ideas for what they do.

To prevent this problem from cropping up again as the project progresses, plan on adding prototypes and site examples into the project plan. For future initiatives, educate stakeholders on what support sites

Table 10.5 "We don't know what we want on the support site. Just do what you think is best."

Symptom	Stakeholders don't know what they want.
Eventual Results	The site will not meet stakeholder requirements. Customers may not use the site and may go elsewhere.
Possible Causes	Stakeholders are not familiar with the concept or capabilities of Web-based support.
Prognosis and Suggestions for Recovery	The prognosis is good if a problem is acted upon early. Show customers other support sites and also prototypes.
Prevention	Put prototyping and site examples into the project plan. Get site stakeholders involved in the cost justification, and research examples of functions to show how a return is realized.

can do as part of the cost justification process. When you show the return a specific function could have, give an example of a site that uses that function. The extra time it takes you to research sample sites will be well worth the cooperation and interest you get from your stakeholders. Table 10.5 contains a summary of suggestions for addressing the problem of stakeholders who don't know what they want.

Problem Symptoms during Staff Selection and Design

The problems that occur during staff selection and site design are usually based around having unrealistic expectations about what a person in a given role can do and doing a poor job managing outsourced work.

"Jim can set up the knowledge base. He's a whiz at HTML."

This statement is actually one version of many possibilities. Jim could be anyone and HTML could be any technical specialty other than knowledge bases. The danger in this statement is that a person with no understanding of knowledge management is being assigned the task of setting up a knowledge base for a support site. This could have several undesirable results. First, the knowledge base might be built, but it might not work. Customers would not get the answers they require or they might not understand the answers that they did get. Second, the person might not be able to complete the knowledge base, in which case you would have to scramble to find someone that could put the knowledge base together. The support site would then be late and over budget.

If someone with no understanding of knowledge management is not assigned the job of setting up the knowledge base, then the prognosis for recovery is good. You need to convince whoever made the suggestion that Jim is not a suitable candidate and you need to find a candidate who can do the job, or you need to give Jim some training. This means you need to have some understanding of the skills necessary to set up the knowledge base. You can get this information from a third party, such as the vendors of the knowledge base software you are using, the vendors of an outsourcing service for knowledge management functions, or from a training provider. If the suggestion of training is unacceptable and you don't have the required skills in house, you may have to consider outsourcing the job of setting up the knowledge base.

The reason why someone would suggest having a technical wizard set up the knowledge base is because of the perception that he or she can do anything or it's due to a poor understanding of knowledge management. Setting up a knowledge base requires an understanding of the problem domain, an understanding of how the knowledge base tool works, and an understanding of how customers will access the knowledge. A very technical person may not necessarily have this understanding.

The way to prevent such suggestions in the future, when you may not be around to stop them, is to do some knowledge management training. Identify key technical players or their managers and invite them to a knowledge management seminar courtesy of your knowledge base software vendor. Define a specific position for managing or maintaining knowledge bases even if that position is outsourced. Also identify some training sources for knowledge management positions. Table 10.6 is a summary of how to prevent someone without the proper training from setting up knowledge bases for the support site.

Table 10.6 "Jim can set up the knowledge base. He's a whiz at HTML."

Symptom	The person hired is a technical wizard with no understanding of knowledge bases.
Eventual Results	The knowledge base gives incorrect or unclear answers and the site return is not realized, or the support site project is late and over budget.
Possible Causes	A poor understanding of knowledge management or a perception that technical wizards can do anything
Prognosis and Suggestions for Recovery	This is good if not allowed to go further but is poor if an underqualified person performs the setup. Train the hired person or find a more suitable candidate, outsourcing if necessary.
Prevention	Have appropriate people trained in knowledge management and create a specific position for setting up and updating the knowledge bases.

"Maria can do the design. She's a whiz at Java."

Again, this statement is actually one version of many possibilities. The ability to code Java, HTML, or whatever is not always accompanied by the ability to design a good support site. Witness all of the terrible designs on the Internet. If design is given to someone who has little knowledge of good design concepts, the result could very well be a site that is difficult to use, which means it would not be used and in turn would result in a poor return.

If someone without a strong knowledge of good design concepts is not allowed to do the design, the prognosis for recovery is excellent. If, however, the resident Java whiz is allowed to go ahead with the design, the prognosis is very poor. You will probably have to redesign your site very soon after it is implemented. In order to ensure that you get a good design, you need to convince whoever suggested the Java whiz that site design requires specific skills that he or she does not have. You can use the Internet to show examples of sites that are obviously designed by people without any design skills. You can do some quick prototypes of poor designs versus good designs to show how important design is. You can also refer to the ASP publications *The Year's Ten Best Web Support Sites, 1998 Edition* and *The Year's Ten Best Web Support Sites, 1999 Edition* to find testimonials of the importance of design skills when putting a site together. If none of this works, then research a site design seminar and get the Java wizard signed up. Insist on prototypes and have frequent prototype reviews to get feedback from all stakeholders and to ensure that the design is acceptable.

A Java whiz would probably be suggested for the job of site designer because of a lack of understanding of the role that site design plays in the success of a support site and the perception, as stated earlier, that technical experts can do anything. Sometimes a well-designed site looks so simple and easy to use that it generates the perception that it is also easy to build. An analogy would be designer clothing. Designer clothing may look deceptively simple, but in reality, each line and shape is designed for a specific purpose and must follow strict rules; otherwise, the design falls apart. A way of changing the false perceptions about site design is to give it the importance it deserves by establishing a specific site designer role with associated responsibilities and training. To ensure that a site design is acceptable, creating site prototypes and scheduling prototype reviews should be required tasks in all initiatives involving changes to the support site. Table 10.7 summarizes the suggestions for preventing someone inexperienced in site design be responsible for this task.

Table 10.7 "Maria can do the design. She's a whiz at Java."

Symptom	The person hired is a technical expert inexperienced in site design.
Eventual Results	The site is poorly designed and difficult to use. It will not be used to its full potential and will generate a poor return.
Possible Causes	A poor understanding of the complexity and importance of site design along with the perception that technical experts can do anything
Prognosis and Suggestions for Recovery	Good if the person hired is replaced by someone with good site design skills. It's poor if the person hired is allowed to design the site. You should explain the importance of design; use the Internet and ASP publications. Then replace the Java whiz with a trained designer or train the person hired and monitor his or her work with frequent prototype reviews.
Prevention	Create a recognized site designer role with associated responsibilities and training. Make site prototypes and review the required tasks for all support site changes.

"Oops . . . This isn't what I wanted."

You outsourced your site design and now you're looking at the less than desirable results. The design isn't at all what you asked for or what you expected. You thought you would get a workable design or something that required a few minor modifications, but what you actually got was a totally unacceptable design that will have to be reworked from the ground up. If you go with the disastrous design, all stakeholders will be very dissatisfied. The site return will be extremely poor or non-existent and you could very well be out of a job. If you spend the time and money necessary to get the site design redone, your project will be late and you will be over budget. This is a very undesirable situation to be in; the phrase "between a rock and a hard place" comes to mind.

I'm afraid that the prognosis for recovery in this situation is only fair. You cannot come out of this unscathed unless you are way ahead of schedule and way under budget in your support site project. I suspect you are not. In order to make a decision about what to do, you will have to think about how you got yourself into this situation in the first place. You probably did not manage the outsourced activity. If you had, you would have had frequent reviews of prototypes with the site designer and you would have picked up on any undesirable design feature very early on in the design process. You may not have given the outsourcer enough direction. Perhaps you said something like, "do what you think is appropriate," or you may have made a very poor choice in the third party that you outsourced to. Perhaps you didn't check any references or reference sites.

If you can admit that you did a poor job at managing the outsourced task and you still have confidence in the third party that you outsourced to, you may be able to strike a deal. Admit that you made a mistake and are willing to pay for a redesign of the site. You may be able to negotiate an expedited service so that you can make up some of the time that was wasted. Make sure you allocate time for reviewing the prototype designs. The third party doing the design will most likely be very interested in doing what it can to keep you satisfied since you are a potential future reference. If you don't have confidence in the third party that you outsourced the design work to, you are going to have to find another source for your site design. Check your sources carefully

Table 10.8 "Oops . . . This isn't what I wanted."

Symptom	The site design you outsourced is poorly done.
Eventual Results	Either you will implement a site that satisfies no one and generates little or no return or the project will be late and you will be over budget.
Possible Causes	A poor management of outsourced activity, no prototype design reviews, or a poor choice of a third party
Prognosis and Suggestions for Recovery	The prognosis for recovery is fair. It may cost you a fair bit of time and money. If the outsourcer is not the problem, arrange a deal in which expedited service is provided and review the work frequently. Otherwise, you will need to find another source for design work.
Prevention	Manage what you outsource, insist on frequent prototypes and reviews, and check the third-party references carefully.

and ask for an expedited service if your budget can handle it. If you explain your dilemma, the third party will probably be very willing to help you out unless they happen to be swamped with other work.

To prevent a recurrence of this situation in the future, allocate some time in the process to manage what you outsource. Also review the outsourced work frequently. Before you outsource any work, check the third party's references carefully and ask to see some sample sites. Table 10.8 summarizes how to address the problem of an outsourced design that does not meet your expectations.

Problem Symptoms Involving Functions and Tools

The problems that you might encounter while selecting functions and tools for your site may include budget issues. The cost of the tools may be more than your budget or management will bear, buy versus build issues may occur, and the wrong people may be involved in the function and tool selection process.

"We've picked out our tools, but management refuses to pay for them!"

After a long and arduous search, you have found the perfect tools for your support site. They have exactly the functionality that you need. You add up the tools' prices, go to management with your sales pitch, and come back empty-handed. Management is not willing to pay for the tools you selected. You now face two main problems here. First, you have already invested significant time in tool research. Investing more time might make your support site late. Second, you may be forced to go with inferior tools that don't deliver the functionality your site needs. This means they may be more difficult to implement or maintain, they may offer less functionality, or they may be more difficult to use. Customers will be less likely to use the functions and the site return will be negatively affected.

How did you find yourself in this situation? You may not have carried out a cost-benefit analysis or the analysis that you did was perhaps inaccurate. You may not have done enough research on the price of tools or on tool functionality. You may not have had a detailed enough understanding of the functionality that was required to generate the return you projected.

The prognosis here is only fair. Tools are a capital cost and funding for capital costs is typically limited. If the cost wasn't included in your original budget, you may have a problem getting it. If you did not do a cost-benefit analysis previously, you may try putting one together in order to receive the funding you require. If you can show management the return your chosen tool can generate, you may get the money you need. If you did a cost-benefit analysis previously but it was inaccurate, redo your analysis replacing your projected costs with the actual costs of the tool. Again, you may be able to get the funding you need. If you cannot get the extra funding, you'll have to go with a tool you can afford. This tool may require extra work on your part in terms of extra processes or more clear instructions on the site. Make sure that you identify all the extra processes that you require for the tool and include them as part of the process definition phase of your project. Design the function into your site in such a way as to minimize its shortcomings if at all possible.

Table 10.9 "We've picked out our tools, but management refuses to pay for them!"

Symptom	The tools cost more than management is willing to pay.
Eventual Results	The project is late and over budget. The site functions are not easy to use or maintain, and the site generates a poor return.
Possible Causes	No cost justification was done or an inaccurate cost justification was done.
Prognosis and Suggestions for Recovery	The prognosis is fair. Try to get the required funding with an accurate cost justification. If this is not possible, go with the next choice and be careful to build in all the required processes.
Prevention	Cost-justify everything. Research the tool prices and functionality until you are confident in your cost projections.

To prevent this situation in the future, always cost-justify your projects. Do enough research so that you have a good level of confidence in your projected costs and estimates. Get actual costs from several vendors so that you have a good idea of the range of prices. Also make sure you understand the functionality of the tools you are getting prices for. You can see a summary of the problem of selecting a tool that management is unwilling to pay for in Table 10.9.

"Let's build our own tools. It can't be that hard."

Vendors of support site tools such as knowledge bases, call-tracking software, and so on put a lot of time and effort into researching, developing, marketing, and maintaining these tools. A huge variety of tools is available at all price levels and with varying degrees of functionality. Getting into the business of developing support site tools doesn't make very much sense unless you have a very specialized or unique application, yet some organizations still insist on developing their own tools and are then forced to live under the constraints they impose.

The main reason that organizations make inappropriate decisions to build software rather than buy it is a lack of understanding of the software requirements. I'll use an accounting system as an example. At first, the system looks fairly easy. Various registers need to be maintained, so building the accounting system seems fairly straightforward. Then as you get deeper and deeper into the functionality of the tool, into all of the rules around every financial transaction, the system starts to look much more complex and suddenly the idea of building the system becomes much less attractive. The tool is not completely understood, so it seems easy to develop. If you decide to build your own support tools, you may be very surprised at the complexity, at how long it takes you to build and test the tools. You will also be forced to maintain the tools as your support requirements change and as technology changes and you will discover that maintenance costs are high.

If you do make an inappropriate decision to build any of your support site software, your project may be late and over budget. You may end up with a tool that does not have the required functionality. Your site's ROI could be less than planned because the site maintenance costs will be higher than planned. The return of your site will be negatively affected.

If you have not started to build yet, the prognosis is good for avoiding disaster. Unless the functionality you require is very unique, rethink your decision and purchase a tool. If you aren't convinced, then take some time to do a more in-depth analysis of what the tool you are thinking of building must do and hopefully that will convince you of the value of purchasing a packaged tool. If you have already started to build your own tool, the prognosis for success is poor, but you have a few choices. You can scrap the work that you've done and purchase an appropriate tool. This will make your project late and perhaps over budget, but it can save you much grief later on. If the end date is critical, you may need to outsource some help to get your project done on time. Another choice is to continue and complete the tool. If you choose this route, you need to take the time to do the appropriate analysis to make sure that the requirements for the tool are understood and are met. If you do a good job in developing the tool, you may consider selling the code to a software vendor. You have the tool you want, but someone else will maintain it.

The way to avoid getting into trouble when building your own tools is to always do a thorough analysis of what the tool must do and get a good understanding of how complex the required functionality will be to create. Once you understand what it will take to build the tool you need, create a realistic estimate of what it will cost to maintain the tool. Compare your estimates against what buying a tool would cost. You should not proceed with building until you have completed all of these analyses. Table 10.10 summarizes the problem of making an inappropriate build decision.

Table 10.10 "Let's build our own tools. It can't be that hard."

Symptom	You want to create support site tools, rather than buy them.
Eventual Results	The project is late and over budget. The site return will then be negatively affected.
Possible Causes	A lack of understanding of tool functionality and complexity
Prognosis and Suggestions for Recovery	The prognosis is good if you have not started to build and poor if you have started to build. If you have started, you can scrap it and buy something or you can continue but put in the required time and analysis to do a good job.
Prevention	Do a thorough analysis of the tool requirements, its complexity, and the required maintenance costs before considering to build.

"We didn't have to get the customers involved. Our techies did a great job designing the functions."

Functions that are designed by technical staff without customer input tend to be rated very highly by technical staff, but not as highly by customers. Non-technical customers might find such functions difficult to use or they may find the information that the functions provide too technical to comprehend. Customers will thus not be able to get the help they need from the site and will end up calling the Help Desk instead. Ultimately, the site will not generate the projected return.

Customers might be excluded from providing input to the function design for several reasons. The support site project might have a very tight deadline and the project manager might see this as a shortcut in the function creation process. Perhaps the environment is one in which not enough importance is placed on the customers' requirements and preferences. If the technical staff have already designed the functions without customer input, then the prognosis for recovery is poor. The damage has been done and unless the technical staff had a very good understanding of client requirements, they will have to make changes as problems emerge, but this time with client input. If problems occur with the functions, then customers must be surveyed to find out what the problems are and what solutions are acceptable. A site log analyzer can be used to help analyze the problems with the function in terms of paths to and through the function.

Table 10.11 "We didn't have to get the customers involved. Our techies did a great job designing the functions."

Symptom	The technical staff designed the site functions with no input from customers.
Eventual Results	The functions may be difficult to understand or to use and the site will have a poor return.
Possible Causes	The project deadline is very tight and not enough importance is placed on the requirements and preferences of the customers.
Prognosis and Suggestions for Recovery	The prognosis is poor if the function design has been completed. Customers must be surveyed and the functions should be redesigned.
Prevention	Have customer representatives involved in the function design and review. Test content out on customers and show the impact of cutting corners in terms of diminished returns.

To prevent this problem in the future, customer input must be solicited for the design of all the site functions that customers will be using. Customer representatives should review any sample function content. If deadlines are tight, then deliverables should be negotiated rather than having quality compromised by shortcuts. A project manager can show the impact of cutting corners in terms of a diminished site return and the cost of having to go back and update the function with modifications that will make it more usable by customers. Table 10.11 shows the impact of having a technical staff design site functions without any customer input.

Problem Symptoms Involving Processes and Implementation

Problems involving processes are typically problems caused by not defining processes in the first place. Any site development and implementation trouble often stems from a lack of appropriate testing.

"We'll let whoever is not busy handle email."

Leaving the handling of email to whoever happens to have extra time is a symptom that occurs far too often. A task that is not assigned to a specific individual or position is a task that probably won't get done. Also, the assumption that anyone on the support staff will have spare time is probably false.

Neglecting to assign the handling of email to a specific person or position will result in email not being handled. This means that customers will not get timely responses to their email inquiries or problems. In turn, this will result in a flood of complaints, calls to the Help Desk will increase, and when the email issue is resolved, it will be very difficult to convince customers that sending email is a viable support option. The prognosis for recovery depends on how quickly effective email-handling processes and assignments are developed and put into place. If processes are put into place quickly and customers get an apology and an explanation, the prognosis for recovery is good. If email is allowed to get out of control for a significant amount of time, then the prognosis for recovery is fair to poor. Once you have destroyed customer confidence in email, it is very difficult to get it back. You may need to totally change the email function so that it looks like a different function and you will have to undertake various marketing initiatives to try to convince your customers to use email again. You may need to market email as a new function, a replacement of the old email function, rather than as just an improvement.

Neglecting to assign someone to handle email could be the result of staff not wanting to do this task. The manger might not want to make an unpopular decision and may choose to leave the email up for grabs, hoping that a miracle will happen and someone takes responsibility for it. The problem could also be the result of not enough importance being placed on the development of processes or of simply poor planning and project management. Perhaps no one planned for email processes or no one checked to make sure that processes were in place and assigned.

To prevent the problem in the future, email handling needs to be a defined process, planned for and managed. If handling email is a task that the staff does not enjoy, then find out why. Do what you can to make it easier to respond to email, such as setting up templates. Channel email so that it gets sent to the appropriate place and the staff is not forced to spend time dispatching messages to various locations. Make handling email a rotating responsibility so that no one spends longer than a day at a time on it. Table 10.12 summarizes the problem of unassigned email-handling processes.

Table 10.12 "We'll let whoever is not busy handle email."

Symptom	The email-handling processes are not assigned to specific people.
Eventual Results	The email response time is too high, so customers will complain and call the Help Desk. The site return will thus be negatively affected.
Possible Causes	The staff does not want to handle email, a poor understanding of the importance and the processes exists, or poor planning and management has occurred.
Prognosis and Suggestions for Recovery	The prognosis is good if the problem is caught early. Effective processes should be put into place quickly and customers should be sent an explanation and apology. The prognosis is fair to poor if the problem is allowed to go on for any length of time. You may need to change the email function and you will need some marketing initiatives.
Prevention	Make email a defined process and make it easier to handle. Set up templates for responses, channel email to the appropriate locations, and make email a rotating responsibility.

"We can do processes later when things settle down."

What this phrase means is that you are going into site implementation without processes. You have not defined how the site information sources will be updated, how email will be handled, how feedback will be gathered, and so on. In short, you haven't defined how you will run your site, yet with the incredible optimism of IT people that no amount of disasters seems to diminish, you probably still expect your site to be successful. What will more likely happen is that your site will break down function by function as required processes are not carried out. Your site return will become negative. Things will never settle down because you don't have any processes in place.

If you have finished your site and are about to make it available to customers, your prognosis for recovery is poor. You will go into production without processes. Everything you should have had a defined procedure in place for will need to be manually initiated by you or by someone who happens to think about it. Knowledge updates will be hit and miss and your email queues may start backing up alarmingly. Customers will start complaining and calls to the Help Desk will increase. You will be forced to try to develop processes while you are trying to handle the problems caused by not having them. If you are in this situation, it might be a good idea to hire extra help to handle the site while you get your processes into place. The stability that processes will bring to your site will be well worth the extra cost. You will also need to take some time to create a marketing initiative to convince customers that your site is back on track.

Why would a site or project manager put a support site into production without processes? Perhaps the project deadline was too tight so something had to go. Maybe the importance of processes was poorly understood so processes were dropped. Project management may have been poor or lacking so that the project was not kept on track and again processes were eliminated. To prevent this problem in the future, the development of site processes must be recognized as a critical success factor in effective support site implementation. It should be a required phase in all support site maintenance. All appropriate staff should be trained in effective project management techniques. The problem of no site processes is summarized in Table 10.13.

Table 10.13 "We can do processes later when things settle down."

Symptom	No processes are developed for site maintenance and management.
Eventual Results	The site functions will break down and the return will become negative.
Possible Causes	It is due to tight deadlines, the importance of processes being poorly understood, or poor project management.
Prognosis and Suggestions for Recovery	The prognosis is poor if you have completed your site and are ready to implement. Outsource extra help while you develop processes and create a marketing initiative to lure customers back.
Prevention	Recognize support site development as a critical success factor in support site implementation. Make it a required phase in all support maintenance and train all appropriate staff in project management.

"We can't really test this stuff until our site is up."

What this phrase really means on too many occasions is, "We don't know how to test all aspects of our site," or, "We don't want to put the effort required into testing," or, "We don't have time for testing." These are often the causes of inadequate testing. Analyzing what needs to be tested is not an easy task and the actual testing can be monotonous and time-consuming. If a support site project has a short deadline or is running behind schedule, then testing is often dropped.

A site that is untested is a site that will behave unpredictably. Some functions may not work with certain customer technology or when subject to high traffic volumes. Some functions may have a high response time, they may crash, or they may generate incorrect results. Customers won't be able to get the help they need and will turn to the Help Desk for support. The site return will then fall.

If you have put your site into production without adequate testing, then the prognosis for emerging unscathed is poor. You will be troubleshooting complaints and problems until you get stabilized. If you are in this situation, you may want to outsource some extra help while you do a thorough testing of your site, flushing out as many problems as possible in as short a time as possible. You may have to do some marketing to get customers back to your site.

In the future, you need to make thorough testing a mandatory part of each site iteration. Test plans need to be created and as many customer configurations as possible should be duplicated. Chapter 7, "Processes and Implementation," will help you define what is effective testing. If you can afford it and if you can find something appropriate, try purchasing an automated testing tool to relieve the monotony of testing. If a tool does not make sense to you, rotate the testing responsibility among employees or break testing up into more palatable portions. The information in Table 10.14 summarizes the problem of inadequate site testing.

Table 10.14 "We can't really test this stuff until our site is up."

Symptom	The site is put into production without all the functionality tested.
Eventual Results	Customers experience problems with site access or performance. They turn to the Help Desk and the site return is negatively affected.
Possible Causes	You don't know how to test all aspects of the site, or you're not willing to put the required effort into testing. A deadline could also be tight, so testing is dropped.
Prognosis and Suggestions for Recovery	The prognosis is poor if the site is put into production without adequate testing. Outsource extra help while you thoroughly test to flush out problems. Also read Chapter 7
Prevention	Make testing mandatory for each site iteration. Create test plans and duplicate as many customer configurations as possible. Rotate and break up testing and automate the process where possible.

Problem Symptoms during Site Operation

Problems that appear during site operation might be caused by poor or inadequate site management processes, poor marketing, or by tasks that were carried out poorly during the site creation process. Examples of the latter include poor scope definitions and poor process definitions.

"Jenna can manage the site along with the four other departments she manages."

What this phrase implies is that Jenna, or whoever is managing your support site, has too much to do. She is not being given enough time to dedicate to site management. In Chapter 9, "Site Management," we saw that site management could involve significant effort, depending on the size of the site and the volatility of the problem. If a site manager has too much else to do, the site will not be managed. Negative trends will not be noticed, improvement processes will not be undertaken, processes will not be monitored, objectives will not be set, and performances will not be measured. The site will not reach its full potential in terms of return and its usefulness will diminish over time.

The management in your organization may not understand the quantity and type of work that site management entails, or your organization may simply be short-staffed. If you find yourself in the situation that you, as site manager, do not have enough time to adequately manage your support site, you need to show your management the consequences of neglecting these processes. In effect, you need to cost-justify the site management function. If you can do so fairly quickly, the prognosis for recovery is good. If the site is left unmanaged for too long, the prognosis for recovery is poor and it will take a lot of cleanup work to get the site back on track.

To prevent this problem in your organization, you need to market the importance of site management from the very start of the project. It is also important to define the site management processes and create a job description around these processes. Be sure to include time for site management in the cost justification of your site and educate management in the factors that affect site return: management, functions, and tools. Table 10.15 summarizes the problem of inadequate site management.

"Why are our traffic volumes so low?"

The symptom here is site traffic that is lower than expected. Too few customers are using the support site, which means in terms of site impact that the return will be less than projected and calls to the Help

Table 10.15 "Jenna can manage the site along with the four other departments she manages."

Symptom	The site manager is given inadequate time to manage the site.
Eventual Results	Diminished return and usefulness
Possible Causes	A lack of understanding of the type and quantity of work involved in site management. The organization may also be short-staffed.
Prognosis and Suggestions for Recovery	The prognosis for recovery is good if management processes are put into place quickly; otherwise, it is poor. Create a cost justification of the site management function to convince your management of its importance.
Prevention	Emphasize the importance of site management and include it in your cost justification. Define the management processes and create a job description around these processes.

Desk will probably not be reduced to the level anticipated. This situation is probably caused by one of two factors: poor marketing or poor scope definition. If the cause is poor marketing, then the problem is not serious. Customers were simply not told or not told enough times and via an appropriate media that the site is in place. The prognosis for recovery, however, is good. The site manager has to put together a marketing plan covering all the appropriate segments and then implement the plan. One idea might be to start letting all callers to the Help Desk know about the site. As customers get the message, site traffic should increase.

If the cause is poor scope definition, then the problem is much more serious; the site is not structurally sound. The prognosis for recovery is poor. The site stakeholders' requirements will need to be reanalyzed and the required changes should be identified and carried out. This could involve a significant cost.

Preventing low site traffic is a two-fold process. First, ensure enough time and effort is dedicated to defining the scope. Also make sure all stakeholders are involved. Second, create a thorough marketing plan before implementation, ensuring that marketing activities are in place to let customers know about the site and that they cover all customer segments. Chapter 8, "Marketing," will help you. The problem of low site traffic is summarized in Table 10.16.

Table 10.16 "Why are our traffic volumes so low?"

Symptom	The site traffic is lower than expected.
Eventual Results	The return is less than projected and too many calls are going to the Help Desk.
Possible Causes	Poor marketing and a poor scope definition
Prognosis and Suggestions for Recovery	If marketing is the problem, the prognosis is good. Create and carry out a marketing plan targeting all customer segments. If a poor scope definition is the problem, the prognosis is poor. You need to reanalyze the requirements of the site stakeholders and make the required adjustments.
Prevention	Create a marketing plan before the implementation, targeting all customer segments at the appropriate timeframes. Ensure enough time and effort is dedicated to the scope definition.

"Hey, we've got this great site, yet Help Desk calls keep increasing!"

This symptom can be very discouraging. You've implemented a support site that should cause a decrease in Help Desk calls, yet calls to your Help Desk are increasing. This situation could very quickly generate a negative return for your support site, not to mention that it could overload your Help Desk so that customers have long wait times.

The most probable cause of this situation is a support site that has one or more components that are difficult to understand. Instructions on some functions might be unclear, so customers may be calling in to get some clarification. Functions that should be self-explanatory are not. If the problem instructions are at the surface level, on the main pages of the offered functions, then the prognosis for recovery is good. The instructions can be cleaned up fairly quickly. If the problem instructions are sprinkled throughout the functions, the prognosis for recovery drops to fair. Identification and cleanup could take longer, so it may take a while for site return to stabilize.

The way to prevent this problem is to test sample instructions on customer representatives. Don't leave this up to the technical staff; they have a very good understanding of the problem domain, but they will not necessarily be able to effectively see how the customer might view the material. Also, information that is too technical for the customer may seem just fine to the technical staff. Table 10.17 summarizes the problem of increasing Help Desk calls.

Table 10.17 "Hey, we've got this great site, yet Help Desk calls keep increasing!"

Symptom	Help Desk calls increase after a support site is put into production.
Eventual Results	A negative site return and an overloaded Help Desk. Customers experience long wait times.
Possible Causes	One or more components have unclear instructions or functionality.
Prognosis and Suggestions for Recovery	The prognosis is good to fair depending on the extent of the problem. Unclear instructions need to be identified and updated as soon as possible.
Prevention	Test sample instructions on customer representatives.

"We're too busy to keep the site up-to-date."

If support staff are too busy to keep a support site up to date, then that support site will soon start losing customers. Calls to the Help Desk will increase and the site return will decrease. Once a site reaches the point of losing customers, the prognosis for recovery from this problem becomes poor. Even after the problem is rectified, significant marketing efforts might be required to try to get the customers back and success will depend on how much competition that site has.

The probable causes of an overworked support staff include a lack of processes, poorly defined processes, or a lack of staff. If processes are the problem, then the site manager must take the time to put adequate processes into place. Outsourcing may be necessary to get extra help to handle the workload while processes are developed. An aggressive marketing plan must be put into place to convince disillusioned customers that the site is current and will stay current. If you have an inadequate support staff, then the site manager must put together a cost justification for additional staffing, showing the impact on site return if staff members are not added. Contract resources may be the way to go if adding headcount is a problem.

Table 10.18 "We're too busy to keep the site up-to-date."

Symptom	The support team is too busy to keep the site up-to-date.
Eventual Results	Customers will stop using the site, calls to the Help Desk will increase, and the return will decrease.
Possible Causes	Non-existent or poorly defined processes, or inadequate staffing
Prognosis and Suggestions for Recovery	The prognosis is poor once the site starts losing customers. Processes must be defined and an aggressive marketing plan must be put into place. If staffing is inadequate, extra staff must be justified and outsourced or hired.
Prevention	Ensure that update processes are developed before the site is implemented and that they are monitored after implementation. Also ensure the original cost justification includes adequate resources.

To prevent this problem, the site manager must ensure that processes for all aspects of updating the site are developed before the site is put into production and that they are followed. The site manager must also ensure that adequate staffing is included in the original cost justification and that he or she is not tempted to skimp on resources to improve the return. The problem of a support team that is too busy to keep the support site up to date is covered in Table 10.18.

"Wanna come to an email-answering party?"

The symptom here is an overwhelming amount of email generated by the support site. Too much, in fact, to be handled by the available staff. If this problem is not addressed, email response times will skyrocket, causing disgruntled customers to go elsewhere or to call the Help Desk. The site return will consequently plummet.

Two of the possible causes for this situation are lack of effective email-handling processes and a scope that does not adequately cover customer requirements. If the cause is a lack of effective email-handling processes, then the prognosis for recovery is good if the problem is caught early. The site manager needs to put some processes for managing email into place and then must create a marketing plan to let customers know about the improvement. If the cause is a scope definition that does not adequately meet the customer requirements, then the problem is much more serious and the prognosis for recovery is poor. The requirements of the customers need to be reanalyzed and changes must be planned accordingly. Changes involving the scope could be extensive and expensive. Once the changes are in place, an intensive marketing initiative must be developed and carried out to let customers know about the changes to convince them to visit the support site again.

To prevent this email problem, the project manager must ensure that the scope definition is carried out for all site stakeholders. The resulting scope summary should be reviewed with stakeholders for completeness. Processes for email handling need to be defined and put into place before the site is in production so that the email will be handled correctly from day one. The problem of too much email is summarized in Table 10.19.

Table 10.19 "Wanna come to an email-answering party?"

Symptom	The site generates an overwhelming amount of email.
Eventual Results	Email response times skyrocket, disgruntled customers go elsewhere or call the Help Desk, and the site return plummets.
Possible Causes	Customer requirements are not adequately covered by the scope or a lack of effective email-handling processes exist.
Prognosis and Suggestions for Recovery	If the problem is the processes, then the prognosis is good if caught early. Processes need to be put into place and some marketing should be carried out to get customers back. If the problem is poor scope definition, then the prognosis is poor. The scope needs to be reanalyzed and the site may have to be redesigned.
Prevention	Ensure that the scope definition is carried out fully and that a scope summary is generated. Review the scope summary with customer representatives. Also ensure that email processes are in place before the site goes into production.

"Customers keep telling us we aren't delivering answers that are useful to them!"

If customer feedback indicates that customers are not getting the answers they need from your support site, then the eventual result will be that customers will stop using the site and go elsewhere or start calling the Help Desk. The site return will therefore drop. Several causes could be the source of the problem. Perhaps instructions are unclear or the information is too technical and needs to be simplified. Perhaps the site just doesn't cover all the problems that customers might encounter.

If the problem is unclear instructions at a surface level, then the prognosis for recovery is good. You need to get all the instructions clarified and reviewed by a customer representative. If the problem is language that is too technical, the prognosis becomes fair. You thus need to work through all of your site's information, making the text easier to understand. If the problem is that your problem domain is too narrow, then the prognosis for recovery is poor. You will have to reanalyze your customers' problem domain and add to your site's information as required. The cost in terms of effort could be significant. In all cases, you need to undertake some marketing to make sure your customers know about the improvements.

Table 10.20 "Customers keep telling us we aren't delivering answers that are useful to them!"

Symptom	Customers aren't getting the answers they need.
Eventual Results	Customers will stop using the support site and will call the Help Desk. The site return thus will fall.
Possible Causes	Instructions are unclear, the information is too technical, or the problem domain is too narrow.
Prognosis and Suggestions for Recovery	The prognosis is good if the problem is unclear instructions. The instructions should be clarified and reviewed by customer representatives. The prognosis is fair if the problem is language that is too technical. Make all information is easier for customers to understand. The prognosis is poor if the problem domain is too narrow. The domain must be reanalyzed and additional information should be added. Marketing must also be undertaken to let customers know about the improvements.
Prevention	Involve customer representatives in reviewing instructions and information. When defining the scope, make sure you understand your customers' problem domain and review it with customer representatives. Also measure the problem domain on an ongoing basis.

To prevent this problem, have customer representatives review some sample instructions and examine the site's information. Also, at scope definition time, make sure that you understand your customers' problem domain and review it with some of your customers. Once your site is up and running, you need to measure and monitor your site's problem domain to ensure that it keeps up with changing customer requirements. Chapter 9 will help you do this. Table 10.20 summarizes the problem of customers not getting the answers they need.

Key Points

This chapter presents 20 problem symptoms that you may encounter during the planning, development, and management of your Web-based support site. For each of the 20 symptoms, the negative impact is described and events that may have caused the situation are explained. A prognosis for recovery is given and suggestions for addressing the problem are also made. Prevention tips for avoiding the problem or any recurrences of it are discussed as well.

PART FIVE

Examples

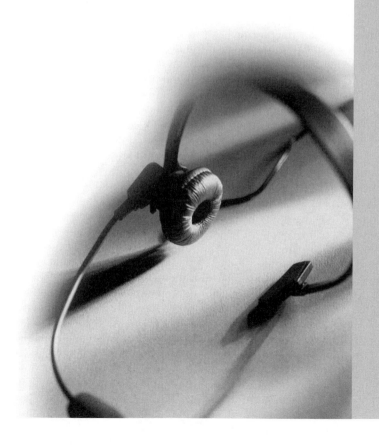

CHAPTER 11

A Support Site That Provides Unattended Operations Knowledge

The support site that I discuss in this chapter is somewhat different from the examples that we discussed in the previous chapters. The site is Farber/LaChance Online (www.farberlachance.com), the online arm of a consulting firm that specializes in data-center automation, or unattended operations. The partners in the firm travel around the world helping various organizations automate their data centers. Unlike the sites that we have discussed in our previous examples, this support site does not provide an instant response to a problem that someone might encounter during the work day. Instead, it focuses on providing a base of information and education to those organizations interested in some aspect of unattended operations. Organizations will use this site for research on processes, tools, and new developments.

Users of this site can save significant time by not having to go through the painstaking research that would have been necessary without this site. This site will educate them in various aspects of unattended operations or will broaden their knowledge of the topic. What this means to Farber/LaChance is that it can shift its focus from onsite consulting for individual organizations to mass education. The support site therefore provides a medium for reaching a much larger audience. The site also hosts paid sponsorships and ads from vendors of products and services related to the unattended operations field.

In this chapter, I discuss which aspects of this site are particularly interesting, the site content, the marketing that was and will be done to promote the site, the challenges the site faces, and plans for enhancements or other activities. The specific topics to be covered are as follows:

- Particularly interesting aspects of the Farber/LaChance Online site
- Site content
- Information and marketing versus support
- Planning, site development and marketing
- Challenges and future plans
- Key points

Of Particular Interest

Of particular interest is the degree to which users of this site control the content. The site is organized by the information area based on the various aspects of unattended operations. Each knowledge area collects feedback on what site users want to see via an online survey. The content of the site is a direct result of this feedback. The site is only four months old yet boasts a very high site user return rate. People keep coming back to a resource they know will provide useful information, lots of good stuff for free. A site log analysis tool is used to keep a close eye on the site's traffic patterns. The management of this site carries out evaluation and improvement based on traffic patterns and customer feedback.

Site Content

As Figure 11.1 shows, the site provides articles, white papers, product information, information on various associations, and useful links based on 10 knowledge areas. These information areas are based on the managing of various aspects of data center automation, such as job scheduling, console management, output management, performance management, change management, and so on.

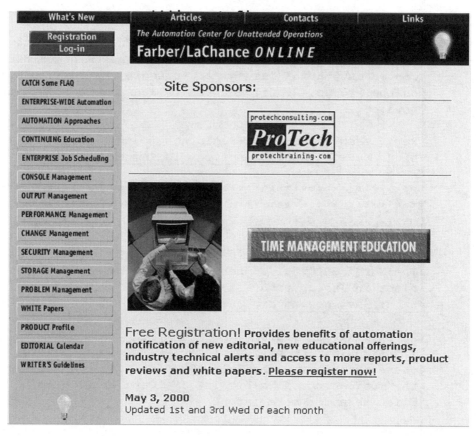

Figure 11.1   The Farber/LaChance Online site.

In order to gain access to all areas of the site, you must first register. Registration is free and once you are registered, you will receive a regular e-newsletter. The newsletter contains information about new articles on topics of interest at the site, upcoming conferences, industry news, and new products. Figure 11.2 shows an excerpt from a Farber/LaChance Online newsletter.

Articles can be accessed by going to a specific information area or by going directly to the articles tab, as Figure 11.3 shows. A What's New section provides information on new developments in various aspects of the data center automation industry.

Each information area offers a survey asking the site user to indicate points of interest or to provide suggestions for that particular area. This is what drives changes to site content. Figure 11.4 shows an example of the survey for the Automation Approaches area.

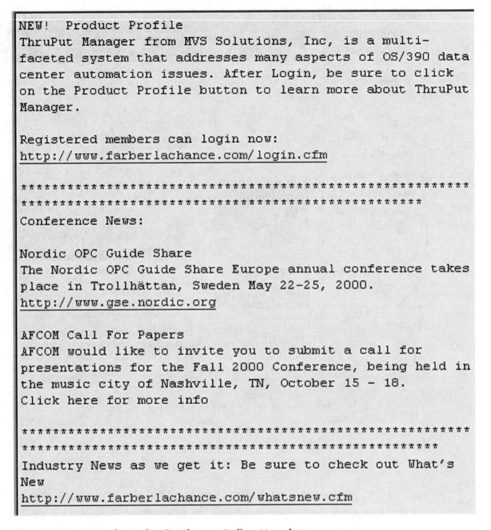

```
NEW!  Product Profile
ThruPut Manager from MVS Solutions, Inc, is a multi-
faceted system that addresses many aspects of OS/390 data
center automation issues. After Login, be sure to click
on the Product Profile button to learn more about ThruPut
Manager.

Registered members can login now:
http://www.farberlachance.com/login.cfm

*****************************************************************
*************************************************************
Conference News:

Nordic OPC Guide Share
The Nordic OPC Guide Share Europe annual conference takes
place in Trollhättan, Sweden May 22-25, 2000.
http://www.gse.nordic.org

AFCOM Call For Papers
AFCOM would like to invite you to submit a call for
presentations for the Fall 2000 Conference, being held in
the music city of Nashville, TN, October 15 - 18.
Click here for more info

*****************************************************************
************************************************************
Industry News as we get it: Be sure to check out What's
New
http://www.farberlachance.com/whatsnew.cfm
```

Figure 11.2 FLO, the Farber/LaChance Online Newsletter.

Each information area also provides articles, lists of software vendors, or links to various associations or sites of interest. Figure 11.5 shows user, discussion, and informational group links for the storage management area.

The site also has a FAQ called FLAQ. The content changes monthly and is provided by Farber/LaChance consultants. Topics are selected based on what the consultants see in their work with various organizations.

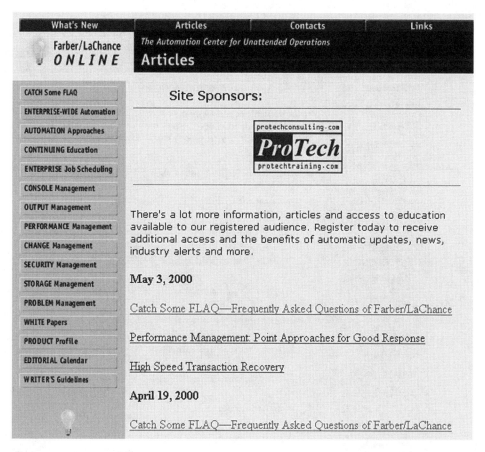

Figure 11.3   FLO articles.

Farber/LaChance Online has also partnered with a training provider to provide a continuing education option on the site. Site users can sign up for online training on a wide variety of topics, technical and non-technical. A fee is charged for this service. The Continuing Education option enables users to log directly into the training provider's site. A survey is also offered that gives Farber/LaChance Online feedback on training requirements.

The site also provides an editorial calendar that contains a schedule of upcoming topics so that users can see when specific topics will be featured. Writer's guidelines are also provided for site contributors.

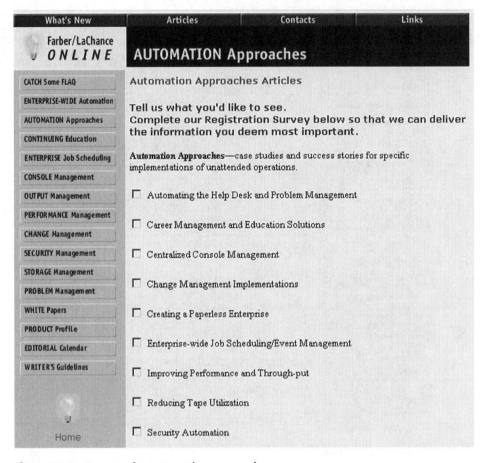

Figure 11.4 A survey for automation approaches.

Information and Marketing versus Support

Don't forget that this is an information and marketing site; it is not designed to provide quick solutions for someone seeking technical support. It begins with an introductory marketing-only page. This would not be appropriate for a technical support site because it creates one more layer and would be unnecessarily time consuming for someone with a dial-up connection. The main page that follows the introduction is very busy and although it is very appropriate for the informational focus of Farber/LaChance Online, it would need to be reorganized for technical support.

**Storage Management
User/Discussion/Informational Group Links**

Common
http://www.common.org
International association of IBM users including AS/400. Site features info about membership and Common educational initiatives with links to publications and other resources.

Optical Storage Technology Association
http://www.osta.org
International trade association dedicated to promoting use of writable optical technology for storing computer data and images.

Tivoli User Groups WorldWide
http://www.tivoli.com
Links to user group sites with information about starting a user group for IBM's Tivoli division products, including Tivoli Storage Manager

E-Storm
http://www.e-storm.org
Web site for E-Storm, a user group for enterprise storage management professionals in Michigan, Ohio and Pennsylvania. Includes news and events, meeting information and resource links.

ADSM.ORG
http://msgs.adsm.org
Discussion database for IBM ADSM users. Discussion tracks include topics such as ADSM performance and volume management.

SearchStorage.Com
http://www.searchstorage.com
Storage-specific portal with weekly updates, chat with storage gurus and many other valuable links.

Figure 11.5 Storage management links.

Planning, Site Development, and Marketing

Before this site went live, a business plan for the site was developed and the market for the site was researched. Traffic projections were also created. The development and hosting of the site were successfully outsourced as well. In short, the site is not a whim, but a carefully planned business venture.

When Farber/LaChance Online first went live in early 2000, it did so with no marketing. Site management wanted to build the site up before announcing its existence to the industry at large. The current marketing plan for the site includes a variety of activities. One of these is co-promotion with various organizations and events such as user groups and conferences. The Farber/LaChance site will also market activities for the organizations and events. In return, the organizations and events will market Farber/LaChance Online. The site will also market its existence through links to other related sites.

Another recent marketing activity involved a direct mail campaign to all Farber/LaChance, Inc. customers. All organizations that had purchased consulting services from Farber/LaChance, Inc. received a mailing containing information about the new site.

Challenges and Future Plans

The biggest challenge the Farber/LaChance site faces is one shared by most sites providing a central source of information for research. Generating content is a full-time activity. Farber/LaChance Online has recognized this and has assigned this work accordingly. Articles must be sourced and edited, information leads must be followed up and researched, and industry trends and events must be identified, described, categorized, and added to the site. Since the business of this site is information, this will continue to be a challenge. Thus, Farber/LaChance Online has to do the research that organizations would do if they wanted information on any of the 10 knowledge areas supported.

Plans for the site include a search engine, a quick poll survey to identify new issues and topics that site members would like to see addressed, and a question of the week to be answered by the Farber/LaChance Online consultants. The site will also be used to take an annual automation survey to tabulate industry practices, trends, and problems. In the past, this survey was carried out manually, but survey administration became overwhelming. The next iteration of this site is already in the works.

Key Points

This section contains some key learning you can take away with you from the Farber/LaChance Online site:

Your customers will tell you what they want to see on your site if you ask them. Surveys and a log site analyzer will help tell you if you have succeeded in providing what they want. Giving customers what is useful to them generates return traffic.

Ongoing evaluation and improvement activities will ensure you keep giving customers what they need. It will also mean that you generate new versions of your site on a regular basis.

Going live quietly makes a lot of sense. Market with a vengeance once your site is fully operational and able to handle the projected volumes.

CHAPTER 12

Simplicity in Boxes

I n this chapter, I examine a support site from a usability point of view. We'll look at how quickly and easily this site provides its users with information. I also discuss techniques used to funnel the site user to a particular topic, techniques used to keep things simple, and a review of the site's available functions. The site examined in this chapter belongs to an Internet Service Provider (ISP), Echo Online (www.echo-on.net). The topics covered include the following:

- Echo Online's noteworthy features
- Site functions
- Navigation and information in a box
- Key points

Of Particular Interest

The two aspects of the Echo Online site that are particularly interesting are its simplicity and ease of navigation. It's a full-function site, but its method of navigation makes it very easy to use. A while ago, I was searching for a new ISP to host my domain. I made my way through several ISP support sites trying to learn which hosting services they offered and how much these services cost. The process was very frustrating. On some sites, I spent a fair bit of time trying to find what I wanted, while on others I could not understand what I found when I did find it. I often ended up calling someone to get the information I needed. The Echo Online site was very different. It is a very tidy, uncluttered site and I could find the information I needed very quickly. The site's functions are organized logically and simply, and site users are not distracted by unnecessary noise in terms of superfluous information, colors, or graphics. The following sections explain how Echo Online achieves this simplicity and focus.

Site Functions

The Echo Online site actually made its first appearance in this book in Chapter 6, "Designing the Site," in a discussion on site navigation. The main page of the site is repeated here in Figure 12.1. It defines a look and navigation that is carried through the whole site. At the top of the main screen are quick access options to functions for checking mail, checking accounts, doing searches, and reading about Echo Online news. These options are accessible from all site pages. Having News as a quick access option keeps the main page uncluttered, easier to navigate, and easier to maintain.

From the main screen, the user can find out about products and services that Echo Online offers and can sign up for services or make changes to the ones he or she is signed up for. This option helps eliminate calls from customers wanting to change services, from potential customers wanting to know what services are offered at what prices, and from potential customers wanting to know how to apply for services. The Download File option enables users to download the most popular browser, email, FTP, and compression software, eliminating many "Where do I find . . . ?" calls. User Services provides functions for checking account information, picking up email, and various site administration functions.

ISP organizations have a unique support challenge in that the services they provide, specifically Internet access and Web hosting, generate a myriad of support questions that are not in the domain that the ISP

Figure 12.1 The Echo Online home page.

supports but which the ISP gets regardless. For example, an ISP might get questions from home users asking how to set up a network so that Internet access can be shared. ISPs are not really in the home networking business, yet to eliminate calls about home networking, they might want to offer links to relevant sites or home networking information on their support sites. The Echo Online Support option offers five categories of support, shown in Figure 12.2. These options include topics that address some of the external support issues.

The first category of support shown in Figure 12.2 is the Business Support option, which in turn offers several categories of business services. The first of these is the "I need help with" category shown in Figure 12.3. This is a FAQ that includes topics such as creating and installing your own CGIs and password-protecting your Web site to handle external support issues. It is not part of Echo Online's business

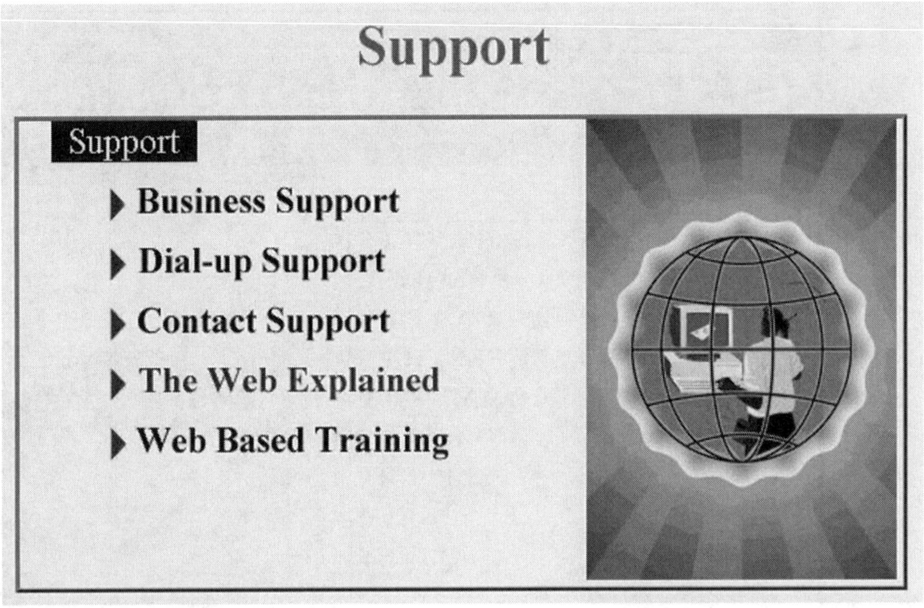

Support

Figure 12.2 Support options.

to provide technical support for these kinds of topics, but the FAQ does provide added value to customers and will eliminate many email support requests. These pages offer no email links to technical support.

The second category of support shown in Figure 12.2 is the Dial Up support option, which leads to four further categories around dial up services, the first two of which you can see in Figure 12.4. These categories also include several topics, such as "What are Newsgroups?," that are designed to handle issues external to support. The "Contact Support" option, the third category of support shown in Figure 12.2, offers the site user support via email.

The fourth support category, "The Web Explained" option, provides a link to a site that is an excellent introduction to the Internet, offering information about the Internet itself, browsers, email, searches, newsgroups, chat functions, games, and more. A "Web Based Training" option, the final category of support in Figure 12.2, offers all kinds of technical and non-technical online training provided by a third-party via a link to the Echo Online site. Interestingly, this third-party training provider is the same organization used by the Farber/LaChance Online site discussed in Chapter 11.

Business Support

I need help with

- Uploading my webpage using FTP
- Publishing your website with FrontPage
- Adding your web site to Search Engines
- Accessing/setting up my email program
- My server names/host names
- Registering a domain name
- CGI Scripts, SSI and ASP's (General Information)
- Using Echo Online Supplied CGI's/Scripts (formresults)
- Creating or Installing your own CGI's
- Creating or Installing your own Active Server Pages (ASP's)
- Sending mail using Simple Mail (NT Hosts)
- Using ODBC databases (NT Hosts)
- Password Protecting your Web Site (Unix Hosts)
- Securing my web site with SSL
- E-Commerce

Figure 12.3   Support for external issues.

Navigation and Information in a Box

One of the reasons for Echo Online's ease of use is its encapsulation of information into boxes. Information is segmented into options or topics, and each segment is stored in a box. The box can help the user to focus on its contents, and it contains what the user needs to make a further decision. A series of these boxes is presented when a user selects a function. Putting information into boxes makes the information easier to read and other information on the page does not distract the user. As an example, let's say a user selects the Dial Up Support option from a support menu that we will see later on in this chapter. In response, the user is presented with four boxes: I need help with, Questions about the Internet, Questions about my account, and Forms and Reference Material. Figure 12.4 shows an example of the first of these two boxes.

Dial-up Support

I need help with

- Configuring my Dialer
- Email & Newsgroups
- Surfing the Internet
- Building my Website
- Other Echo Online Services

Questions about the Internet

- What are Chat Rooms?
- What are Newsgroups?
- How can I protect my children from objectionable material
- Building my Website
- What are "Cookies"
- How secure are online transactions
- What is Spam
- How can I advertise on Newsgroups/Usenet

Figure 12.4 Options in boxes.

Note that no technical support email address is available at this level. Many organizations try to force customers into using online self-help by providing no immediate email links or telephone numbers. This is one way of reducing calls to the help desk, but a few organizations take it to the extreme by not having any direct contact information anywhere on their sites. Obviously, Echo Online wants to encourage customers to seek online solutions to their problems, but they provide an email address at the next level down, as Figure 12.5 shows.

Another reason for Echo Online's ease of use is its very clear navigation. This is initiated by clicking on large, easy-to-read words describing the

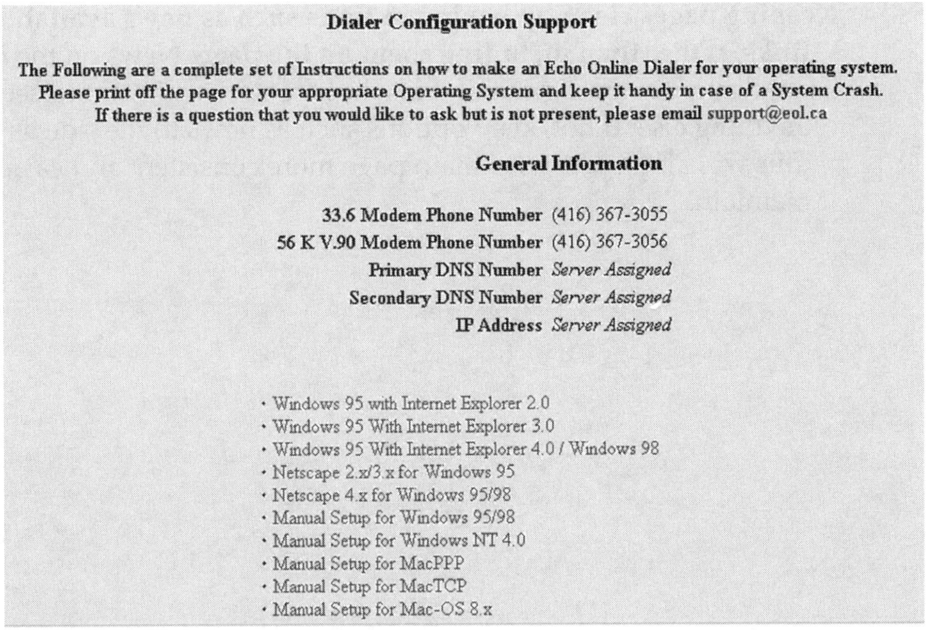

Dialer Configuration Support

The Following are a complete set of Instructions on how to make an Echo Online Dialer for your operating system.
Please print off the page for your appropriate Operating System and keep it handy in case of a System Crash.
If there is a question that you would like to ask but is not present, please email support@eol.ca

General Information

33.6 Modem Phone Number (416) 367-3055
56 K V.90 Modem Phone Number (416) 367-3056
Primary DNS Number *Server Assigned*
Secondary DNS Number *Server Assigned*
IP Address *Server Assigned*

- Windows 95 with Internet Explorer 2.0
- Windows 95 With Internet Explorer 3.0
- Windows 95 With Internet Explorer 4.0 / Windows 98
- Netscape 2.x/3.x for Windows 95
- Netscape 4.x for Windows 95/98
- Manual Setup for Windows 95/98
- Manual Setup for Windows NT 4.0
- Manual Setup for MacPPP
- Manual Setup for MacTCP
- Manual Setup for Mac-OS 8.x

Figure 12.5   An email address is provided.

function being navigated to, as illustrated in the main screen in Figure
12.1, or via topics in a list, such as the Configuring My Dialer topic in
Figure 12.4.

Key Points

The Echo Online site makes use of some effective techniques that you
might be able to duplicate on your own site. They are as follows:

**Visually separating information into distinct areas that users can
focus on without distraction.** Putting a visual frame around the
information, or, simply put, putting it in a box, is an effective way of
doing this. Each box should contain the information and links
required to take the user to the appropriate next location.

Using words or phrases for simpler navigation. This means having
users click on icons that are descriptive words or phrases, rather
than on artistically interesting but meaningless icons.

Keeping pages clean by having options such as news available as links, rather than including them on the page. News on the front page may be appropriate if it is what the user will want to see before anything else. If not, keep options such as news to the side as a link. This will also make your main page more consistent and easier to maintain.

CHAPTER 13

Support Site for a Business Software Manufacturer

I n this chapter, we visit a support site in the prototype stage. The company developing the site, Strategic Connections Inc., www.strat-con. com, is in the process of developing a series of site prototypes. I will discuss the requirements that the site must meet, some of the challenges Strategic Connections faces, and the site functions on the prototype. The topics I will cover are as follows:

- The Strategic Connections site's interesting features
- Site requirements
- Site functions
- Challenges
- Key points

Of Particular Interest

This site is of particular interest for three reasons. First, the site is in the prototype stage. That brings us closer to some of the issues involved.

Second, the site has to serve an interesting mix of users. One group of site users is made up of partners, resellers, and sales agents. Partners work with Strategic Connections to deliver complementary products or services. Resellers and sales agents work to generate sales of Strategic Connections products. Another group of site users is made up of those people installing, administrating, and supporting Strategic Connections products. The third group of site users consists of business users and the end users of Strategic Connections products, which are typically people involved in some aspect of sales and marketing.

The third reason that the site is particularly interesting is due to the nature of this group of business users. These users need help with using the product, but more than that, they need help formalizing their own business processes. They need to define the procedures around carrying out marketing and sales activities. Thus, the site needs to provide business process information to help them do this.

Site Requirements

The requirements of each of the three groups of users are quite different. The partner group needs support in selling products and developing relationships. They also need summary-level documentation that explains what the products do and demonstration files. It is also important that they understand each product's potential. They need to know what's coming in terms of product development, so they can see if a potential customer's requirements might be met by a future release. Partners also need a way of passing feedback to Strategic Connections' management in terms of customer responses to products, product development suggestions, and the quality of support material.

The technical group needs access to software patches, especially for platform-related issues, as soon as they are created. They also need to be able to see key problems or recommendations for each software release as well as to search the knowledge base of logged problems and solutions. Administrators will need to be able to get "how-to" help on the tasks they need to perform, while technical users who are installing new software will need to download new versions or intermediate upgrades. They will also require access to the most recent installation instructions.

The business group has very different requirements. As mentioned previously, they need help in using the software, but they need more help in developing business processes to formalize their marketing and sales activities. The business group also tends to be non-technical, preferring the telephone to any other kind of support. They will thus need incentives to move over to Web-based support.

Strategic Connections management would like to funnel all product problems and requests for enhancements through the support site. Right now, these come through various channels and don't always end up where they should: in support. Management also wants to have a single up-to-the-minute source of all product material so that all their various users can get what they need from the Web, thus avoiding the costs of publishing material that is all too soon out of date. Strategic Connections also wants its various users to be able to get extensive self-help from the support site and make all other support options fee-based. Table 13.1 shows what a scope summary for Strategic Connections might look like.

Site Functions

Strategic Connections has developed a prototype of site functions based on the scope summary in Table 13.1. Each site user group, partners, technical users, and business users has its own place on the site. The site is only accessible to authorized users and a log-in function must be carried out before other site options can be accessed.

Figure 13.1 shows the support page for the partners group. Partners can download current brochures, sales presentations, and product demonstrations. The Information Center function gives them access to news about product recommendations and upcoming product developments. The feedback function enables partners to communicate customer reactions to products, to report on requested enhancements, and to pass on their own suggestions. This function will most likely be a form.

A series of research papers, or white papers, are available to partners on a variety of sales and marketing topics. Partners can use these for self-education and for educating potential customers. Figure 13.2 shows a sample white paper. With the Partners Help function, partners will have a single source for all the support material they need.

Table 13.1   Scope Summary

SOURCE	REQUIREMENT	DATA AND PROCESSING REQUIRED	POTENTIAL IMPLEMENTATIONS
Management	Funnel product problem reporting and requests through the support site	Define the service levels and put processes in place to act on requests. Marketing should be done to encourage site usage.	Email or online forms and online call-tracking functions
	Single source of all product material	The material exists. Decide on the format, make the required changes, and post it. Put processes in place for regular updating.	All material is downloadable from the support site.
	Security by user type. Only registered users will have access to the site.	Need to put security definition processes into place.	Have a separate area for each user group and implement the security by area.
	Provide extensive self-help to all three groups of users for free. Also implement fee-based support for technical and business users.	Marketing initiatives are required to encourage site usage.	Telephone support and other assisted support is to be fee-based and tracked by online call-tracking tool.
Partners	Access to current product sales support material	Decide on the format for the material, make the required changes, and post it. Put processes in place for regular updating.	Downloadable documents
	Access to current product development information	Put processes in place to define who provides this information and how.	A "Product News" bulletin is posted to the site weekly.
	A means of feedback for customer responses to products, requests for enhancements, and suggestions	Processes must be put into place to collect, respond to, and act on this information.	Email from Web site. Might make this form-based to facilitate entry of information

SOURCE	REQUIREMENT	DATA AND PROCESSING REQUIRED	POTENTIAL IMPLEMENTATIONS
Technical users	Ability to download software patches	Need processes for updating patches as soon as they are available.	Downloadable function
	Current information on any issues or recommendations	Define who provides this information and how.	A hot sheet to be issues come up
	The ability to search a database of problems and solutions	Define the processes for updating the call-tracking system to ensure that solution information is consistent.	Online search access to the call-tracking database
	The ability to download new software releases	Need processes for the posting of new software releases and who is authorized to use it.	Downloadable functions
	Current installation documentation	Keep this information up to date.	Downloadable installation information
	"How-to" information for administration issues	Same as above.	FAQ for administrators Downloadable administrator's guide
Business users	Samples and templates to help implement business processes	Examine the support calls and talk to the field support staff to see what kind of examples would be most helpful. Create a process to keep these current.	Downloadable sample campaigns, planning forms, and questionnaires
	Help using the product	Look at support calls and talk to the field support staff to gather a FAQ and determine the topics for any tutorials. Also develop a process to keep these current.	Top 10 FAQ and online tutorials

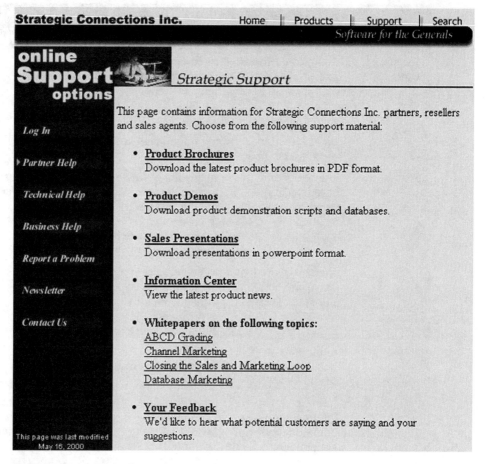

Figure 13.1 Support for partners.

The technical users group also has its own section on the support site called Technical Help, as shown in Figure 13.3. Technical users can download software patches or full upgrades of Strategic Connections' products. They can also view or print product hot sheets that contain up-to-the-minute information on any software issues or recommendations. Technical users can also search a knowledge base of resolved problems and can download current installation instructions.

Administrators of Strategic Connections' products can also get help here. An administrative help option provides them with a FAQ to answer the most commonly asked administrative questions and

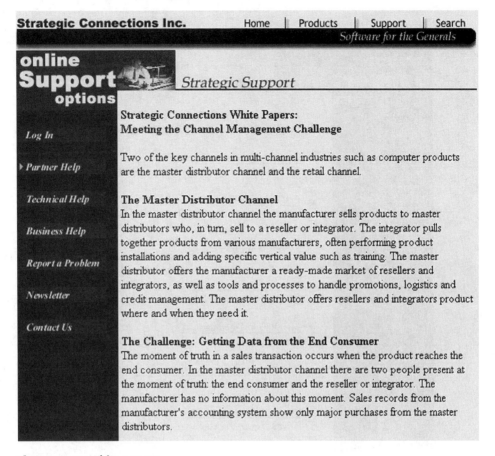

Figure 13.2   White papers.

enables them to download administration documentation. Figure 13.4 shows an example. All technical users can submit requests or suggestions for enhancements via the request enhancement option.

Figure 13.5 shows the Business Help option. Business users can download a variety of samples and templates. They can also download sample campaigns that will be available by business type, planning sheets to help them define processes around their marketing, and sample questionnaires to help them plan out the information they need to gather during marketing activities.

Business Help includes an easy-to-use FAQ as well that will help business users with their most common problems (see Figure 13.6). Business

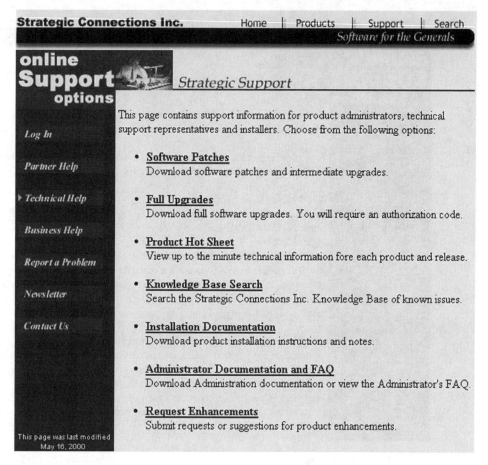

Figure 13.3 Support for technical users.

users also have the option to take a short online tutorial. It will focus on one specific topic, so that business users can get the information they need in a short period of time, rather than sitting in front of an online course for hours. Business users can also submit requests and suggestions for enhancements via the Request Enhancement option.

As well as help for individual groups of users, the site offers an online problem-reporting function and a general contact option. These are readily accessible from the side navigation buttons, a user-friendly design that is very common on good Web sites. Also, the newsletter option enables users to request an e-newsletter by specifying their email IDs. The newsletter will keep them informed of all current issues, upcoming changes, and product directions.

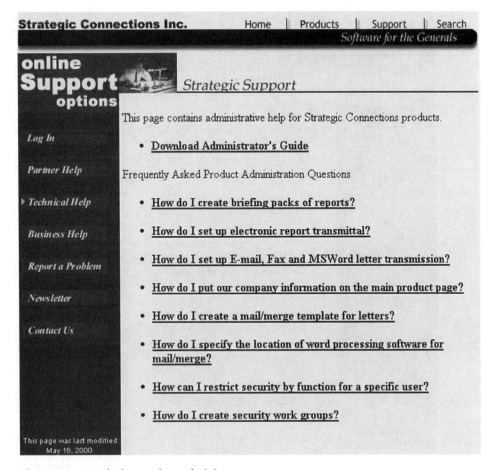

Strategic Connections Inc.   Home | Products | Support | Search

Software for the Generals

online
Support
options

Log In

Partner Help

▸ Technical Help

Business Help

Report a Problem

Newsletter

Contact Us

This page was last modified
May 16, 2000

Strategic Support

This page contains administrative help for Strategic Connections products.

- **Download Administrator's Guide**

Frequently Asked Product Administration Questions

- **How do I create briefing packs of reports?**
- **How do I set up electronic report transmittal?**
- **How do I set up E-mail, Fax and MSWord letter transmission?**
- **How do I put our company information on the main product page?**
- **How do I create a mail/merge template for letters?**
- **How do I specify the location of word processing software for mail/merge?**
- **How can I restrict security by function for a specific user?**
- **How do I create security work groups?**

Figure 13.4 Help for product administrators.

Challenges

The major challenges Strategic Connections faces in making its support site successful revolve around getting business users to actually use the site. These potential users typically work in smaller business units and perform several functions. Their culture is very telephone-based and they will need to be encouraged to get the help they need from a support site. Strategic Connections will therefore need to carefully plan out a series of marketing activities to help move the customers from telephone support to the support site before implementing any kind of fee-based support.

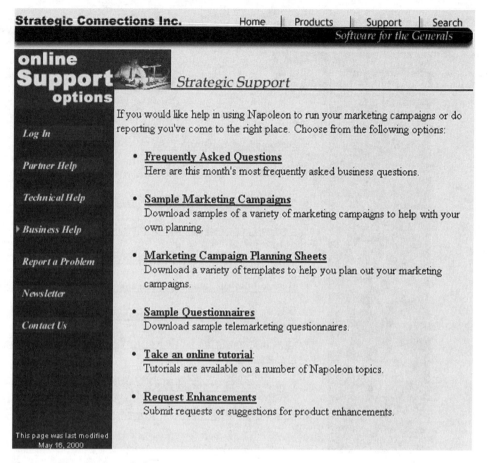

Figure 13.5   Business help.

Key Points

This chapter contained several notable points:

If you have customers with very different requirements, consider giving them their own space on your support site. This will keep the options simple for each group of users and will make it easier to implement security.

If your product or service requires that your customers implement new processes or change existing ones, you will need to help them do this. If you don't address this requirement, your products or ser-

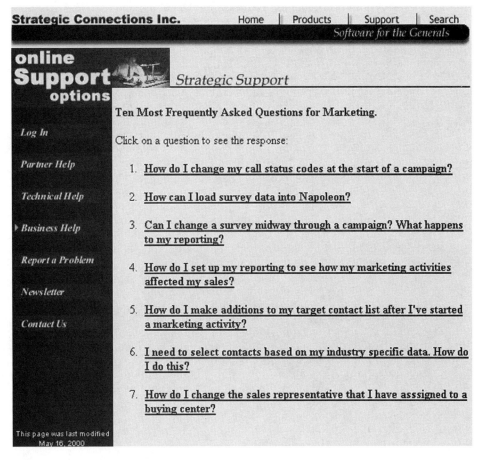

Figure 13.6 Business users' FAQ.

vices may not be successful. Getting people to change the way they do things can be a big challenge.

Don't pull the rug out from under people in terms of what you provide for support. If you are moving to fee-based support, as Strategic Connections is considering, take it slowly. Put self-help options in place, help people get used to them, and give them time to get used to them.

CHAPTER 14

Revisiting the Education Plus Example

I n this chapter, we revisit the fictitious Education Plus example. We'll compare the original requirements with the site that Education Plus planned and built throughout this book. I will discuss how the functions were implemented and how each requirement was met. The topics I will cover are as follows:

- The original requirements
- The new site
- Report card
- Key points

The Original Requirements

Table 14.1 shows the original Education Plus scope summary. I am going to compare each of these requirements against the site Education Plus created to see if and how they were met. I will do this by navigating through the new Education Plus site and referring back to Table 14.1 to see which requirements were satisfied by each specific page or function.

Table 14.1 The Original Education Plus Support Site Requirements

PRIORITY	SOURCE	REQUIREMENT	DATA AND PROCESSING REQUIRED	POTENTIAL IMPLEMENTATIONS
Mandatory	Business/support	Provide all customer support requirements.	Analyze the contract file to determine the information and functions that must be covered. Also put a process in place to keep the data current.	A FAQ, a searchable knowledge base, and course downloads.
Mandatory		Promote professional image.	Research other sites to see the look that is desired.	Hire a site designer.
Desired		Market new products.	Research where the marketing information should be placed on the site and who should provide it. Put a process in place to keep it current.	Online ads in locations accessed by current customers.
Desired		Attract new business.	Same as marketing new products but with collecting customer testimonials and creating course samples.	Add product descriptions, samples, and customer testimonials to the products page.
Mandatory	Customers	Quick responses to email.	Estimate volumes, determine the response times that can be met, and determine the email traffic that can be diverted to self-service options. Also create the required processes.	Implement a one-month pilot.
Mandatory		Download copies of courses.	Ensure that only owners of the courses get access to them. The courses should be stored on a secure server.	A special customer-only function to access the course downloads. It could be part of the call or order management.
Mandatory		High security.	A secure server and sign-in procedures.	The sign-in feature could be part of the call or order management systems.
Desired		Request and track course changes online.	Research information on available call or order management systems.	A Web interface to the call or order management systems.

At the end of the process, we will be able to see whether the site did indeed satisfy all the requirements.

The New Site

Figure 14.1 shows the main support page for Education Plus' new site. We can see at once two requirements that were met. First, the clean, uncluttered lines of the site contribute to its professional image. Second, users are required to log in to the site. Thus, the site controls what each site user can see and do and meets the actual security requirements. We will presume that the server hosting the site also has adequate security.

As we can see in Figure 14.1, the Education Plus site has several sections: a products section, a customers section, and a support section.

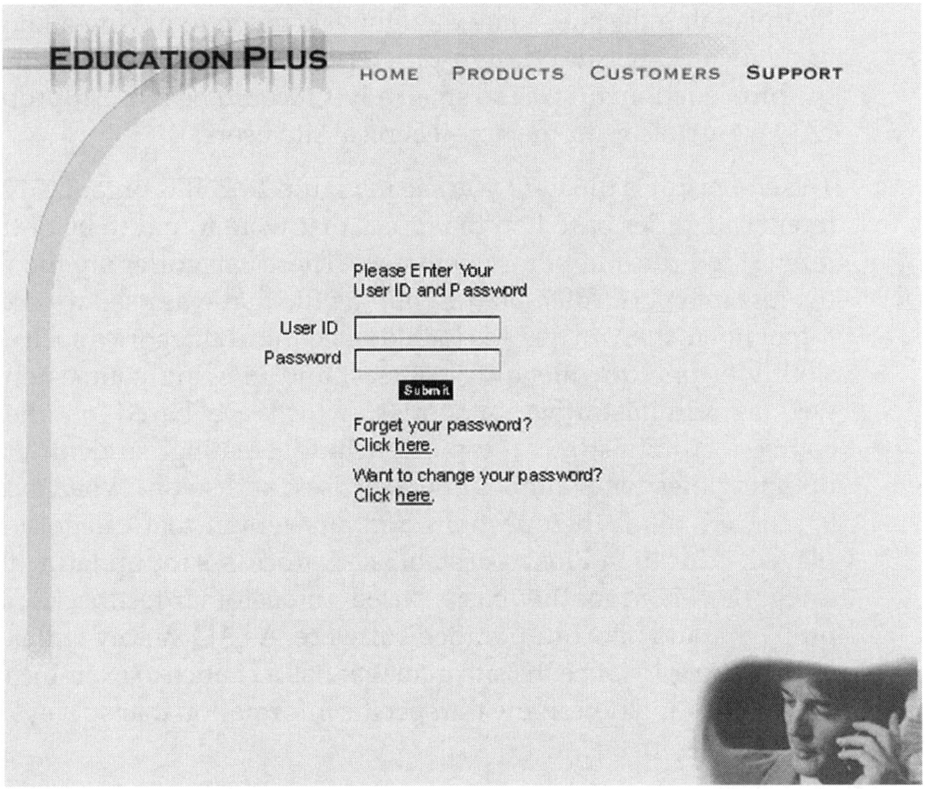

Figure 14.1 The Education Plus support site.

The home page is accessed by clicking on Home. It contains information on Education Plus itself and on any featured products or services, as well as news. The Products section, accessed by clicking on the Products icon, contains information on Education Plus products and services. New products are introduced here. The Customers section, accessed by clicking on Customers, contains customer testimonials and samples of courses created for specific customers. These pages satisfy most of the marketing requirements in Table 14.1.

In Chapter 6, "Designing the Site," we saw the prototypes for the Education Plus screen. One of these prototypes suggested some kind of help function for logging in. The actual site takes care of this by offering options for changing passwords or for retrieving a forgotten password.

Once a user logs into the Education Plus site, the screen shown in Figure 14.2 is displayed. All of the support options become visible: FAQ access, problem- or request-logging options, course downloads, and email. The site defaults to the FAQ option. When Education Plus was first planning the site, some thought was given to having a knowledge base. As analysis and design progressed, it became evident that since the problem domain was so small a FAQ would be more appropriate. A FAQ would also suit the non-technical site users.

The end result is the FAQ you see in Figure 14.2. It is organized into different categories based on the topics that were found to be of the most interest to Education Plus customers. These categories are the result of the research performed on the contract file that was used to record customer interactions. The FAQ includes technical categories such as accessibility errors, downloading courses, and viewing courses online, as well as administrative categories, which are based on the actual courses. Administrative topics include creating student accounts, updating files for examples and exercises, and so on. When a category is selected, all of the questions and answers in that category are displayed. Education Plus has established processes for updating the FAQ categories on a monthly basis, based on customer feedback, customer problems, and new or upgraded software. A FAQ survey will be added to each category once the site manager has a chance to examine the traffic statistics and determine the specific information that surveys need to collect.

Figure 14.3 shows the problem-, request-, and question-logging function for Education Plus. This function is actually a combination of problem

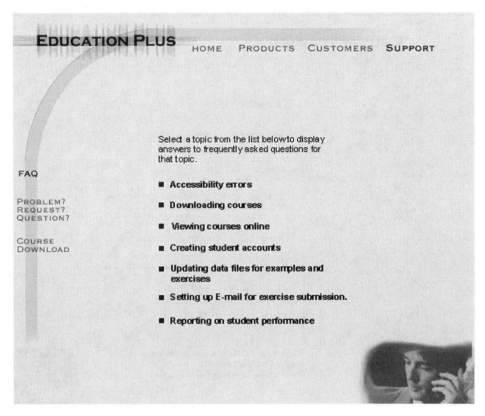

Figure 14.2 The Education Plus FAQ.

logging and email. Note that each support function in Education Plus' support site is accessed by clicking on the appropriate support category at the side of the screen. Navigation is thus very clear.

Education Plus selected a simple logging tool and its implementation on the page, shown in Figure 14.3, is also very simple. Customers have only two tasks to perform. First, they must indicate whether they are logging a problem, making a request, such as a change to a course, or asking a question. Next, they must describe the problem, request, or question. Service levels are indicated right on the screen. Problems or questions will be responded to within four business hours, and requests will be responded to within 48 hours. The processes to ensure that these response times are met, such as frequency of reviewing queues, have been put into place. The staff will also be very clear about letting customers know when they can expect to hear from someone at Education Plus. This screen also shows

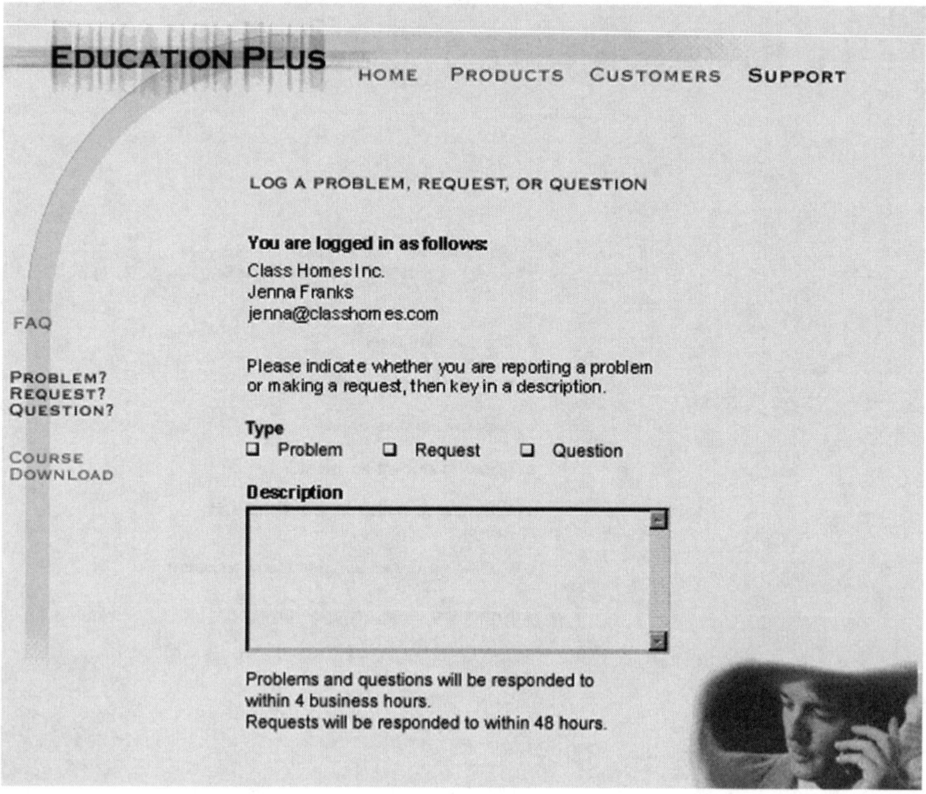

Figure 14.3 Logging a problem, request, or question.

the name, company, and email of the customer who is logged on to the screen. The problem, request, or question will be logged under the name shown and the response will be sent to that person.

This online logging function meets the requirement in Table 14.1 for tracking requests and changes online. It also meets the requirements for quick responses to email. The same processes that are in place for tracking and managing problems and requests will be used for handling any questions that customers might have. The contents of all the logs will be reviewed regularly to determine what additions can be made to the FAQ or what other site improvements can be made. The statistics generated by the logging tool can be used to monitor and manage the advertised service levels. All these activities will be part of the ongoing process of site evaluation and improvement.

In Table 14.1, Education Plus indicates that it would try out a pilot project focusing on quick responses to email for a month. With the final implementation, however, this is not necessary. The ongoing evaluation and improvement will quickly point out any weak spots.

Another customer requirement listed in Table 14.1 is the ability to download specific courses. Customers want to be able to download their own courses, but they want to be sure that their courses are available only to them and not to other customers. Figure 14.4 shows the download function that has been implemented to meet these requirements. Only courses belonging to the person or organization logged in to the support option are available to be downloaded. These courses are displayed for the customer so that the customer can make a selection, click on Start Download, and get the required course.

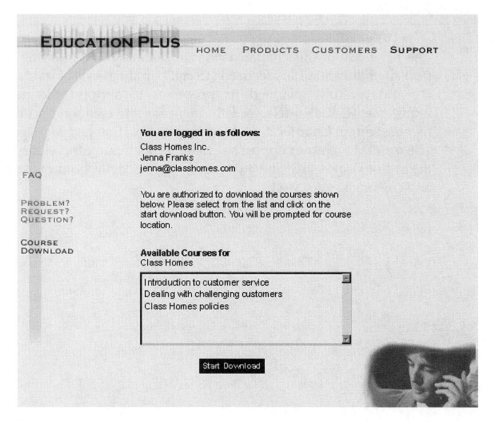

Figure 14.4 Downloading a course.

Report Card

Does the Education Plus support site meet all the requirements in the scope summary shown in Table 14.1? If you go through the table, you will see that it does, save perhaps for one requirement. Education Plus' management thought that it would be a good idea to market products in the support part of the site where the marketing would be seen by the appropriate people. The site manager decided that it would be best to first get the site up and running and use the site log analyzer to see how customer traffic moved.

Overall, I think we can give the Education Plus support site a very good rating for meeting the requirements of the business and customers.

Key Points

The key point of this chapter is that in planning and building its support site Education Plus focused strongly on the needs of its stakeholders and carefully planned its processes to support the necessary requirements. It also followed the map for site creation and management set out in Chapter 2, "A Map for Site Creation and Management." The result is a simple support site that did not incur unnecessary expenditures or complexity and that serves the needs of both management and customers very well.

CHAPTER 15

Revisiting the Trace Software Example

I n this chapter, we go back to the fictitious Trace Software example introduced in Chapter 3, "Establishing Scope." As we did in Chapter 14, "Revisiting the Education Plus Example," we will compare the original site requirements against the site that Trace Software planned and worked on throughout this book, culminating with the resulting site shown in this chapter. I will discuss how the functions were implemented and how each requirement was met. The topics I will cover are as follows:

- The original requirements
- The new site
- Report card
- Key points

The Original Requirements

Table 15.1 shows the scope summary created by Trace Software in Chapter 3. The table lists the business, support, and customer requirements for the support site. I am going to review each of these requirements against the site that Trace Software created to see if and how they were met. I will navigate through the new site and, as I do, I will refer back to Table 15.1 to see which requirements were satisfied by each specific site page or function. At the end of the process, we will be able to see whether the site did indeed satisfy all the requirements.

The New Site

In this chapter, the support pages I will be reviewing pertain only to support for Trace Software's registered customers. Before I start my review, I will take some time to describe the rest of the Trace Software site. Back in Chapter 6, "Designing the Site," Trace Software created some very basic site prototypes. The actual implementation is roughly based on the original prototypes, although the resulting design is much more elegant. The design helps meet the requirement of a new international image.

The Trace software home page offers access to three separate sections. The first section is product information, which contains all product marketing information along with downloads of product trial versions. Some thought was originally given to creating a FAQ to support potential customers using trial versions, but this idea was abandoned. Instead, potential customers downloading a trial version of the software are given a temporary user ID and password that expire at the same time as the trial software. Potential customers can then get a good idea of the quality of support that the Trace Software site provides.

A section on customer implementations is also available from the main site. It consists of case studies describing how various customers have implemented Trace Software security products. This section and the product implementation section, along with the new site design, will work to meet the requirement of promoting international business.

The third section of the Trace Software site is the support section for registered users. Customers must specify a user ID and password before they can access this section. Once they do, they are taken into the FAQ support option, shown in Figure 15.1. The site retrieves user information and displays it in the top-right hand corner of the site. It stays there through all the support pages.

Table 15.1 The Original Trace Software Support Site Requirements

PRIORITY	SOURCE	REQUIREMENT	DATA AND PROCESSING REQUIRED	POTENTIAL IMPLEMENTATIONS
Desired	Business	Reflect the new international image.	Research the support sites of similar companies.	Create a site design committee including an international group to ensure acceptance.
Desired		Promote international business.	Research other sites and obtain information from the international marketing staff.	A products page including descriptions, customer lists, and trial versions
Mandatory		Provide remote support for the European office.	Define the issues that the support office will most likely have and what data will be required to resolve these issues.	Have assisted support options on top of self-service and provide a support staff with adequate remote support tools.
Desired		Eliminate necessity for hiring.	Offloading support	See Offload support
Mandatory	Support	Offload support	Analyze the call data to see which calls can be eliminated to reach the 50 percent goal, which data is necessary to eliminate the calls, and where it can be obtained.	FAQs, an interactive knowledge base, and improved processes for updating resolution information
Desired		Customer training	Get feedback from call data and the support staff to define the training that is required. Also define the training source.	Have Education Plus develop some training modules to be posted to a training page.
Desired		Online problem logging	Research Web interfaces for the current call-tracking product.	Implement a Web interface.
Mandatory	Customers	Emergency support	Define what is an emergency and who can call.	A page can be initiated from the support site.
Mandatory		Improved email support	Analyze the current email content and traffic. Then decide what can be offloaded.	Have customers use an online call-tracking system for all communication: problems, requests, and questions.

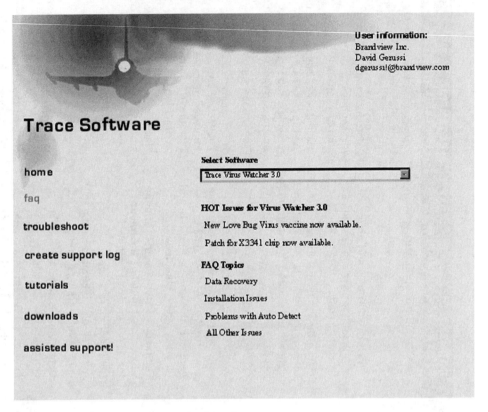

User information:
Brandview Inc.
David Gerussi
dgerussi!@brandview.com

Trace Software

home

faq

troubleshoot

create support log

tutorials

downloads

assisted support!

Select Software

Trace Virus Watcher 3.0

HOT Issues for Virus Watcher 3.0

New Love Bug Virus vaccine now available.

Patch for X3341 chip now available.

FAQ Topics

Data Recovery

Installation Issues

Problems with Auto Detect

All Other Issues

Figure 15.1 The Trace Software support site.

Figure 15.1 shows us the support options that are available, which are listed down the left-hand side of the screen. Similar to the Education Plus site, navigation is carried out by word icons that describe the option being navigated to. Support options include a FAQ, a troubleshooting option, online problem and question logging, online tutorials, software downloads, and assisted support.

In the Trace Software site, FAQs are categorized by software product. The site user is asked to select from a dropdown list of products. When a software product is selected, all support information offered in the FAQ, including troubleshooting and download options, pertaining to that product will be shown. In Figure 15.1, we see that the software product selected is Virus Watcher 3.0. The FAQ displayed includes the current hot issues for the product as well as the product topics that customers are most interested in. In this case, the current hot issues are the availability of a vaccine for the new Love Bug virus and a software patch for the X3341 chip. The FAQ topics for Virus Watcher 3.0 include data recovery, installation issues, and auto detect problems. These issues will be changed on a weekly basis as the most frequently occurring customer questions change. Trace Software has put processes in place to identify and add new topics to the Hot Issues list and to identify new entries in each FAQ category. The site manager has well-defined evaluation and improvement processes in place so that enhancements can be made and new categories can be added as required. The FAQ is doing its part in meeting the site requirement of resolving 50 percent of the customer problems. As we can see in Figure 15.2, the Troubleshooting support option is also doing its part in helping reach the 50 percent problem resolution goal.

The Trace Software troubleshooting option enables a customer to resolve a problem by selecting one or more levels of symptoms and

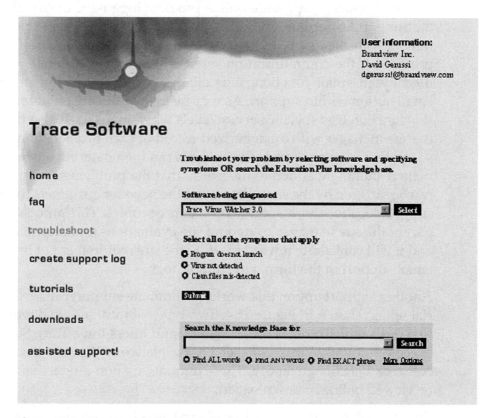

Figure 15.2 The Troubleshooting option.

having the site suggest resolutions. Trace Software has been very aggressive about reaching its call reduction goal and has purchased a fairly sophisticated resolution tool to handle the troubleshooting option. First, a customer is asked to specify a specific software product. If a product is specified in the FAQ option, the troubleshooting option will use it until another product is specified. Then the customer is asked to select one or more symptoms from a list provided. The list is based on the software product selected. When the customer submits the list of symptoms, the system will either start to narrow down the problem by presenting another set of symptoms to choose from or it will present a list of possible solutions. If a list of solutions is presented, the customer is asked if any apply. If not, more symptoms are presented. This process continues until a correct resolution is presented or the customer decides to try something else. A search function is provided for those cases when the customer cannot find the desired answer from the troubleshooting option.

The requirement to provide online problem logging is met by the Create Support Log option, shown in Figure 15.3. This option provides customers with the ability to log problems or questions. It is designed to provide all the communication services that would normally be handled by an email function, thus eliminating the need for a separate email option within support. As we saw in the Education Plus example, this function lists specific service levels when invoked. It also provides the site manager with a categorized record of each problem or question so trends can be analyzed. The analysis can then determine what information should be added to the site so that the problems and questions can be satisfied by the site, eliminating the need for customers to submit support logs for those specific problems or topics. This process will be part of the site manager's ongoing site evaluations and improvements, and it will contribute toward meeting the site requirement of improved email support in the format of support logs.

Another support option that works to eliminate support calls is the tutorial option shown in Figure 15.4. Two types of tutorials are offered. The first deals with Trace Software training and offers three Trace Software-specific tutorials: Virus Watcher basics, Network Watcher basics, and Network Watcher advanced. These tutorials are non-interactive and can be viewed online or downloaded.

The second group of tutorials offered revolves around general networking and security topics. Even though these topics are beyond the

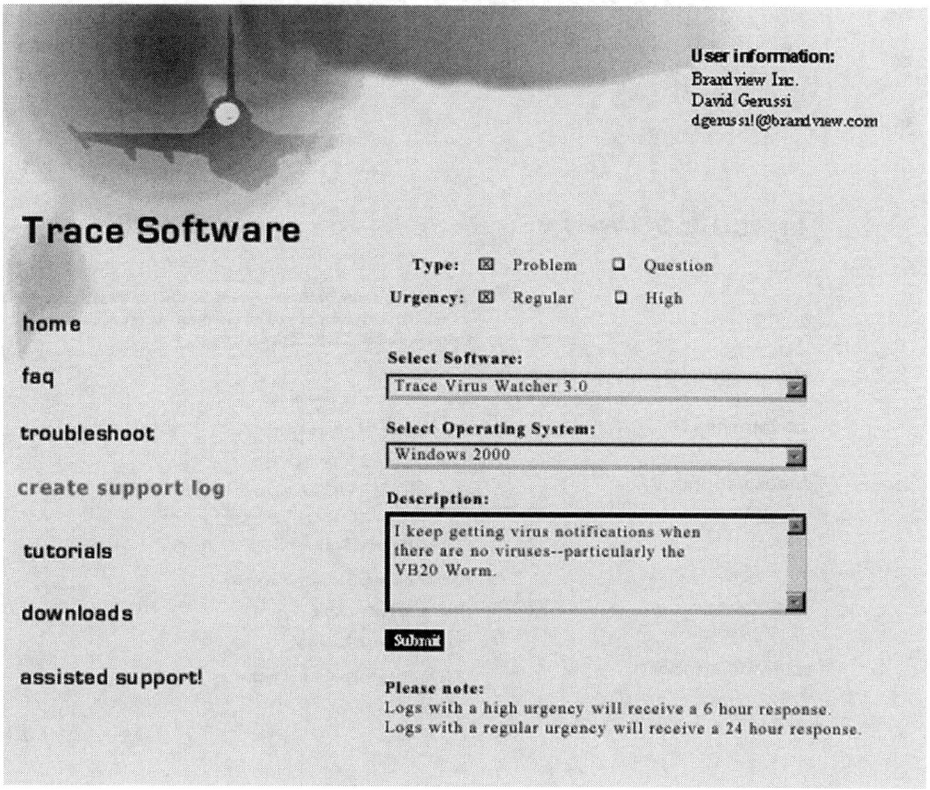

Figure 15.3 Creating a support log.

scope of the support offered by the Trace Software Help Desk, the Help Desk has received a significant number of calls related to networking and security. The tutorials, which can be taken online and are interactive, are directed at eliminating those calls. When the Help Desk receives calls on these topics, it will direct the customers to the support site tutorials. The Tutorials option is a good start at meeting Table 15.1's requirement of providing customer training.

Another support site option that works to eliminate calls is the Downloads option, shown in Figure 15.5. Based on the software product selected, a customer can download a variety of patches and updates. In Figure 15.5, the software product is Virus Watcher 3.0, carried over from the FAQ and troubleshooting options. The downloads available for this product are a vaccine for the Love Bug virus, a patch for a chip X3341 compatibility problem, a software upgrade necessary for a specific operating system version, and a beta version of the next version of

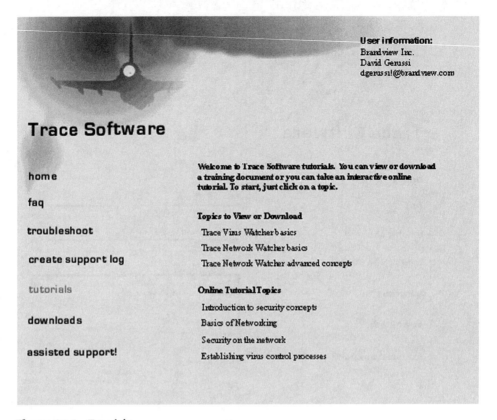

User information:
Brandview Inc.
David Gerussi
dgerussi!@brandview.com

Trace Software

home

faq

troubleshoot

create support log

tutorials

downloads

assisted support!

Welcome to Trace Software tutorials. You can view or download a training document or you can take an interactive online tutorial. To start, just click on a topic.

Topics to View or Download

Trace Virus Watcher basics

Trace Network Watcher basics

Trace Network Watcher advanced concepts

Online Tutorial Topics

Introduction to security concepts

Basics of Networking

Security on the network

Establishing virus control processes

Figure 15.4   Tutorials.

Virus Watcher. Selecting a different product will result in a different list of available downloads. The customer selects one or more items for download and then clicks on Submit to initiate the download process, which will prompt the customer for any required information and will provide all the required instructions.

Another important requirement for the Trace Software site is the capability to provide remote support for all remote users and emergency assisted support. The site meets this requirement with its assisted support option, shown in Figure 15.6. To initiate assisted or emergency support, a customer clicks on the Assisted Support! option at the left of the screen. If the request is initiated after regular hours, a Trace Software support person is paged and immediately logs into the system via the Internet to handle the support request. The customer receives a message saying the support practitioner has been notified and will

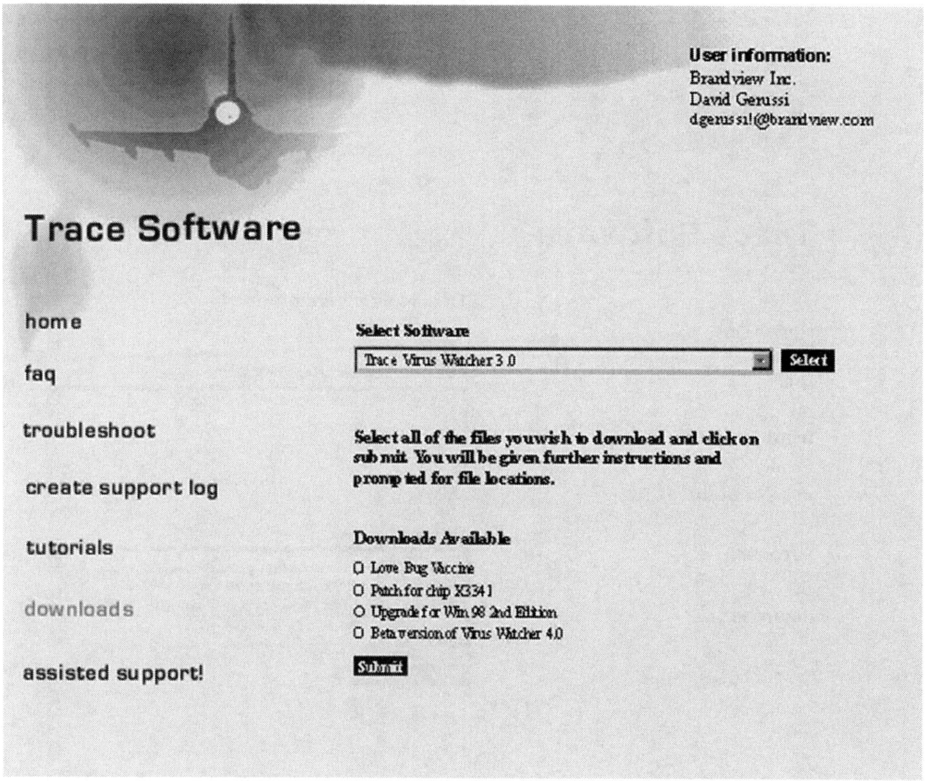

User information:
Brandview Inc.
David Gerussi
dgerussi!@brandview.com

Trace Software

home

faq

troubleshoot

create support log

tutorials

downloads

assisted support!

Select Software

Trace Virus Watcher 3.0   **Select**

Select all of the files you wish to download and click on submit. You will be given further instructions and prompted for file locations.

Downloads Available

O Love Bug Vaccine
O Patch for chip X3341
O Upgrade for Win 98 2nd Edition
O Beta version of Virus Watcher 4.0

Submit

Figure 15.5   Software downloads.

respond shortly. During regular office hours, requests for assisted support are responded to immediately or on a first-in, first-out basis if all support practitioners are busy.

When a support practitioner picks up a request for assisted support, a well-defined procedure for call-handling is followed. The first step in this procedure is to send the customer an opening message such as, "Hi, Jeff Martin here, what can I do for you?," shown in Figure 15.6. This enables the customer chat function. The customer describes the problem and clicks on Submit. The conversation continues with the practitioner employing whatever remote control tools are required. A set of escalation procedures defines what the practitioner is to do if the problem cannot be resolved. At the end of the assisted support session, the support practitioner will thank the customer, ask if he or she has any other questions or problems, and will then email the customer a transcript of the session

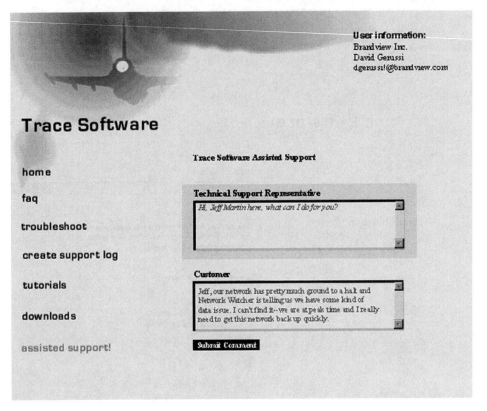

Figure 15.6 Assisted support.

along with any supporting materials, such as some instructions clipped out of the product documentation. During the interaction, the support call is logged so that the information in the call is automatically fed into the evaluation and improvement process.

Report Card

Does the Trace Software support site meet all of the requirements in the scope summary shown in Table 15.1? If the support options reviewed in this chapter and the processes behind them are as good as they seem, then we can assume that all requirements will be met. The one requirement that I have not yet discussed is elimination of the need for additional support staff. Again, if Trace Software's support site options are as good as they seem, then enough calls will be eliminated so that additional Help Desk staff will not be required. The Trace Software support site appears to have done a very good job of meeting the requirements of its site stakeholders.

Key Points

The key point of this chapter repeats that offered in Chapter 14. In order to be successful at planning and building a support site, you must focus on the needs of the site stakeholders. You must analyze, plan, and design the site around these requirements. You must define processes around site maintenance and management. If you follow the map for site creation and management described in Chapter 2, and let yourself be guided by the details in the remaining chapters, your site will be successful, as the Education Plus and Trace Software examples illustrate.